# You Got This!

# You Got This!

*A Straightforward, No-Nonsense Playbook for
Crushing 130+ Workplace Challenges*

HEIDE ABELLI

PALMETTO
PUBLISHING
Charleston, SC
www.PalmettoPublishing.com

Copyright © 2023 by Heide Abelli

All rights reserved

No portion of this book may be reproduced, stored in a retrieval system, or transmitted in any form by any means–electronic, mechanical, photocopy, recording, or other–except for brief quotations in printed reviews, without prior permission of the author.

Hardcover ISBN: 979-8-8229-2693-6
Paperback ISBN: 979-8-8229-2694-3
eBook ISBN: 979-8-8229-2695-0

# Dedication

To Carlo and Alessandra for being the most wonderful children any mother could ever hope to have.

# Contents

**Preface** . . . . . . . . . . . . . . . . . . . . . . . . . . . . . . . . . . . . . . . . . . . xiii
**Section 1—The Game-Changers** . . . . . . . . . . . . . . . . . . . . . . . 1
    Embracing a Growth Mindset . . . . . . . . . . . . . . . . . . . . . 3
    Developing Grit in Your Professional Life . . . . . . . . . . . . . . . 6
    Tackling Everyday Challenges With Gusto . . . . . . . . . . . . . . 10
    Controlling Your Emotions at Work . . . . . . . . . . . . . . . . . 12
    Becoming a Conscientious Employee . . . . . . . . . . . . . . . . 15
    Finding Daily Purpose in Your Work . . . . . . . . . . . . . . . . 18
    Being Open to Others' Ideas . . . . . . . . . . . . . . . . . . . . . 21
    Collaborating With Others for Success . . . . . . . . . . . . . . . 24
    Being a Good Team Player . . . . . . . . . . . . . . . . . . . . . . 27
    Becoming a Proactive Networker . . . . . . . . . . . . . . . . . . 30
**Section 2—Amplifying Your Game** . . . . . . . . . . . . . . . . . . . 33
    How To Face Uncertainty at Work . . . . . . . . . . . . . . . . . 35
    How To Handle Disappointing News With Grace . . . . . . . . . . 38
    How To Learn From Failure at Work . . . . . . . . . . . . . . . . 41
    How To Own Your Mistakes at Work . . . . . . . . . . . . . . . . 44
    How To Get to the Root of a Problem . . . . . . . . . . . . . . . 47
    How To Make Sound Decisions at Work . . . . . . . . . . . . . . 50
    How To Take Initiative at Work . . . . . . . . . . . . . . . . . . . 55
    How To Respond to Questions at Work . . . . . . . . . . . . . . 58
    How To Speak Up in Meetings . . . . . . . . . . . . . . . . . . . 61
    How To Own the Details . . . . . . . . . . . . . . . . . . . . . . 64
    How To Demonstrate Charisma at Work . . . . . . . . . . . . . . 67
**Section 3—Unleashing Your Inner Titan:**
       **Breaking Barriers Within** . . . . . . . . . . . . . . . . . . . 71
    Eliminating Negative Thought Patterns at Work . . . . . . . . . . . 73
    Overcoming Self-Doubt at Work . . . . . . . . . . . . . . . . . . 79
    Accepting Less Than Perfection at Work . . . . . . . . . . . . . . 82

Letting Go of What Other People Think About You.......... 85
Being Receptive to Feedback............................ 88
Overcoming the Fear of Trying New Things on the Job ....... 91
Changing Behaviors That Hold You Back at Work .......... 94
Developing New Work Habits ........................... 98
Finding a Sense of Purpose in Your Job................... 101
Becoming More Confident at Work ...................... 104
Keeping Your Word on Work Commitments .............. 107
Maintaining Your Composure at Work.................... 109
Being More Patient With Others at Work.................. 111
Succeeding at Work as an Introvert....................... 114
Changing Others' Perceptions of You .................... 117

**Section 4—Synching With the Squad:
Navigating Coworker Dynamics** ................ 121
Building Relationships With Peers ...................... 123
How To Deepen Your Workplace Relationships ............ 126
Maintaining Professional Relationships With
Personal Friends at Work ............................. 129
Getting on the Same Page With Your Coworker............ 132
Engaging in Challenging Conversations at Work ........... 135
Creating Boundaries for Chatty Colleagues ................ 138
What To Do When a Coworker Annoys You .............. 141
What To Do When Your Coworker Is the Slacker........... 144
How To Deal With Coworkers Who Are
Always Asking for Help .............................. 148
What To Do When Coworkers Gossip About You at Work ..... 151
Counteracting Coworkers' Negativity..................... 153
Dealing With Conflict on the Job........................ 156
What To Do When a Coworker Dislikes You .............. 160
Dealing With a Toxic Coworker ........................ 163
What To Do When You Are Jealous of a Coworker.......... 169
Mending Relationships at Work ........................ 172

How To Handle Dating a Coworker.....................175
What To Look Out for When You Go From "Buddy" to "Boss"..179
Meeting Colleagues Face-to-Face for the First Time.........183
Interfacing Virtually With Coworkers....................185

**Section 5—Navigating Boss Issues** .......................189
Building Rapport With Your Boss........................191
Getting Off to a Good Start With a New Boss.............195
Getting Comfortable Around Senior Leaders..............198
Bringing a Problem to Your Boss .......................201
Fighting To Be Heard When Your Boss
Doesn't Listen to You.................................203
Coping With an Unpredictable Boss.....................206
Handling a Boss Who Can't Show Empathy ..............209
Handling a Boss Who Gaslights You ....................212
Managing an Abrasive Boss............................215
Handling a Rude Boss ................................219
Feeling Supported If Your Boss Doesn't Back You Up........221
Navigating a Boss Who Is Jealous of Your Success...........224

**Section 6—Advocating for Yourself at Work** ...............227
How To Be Your Authentic Self at Work..................229
How To Assert Yourself in the Workplace.................232
How To Garner Respect at Work .......................235
How To Take Initiative in the
Performance Appraisal Process ........................239
How To Ask for Feedback From Your Boss...............242
How To Get More Constructive Feedback ...............245
How To Play Up Your Achievements at Work............247
How To Ask for a Promotion at Work ..................250
How To Ask Your Boss for a Raise .....................253
How To Handle Not Getting the Promotion .............257
How To Deal With Unfair Treatment at Work ...........259
What To Do When Someone Takes Credit for Your Work....261

How To Shoulder and Prevent Unfair Blame at Work. . . . . . . . 264

**Section 7—Making Strides in Your Career** . . . . . . . . . . . . . . . . . . . 267
    How To Activate Your Company Intelligence Radar . . . . . . . . . 269
    How To Identify the Hidden Keys to Success at Work . . . . . . . 271
    How To Keep Your Skills Current in
    Today's Changing Workplace . . . . . . . . . . . . . . . . . . . . . . . . . . 273
    How To Sell Your Ideas at Work . . . . . . . . . . . . . . . . . . . . . . . . 276
    How To Capture the Attention of Senior Executives. . . . . . . . . 278
    How To Find a Great Mentor . . . . . . . . . . . . . . . . . . . . . . . . . . 281
    How To Become More Visible at Work. . . . . . . . . . . . . . . . . . . 286
    How To Build Personal Power at Work . . . . . . . . . . . . . . . . . . 289
    How To Challenge the Status Quo in Your Workplace . . . . . . . 292
    How To Become an Intrapreneur at Work . . . . . . . . . . . . . . . . 295
    How To Grow in a Dead-End Job. . . . . . . . . . . . . . . . . . . . . . . 298

**Section 8—Upping Your Productivity Game** . . . . . . . . . . . . . . . . . 301
    Asking Your Boss for Clarity in Your Role . . . . . . . . . . . . . . . . 303
    Clarifying Expectations at Work. . . . . . . . . . . . . . . . . . . . . . . . 306
    Asking for Help at Work. . . . . . . . . . . . . . . . . . . . . . . . . . . . . . 309
    Avoiding Procrastination on the Job . . . . . . . . . . . . . . . . . . . . . 311
    Staying Focused on the Job. . . . . . . . . . . . . . . . . . . . . . . . . . . . 314
    Upping Your Task Completion Game. . . . . . . . . . . . . . . . . . . . 317
    Meeting Deadlines and Completing Tasks on Time . . . . . . . . . 320
    Accomplishing More at Work. . . . . . . . . . . . . . . . . . . . . . . . . . 323
    Maximizing Productivity When Working Remotely . . . . . . . . . 326
    Getting Through a Busy Time at Work. . . . . . . . . . . . . . . . . . . 329
    Handling More Work When a Coworker Quits . . . . . . . . . . . . 333
    Combatting Job-Related Boredom . . . . . . . . . . . . . . . . . . . . . . 336
    Succeeding Without Working Long Hours. . . . . . . . . . . . . . . . 339

**Section 9—Nailing Your New Role:**
    **Taking Charge of the Next Chapter**. . . . . . . . . . . . . . . . 343
    How To Make the Decision To Take a New Position. . . . . . . . 345
    How To Ask the Right Questions To Ensure a Job Match. . . . . 351

How To Negotiate Compensation for a New Position. . . . . . . . 354
How To Succeed in the First Week at a New Job. . . . . . . . . . . 357
How To Tackle a New Role With Confidence. . . . . . . . . . . . . . 360
How To Set Yourself Up for Success in a New Role. . . . . . . . . 362
How To Integrate Seamlessly Into a New Team. . . . . . . . . . . . 365

**Section 10—Staying Sane: Workplace Zen** . . . . . . . . . . . . . . . 369
Optimizing Your Workplace Well-Being. . . . . . . . . . . . . . . . . . 371
Achieving Work-Life Balance . . . . . . . . . . . . . . . . . . . . . . . . . . 374
Keeping Yourself Motivated at Work. . . . . . . . . . . . . . . . . . . . 378
Setting Limits When You Are Pushed Too Far. . . . . . . . . . . . . 381
Saying No to Additional Work . . . . . . . . . . . . . . . . . . . . . . . . . 384
Pushing Back When Everything at Work Is "Urgent" . . . . . . . 388
Managing Stress in the Moment. . . . . . . . . . . . . . . . . . . . . . . . 391
Handling Times When You're Anxious at Work . . . . . . . . . . . 395
Taking Steps To Reduce Your Burnout . . . . . . . . . . . . . . . . . . 398
Managing Burnout When You Work Remotely. . . . . . . . . . . . 402
Getting More Support at Work. . . . . . . . . . . . . . . . . . . . . . . . . 404
Staying Sane in a Toxic Work Environment . . . . . . . . . . . . . . 406

**Section 11—Handling Special Situations in the Workplace** . . . . 409
How To Know When To Complain About Something
Versus Keeping Quiet. . . . . . . . . . . . . . . . . . . . . . . . . . . . . . . . 411
How To Stay True to Your Ethics and Principles at Work . . . . . 414
How To Respond When Others
Violate Ethical Standards at Work. . . . . . . . . . . . . . . . . . . . . . 417
How To Handle Gossip at Work. . . . . . . . . . . . . . . . . . . . . . . . 419
How To Survive Office Politics. . . . . . . . . . . . . . . . . . . . . . . . . 421
How To Handle Being Excluded at Work . . . . . . . . . . . . . . . . 424
How To Handle Being Stereotyped at Work. . . . . . . . . . . . . . . 427
How To Handle a Workplace Bully. . . . . . . . . . . . . . . . . . . . . . 430
How To Handle Harassment at Work. . . . . . . . . . . . . . . . . . . . 433
How To Overcome Embarrassment at Work. . . . . . . . . . . . . . 436
How To Talk to Your Boss About Your Mental Health . . . . . . . 438

How To Handle Anxiety About Potential Job Loss . . . . . . . . . . 441
How To Make Two Jobs Work for You . . . . . . . . . . . . . . . . . . 443
How To Cope When You Survive a Layoff . . . . . . . . . . . . . . . 446
How To Cope With a Beloved Team Member's Departure . . . . 449
Index . . . . . . . . . . . . . . . . . . . . . . . . . . . . . . . . . . . . . . . . . . . 453

# Preface

Embarking on your professional journey can feel like walking an unfamiliar path with a confusing map and a backpack full of tools you don't know how to use. Whether you're stepping into the corporate realm for the first time or navigating its twists and turns after a decade, the challenges remain real and the pursuit of success ever-evolving. But here's the thing: you are not alone.

This book gives you a steadfast companion, a guide as you maneuver through the maze of the modern workplace. You'll benefit from my years of educating and training people just like you. I've distilled my advice into eleven potent sections, a blend of firsthand experiences, proven strategies, action steps, practical tips and invaluable recommendations. It's not just about surviving; it's about thriving. And this book helps you do just that.

Before diving into professional conundrums, you need to understand the book's blueprint. The initial sections arm you with fundamental skills; the bedrock of professional success. Later sections transition from internal mindsets to external interactions, from individual pursuits to team and boss dynamics, from harnessing productivity to ensuring well-being and, finally, to navigating the unexpected.

Each section mirrors the trajectory most professionals traverse, from personal growth and development to collaboration and beyond. However, the beauty of this guide is its flexibility. Instead of reading and forgetting it, keep in on your desk. Reference it when you need a reliable coach to consult in moments of uncertainty.

You can hop from one section to another or from chapter to chapter, depending on your immediate needs or challenges. It's about navigating the ebb and flow of professional life, as unpredictable as it can be. There will be times when you're struggling to get along with your boss one week, grappling with an annoying coworker the next, or contemplating how to better advocate for yourself thereafter. In those moments, this book is your steadfast ally. The chapter headings describe their contents, and there's a handy index, aiding your search for quick answers.

With this guide by your side, you'll not just walk the professional path; you'll stride with confidence, purpose and poise. Keep it within arm's reach, for those moments when you need guidance, inspiration or simply a reassuring voice telling you, "You got this!"

## Section 1

# The Game-Changers

Welcome to your go-to manual for no-nonsense professional advice. Drawing from my deep well of accumulated experience, I'm on a mission to turbocharge your path to success. This kick-off section dives into ten competencies I've dubbed the "game-changers". The core tenets of professional success and personal growth often revolve around mindset, collaboration and resilience. These competencies are mission-critical for success in the workplace.

Being a conscientious employee, open to others' ideas and collaborating for success underscores the importance of teamwork and adaptability in today's workplace. Working harmoniously within a group paves the way for effective communication, productive problem-solving and the synthesis of diverse ideas. Embracing a growth mindset encourages continuous learning and adaptability in the face of change. Controlling your emotions, especially in high-pressure situations, ensures that you're able to maintain positive relationships at work and make rational decisions. Being proactive in networking expands your professional horizons and opportunities. Purpose in work gives direction and meaning to your daily tasks. Grit and perseverance in your professional life, coupled with a zeal to tackle everyday challenges with enthusiasm, ensure that obstacles become stepping stones to success rather than insurmountable barriers. These are *The Game-Changers* that make the difference on the road to professional success.

Are you with me? Let's get started.

# Embracing a Growth Mindset

"Whether you think you can or you think you can't, you're right."
*Henry Ford*

If you've spent any time in the business world, you've probably heard the term *growth mindset*. Lots of professionals like to throw it around, but some don't fully understand what it actually means.

A growth mindset isn't simply positive thinking or an upbeat attitude. It's not *just* about being flexible and open-minded. It isn't just random effort or your parent/professor/mentor telling you, "You can do anything you set your mind to." Don't get me wrong: those are great, but they won't take you far.

In a nutshell, a growth mindset is the self-belief that you can continue to learn and grow; that your skills and abilities are not fixed, but can improve over time.

## Why Does It Matter?

A growth mindset allows you to be open to possibilities throughout your life. Moreover, it builds confidence in your ability to learn and grow, enabling you to be the person you want to be in the larger world—not just your professional microcosm. It means knowing you can overcome challenges. Cultivating a growth mindset empowers you with an internal locus of control, transforming challenges into exciting opportunities rather than obstacles to avoid.

To use a cliché, having a growth mindset makes the world your oyster.

## Action Steps

Almost no one is born with a growth mindset. Every person who currently has one had to develop and foster it themselves—meaning you can, too. Here are some steps to developing a growth mindset.

- **Be perseverant, purposeful and patient.** You might never shred at Madison Square Garden, but you can become a proficient guitar player. Or a programmer. Or a data analyst. Or a marketing manager. Devote the time, effort and self-discipline and just keep at it, even when your fingers hurt, when you knock over the orange cones on the driving course or when your software program crashes. Stay committed to your goals by pushing through obstacles and setbacks as they arise.
- **Build relationships.** What every good student needs is good teachers. Chances are, you know some already. Don't be afraid to knock on the doors of coworkers. They are a fountain of skills, talents and information. Be willing to reciprocate with the skills and knowledge you have! Lastly, embrace any feedback you receive, learn from it and use it to improve yourself.
- **Embrace failure**, but not as a lifestyle. Developing a growth mindset requires cultivating a love of learning. When you embark on new lessons and challenges, you invite the chance of failure. Because most of us have been socialized to avoid failing, it's often seen as something to be ashamed of. But there is no learning without failure. Rather than seeing failure as a sign of limitations or as something to be ashamed of, view failures as opportunities to learn and improve.
  - Of course, you need to actually learn from your failures so that you can move forward toward success. Failure without learning *is* lame. It's no way to live your life, and it doesn't build a growth mindset.
- **Pass it on**. Almost any middle school or high school teacher will tell you that the best way for students to learn something is to make them teach it to someone else. If you have a willing friend or coworker who will learn a new skill from you after *you've* learned it, both of you will have the chance to

develop a growth mindset together. It also helps build your confidence in what you're learning with the added benefit of creating the potential for cooperation and collaboration.

Having a growth mindset gives you the confidence in your ability to learn new skills and competencies that will make you the best candidate for new jobs or promotions. You can finally make enough to pay off those loans, get an office with a door or see a path to that next job you covet. Those are all good things that are much harder to achieve without pushing yourself to see what you're capable of doing.

# Developing Grit in Your Professional Life

> "Above everything else I've done, I've always said
> I've had more guts than I've got talent."
> *Dolly Parton*

Bill Gates. Serena Williams. Nancy Pelosi. Lin Manuel Miranda. Four highly successful, unique people who each possess natural talents in their chosen fields. More than their natural abilities, they have the most defining character trait of high achievers: **grit**. Grit is also defined using other words such as nerve, guts or moxie.

Grit is the bridge between having talent and achieving success. It's about possessing the dogged determination and the relentless drive to pursue your goals despite failure and having the ability to maintain a positive attitude and sense of purpose throughout your journey.

What goes into making someone "gritty" varies by individual, but generally five characteristics are commonly found in those who rate high on the grit scale.

1. Perseverance
2. Passion
3. Resilience
4. Courage
5. Conscientiousness

## Perseverance

The leading characteristic in gritty people is perseverance. It's the willingness to stick with something—no matter how difficult it is and how many times you fail. Gritty people find a way to continue working in pursuit of their goals, even if they have to temporarily give up some personal time to keep momentum going.

Perseverance also requires having a spirit of active optimism. Active optimists aren't willing to wait around until things improve; they're the people who proactively make improvements happen.

## Passion
The key to perseverance lies in intentional practice, guided by a specific purpose and context. Ask yourself a few questions. What is your dream? What motivates you? What takes up your thoughts and energies? If your answer is consistent across these questions, you've identified a true passion—a goal so meaningful to you that it directs and infuses purpose into your efforts. Once you're clear about your passion, grit becomes the driving force that propels you to work tirelessly toward achieving it.

## Resilience
We all know that one person who seems to always recover quickly from difficulties, setbacks or failures. That person is the definition of resilience. Resilience enables you to adapt to and recover from setbacks and failures, turning them into opportunities for learning and growth. Without resilience, setbacks become destructive and cause people to give up on their goals. The more resilient you are, the better you can control the stress, anxiety and disappointment that comes from failure.

## Courage
Being brave enough to take on challenges knowing that you might fail is the essence of courage. To have courage, you must develop the ability to manage your fear of failure—otherwise, you create obstacles to your progress. Courageous people are willing to endure setbacks, failures and obstacles without losing hope or becoming discouraged. Without courage, it's difficult to maintain the level of persistence and determination you need to achieve your goals.

## Conscientiousness

Conscientiousness is the willingness to work tirelessly, remain focused on doing your best work and follow through on tasks. It isn't about achieving perfection; it's about striving for excellence because that feeds your passion. Excellence is forgiving because it allows for disappointment and embraces failure as part of the quest to improve.

## Why Does It Matter?

As workplaces continue to evolve and offer more opportunities to work remotely, employers will be looking for people who are focused, tenacious high achievers. Give yourself the edge by developing your grit.

Hard work means setting goals that are focused on your growth and that require that you stretch yourself to achieve them. It's not a sprint to the finish. It's often a long, slow, deliberate climb. To make progress, you may have to assume tasks or take on projects that don't spark your passion. Don't look at them as a waste of time. Instead, see them as stepping stones to greater challenges and resolve to get as much value out of them as you can.

## Action Steps

If you're wondering if you have any "gritty" tendencies, you can search for "grit scale" online and take a short quiz to rate yourself. The higher your score, the "grittier" you are—but even if you rate low on the grit scale, you're not doomed to stay there. No one is born with a larger amount of grit. Grit has to be developed and you can work on increasing your grit level at any point.

You can develop your grit in a few ways. Maintain a positive attitude throughout setbacks. When negative thoughts creep in, use positive self-talk to turn them into optimistic ideas. Build your sense of self-awareness by reflecting on how you're feeling and why you're feeling that way. Proactively seek out new experiences and new hobbies. When you're challenged or even fail, you'll have a new chance to manage your feelings of anxiety or disappointment without it being tied to your job. It can be a safe way to discover which techniques for bouncing back work best for you.

Grit is the unsung hero of the workplace. Having grit enables you to turn setbacks into comebacks. It helps you power through challenges when others throw in the towel.

# Tackling Everyday Challenges With Gusto

*"The greater the obstacle, the more glory in overcoming it."*
*Molière*

Work is full of challenges, both great and small. Sometimes it's taking on a difficult new project. Other times, it's figuring out what you will order for the team lunch meeting. Whether complex or straightforward, the challenges must be met and overcome.

And that process can be daunting.

Challenges take many forms but the basics of how to persevere and overcome them are applicable to almost any situation.

## Why Does It Matter?

You have a job and, chances are, you do it reasonably well. This likely means you've already faced at least a few job-related challenges and successfully overcome them. It's not your first rodeo, and it won't be your last. Therefore, rather than viewing challenges as potential stumbling blocks, see them as invaluable learning experiences that enrich your professional toolkit. Each new hurdle provides an opportunity to expand your skill set and deepen your reservoir of experience. So, the next time a challenge comes your way, you'll be better equipped to tackle it head-on, drawing from the wealth of experience that you've been steadily accumulating.

## Action Steps

Tackling challenges with gusto comes down to your reaction in the moment. Each situation may look a little different, but the following best practices can help you define how you'd like to respond.

- **Take your time to analyze and define the situation.** Make sure you adequately understand the nature of the challenge. Some challenges can have a lot of extraneous noise that can make them seem more complex than they really are. Lift the hood and have a good look around the engine. What's the problem, *really*?
- **Keep asking questions.** What skills do you need to overcome this challenge? What further information is required? What help do you need and who can provide it?
- **Ask for help if you need it.** Don't be shy about getting the help you need to solve challenges. Even the most accomplished people on the planet aren't experts at everything, and they don't have all the answers. Even interpersonal challenges can benefit from the experience and expertise of other people.
- **Break down your challenges into a series of smaller tasks.** When facing challenges, avoid succumbing to the mental stress that comes with trying to leap tall buildings in a single bound. Slice up your big picture challenge and reframe it as a series of smaller ones that you can tackle one chunk at a time. Now you can attack it *as you can, where you can, when you can*. Overcoming challenges is a multi-step process—so treat it like one.

At the end of the day, conquering challenges builds confidence and allows you to establish a track record of success. And at the end of every challenge lies a treasure trove of experience, equipping you with valuable insights for the next challenge your boss presents to you.

# Controlling Your Emotions at Work

> "Engage your emotions at work. Your instincts and emotions are there to help you."
> *Richard Branson*

There is a widespread tendency to be uncomfortable with emotions at work. We try to deny them, bury them and pretend they play no part in our work lives where we often want to be perceived as stoic and invulnerable.

This is nonsense.

Controlling your emotions isn't about denying or ignoring them. It's about finding ways of using them effectively rather than letting them use you. Your emotions **are** there to help you. You just need to use them in the right way.

The least useful response to your emotions is to try to belittle them or shun them. *"I shouldn't feel this way!"* is a dead end. It's a temporary burial. We all know those emotions are going to come back up again sooner or later. Probably sooner.

## Why Does It Matter?

Screaming at the guy who talked over you in the meeting or the boss who told you that the report you spent days slaving away on isn't good enough may feel good for thirty seconds. Everyone who's let their emotions get the better of them at work knows you'll regret it almost immediately after the words have left your mouth.

Learning to control your emotions makes you a more pleasant and effective colleague. At the most basic level, letting your emotions control you at work is immature and annoying. The teammate everyone avoids is the person who doesn't know how to politely and professionally communicate their feelings with the rest of the group. They're not trusted with responsibilities that might "set them off" if something goes wrong. They're also not picked to lead teams because if they can't take care of themselves, how could they take care of others?

Being in charge of your emotions, and not the other way around, allows your skills to shine through and your feelings—which are fleeting anyway—to take a backseat until it's appropriate to discuss them.

## Action Steps

The secret to controlling your emotions isn't in denying them. It's in responding to them in productive ways. Write that down.

Learning how to control your emotions is easier said than done. It's a delicate balance of self-reflection and authentic communication. First, it comes down to identification. As closely as you can, *identify what you're really feeling* and what's causing you to feel that way. You may have a mix of emotions. Acknowledge all of them.

Once you've identified them, own your emotions. Use emotional language and appeals in responding to the situation. Advertisers do this all the time when trying to sell you something you probably don't need. Employ emotions to make your point and explain how you feel about the situation.

Once you know what you're feeling and why, you're ready to reappraise the situation. Then, let your emotions work for you, thinking of them as an internal guidance system. They can help you when you don't try to fight them.

Try to follow these best practices when faced with difficult situations at work that heighten your emotional threshold.

- **Recognize that emotions are a part of you.** You're not a robot. Human beings have feelings and we react differently in varying situations. There's no right or wrong way to feel; there's simply the way *you* feel.

- **Get a little distance.** Step away, take a few deep breaths, excuse yourself and go to the bathroom. Do whatever it takes to avoid an immediate, unproductive response. However, don't take this action to avoid the emotion. Use it to process the situation and buy some time to respond productively.
- **Broaden your vocabulary.** This helps when thinking and talking about how you're feeling. You may think you're sad, but are you really disappointed or dismayed? Are you angry or are you annoyed or disgusted? Are you embarrassed because you feel guilty or because you're confused?
- **Think about the issue as a challenge rather than a threat.** Concentrate on finding a satisfactory resolution and the steps necessary to make it happen. Reappraising and reframing an emotional situation is a good way of building your resilience to emotional stress. Work will always trigger emotions. Learning to reassess and reappraise helps you now and in the future.

The details of your own emotionally charged situations will vary, of course, but you get the idea. Be polite. Be professional. But be honest. You don't need to hide how you feel.

# Becoming a Conscientious Employee

"Conscientiousness is the quiet power within that drives us to act not out of obligation, but because it's right."
*Anonymous*

What does it mean to be conscientious? Does it mean being a "good employee" all the time or simply consistently choosing to do what is best for the company we work for?

Turns out, it's a bit of both—with a few other important indelible qualities peppered in. Conscientiousness has nothing to do with how smart you are. Instead, it's an indicator of your tendency to be organized, responsible and dependable.

A conscientious employee, then, is a reliable, diligent, and hardworking person—a careful planner who is detail-oriented in their approach to tasks and remains motivated by a strong sense of duty.

## Why Does It Matter?

Research demonstrates time and again that developing this trait is one of the strongest predictors of success in the workplace. Why? Because it's a measure of not only how much you care, but how much effort you'll consistently put into the work you're assigned. More effort often equates to better results on the job, which, in turn results in greater success.

## Action Steps

If you struggle with completing your work on time or you lack motivation because you feel the work you're doing is unimportant, don't fear. You can develop conscientiousness through adopting these six habits.

- **Develop your work ethic.** Conscientious people demonstrate their work ethic through their actions. It's baked into the core of their being to work hard; it's not a skill they remind themselves of or a mantle they dawn each morning. It feels unnatural to *not* work hard. To become more conscientious, you need to find your core motivation to be a disciplined, motivated person who does their work flawlessly. In turn, this helps you build a reputation as a person who takes pride in completing your work and does so always to the best of your ability.
- **Recalibrate your approach to your job.** Becoming more conscientious includes developing a passion for detail-oriented work. When you attach importance to your work, it gives you an incentive to pay attention to the details. As you adopt the mindset that every task, even a small one, is important to do your best on, you'll regard your work with greater importance. Chances are that you'll also double-check your work for accuracy and completeness and take responsibility for mistakes.
- **Get yourself organized.** Conscientious people are efficient because they prioritize being organized and better organization saves time. They care where their work sits on their desk or how important emails are filed in digital folders. If you feel notoriously disorganized, develop a routine for your workday that blocks out time for tasks such as checking email, making phone calls and completing administrative to-dos. Itemize your task list in order of priority and tackle them one at a time. This will help you stay focused, avoid distractions and use every minute to the best of your ability.
- **Be on time and reliable.** Punctuality shows respect for other people's time. A tenant of becoming conscientious is understanding how your actions affect others. Consistently being

on time and delivering on what's expected of you demonstrates reliability. As colleagues begin to see you as a reliable person, you'll develop a reputation as a productive and valued team member.

- **Set clear goals**. Conscientious people are mindful about spending their time wisely. Goals are intimidating—especially lofty ones that don't seem attainable on your worst days. You don't have to crush a goal with a single blow, though. Just like building a house brick by brick, you can tackle any task by breaking it down into smaller, manageable steps. This creates a roadmap for success that curbs feelings of anxiety rather than exacerbating them. While building this road map, identify potential obstacles you might encounter. Once you have your plan, you can allocate your time and may realize a more efficient course of action will get you where you want to go better or faster.

- **Get to know your colleagues**. Becoming a conscientious employee doesn't mean it's all work and no play or that you need to be a stick in the mud around the water cooler. On the contrary; studies show that building friendly relationships with your colleagues both inside and outside of work makes you *more* conscientious on the job. When you respect and care more about the people you work with, you'll have natural motivation to work to support and help them.

If you're feeling like you don't care about your work; as if you don't know why you're doing what you're doing but want additional responsibilities or opportunities to grow, consider how conscientious you are. If you think your conscientiousness could use some work, adopt these habits. Soon, you'll become the conscientious employee that every workplace cherishes.

# Finding Daily Purpose in Your Work

*"Your work is going to fill a large part of your life, and the only way to be truly satisfied is to do what you believe is great work. And the only way to do great work is to love what you do."*
*Steve Jobs*

Do any of the following phrases sound familiar?

- "I feel like I'm just going through the motions."
- "I don't see how my work makes a difference."
- "I'm not motivated to come to work."
- "I feel like my work is meaningless."

If these phrases resonate with you, you are not alone. According to Gallup, two out of three workers report a lack of enthusiasm for their work. Despite the commonality of this feeling, it's important to strive for a greater sense of purpose in your work for the numerous benefits that purpose can bring.

For certain roles, it's obvious how the work ties directly to a greater purpose. Nurses and doctors play an essential role in treating people's illnesses. School teachers bear enormous responsibility for ensuring children receive the education they need. You may think the barista at the local coffee shop simply prepares your morning cup of coffee, but his attitude can help your day start off well. The truth is that no matter what role you play in your organization, there is always a way to connect it to the greater purpose of your company.

## Why Does It Matter?

Your work has the power to bring meaning and purpose to your life. It's not just a means to pay the bills, but an opportunity to make a difference, grow, learn and impact the world in a positive way.

Having a sense of purpose in our work also increases our motivation and engagement, leading to improved performance and productivity. And having a sense of purpose positively impacts our well-being, sense of satisfaction and mental health, while reducing stress and burnout.

## Action Steps

Not all of us can have jobs that make headlines by saving lives or reshaping the world. That's setting the bar just a little too high. The good news is that simple steps can help you discover a deeper sense of purpose in your work, shining a spotlight on the significance of your contributions and why they matter.

- **Connect with your company's overall purpose.** Make an effort to understand your organization's larger societal purpose. Nearly every company has an explicitly stated purpose. Johnson & Johnson's purpose of "Promoting health and well-being for people and the planet" or Unilever's purpose of "Making sustainable living commonplace" or Samsung's purpose of "Empowering people to live better lives through innovative technology solutions" clearly communicate the broader societal purposes these companies are trying to achieve through the everyday actions of their workforces. Reflect on your organization's purpose and connect the dots between it and the specific work you do every day.

- **Develop new skills and take on new challenges**. Regularly ask yourself, *"How am I becoming better each day?"* Take on new responsibilities and develop new skills. Let your manager and colleagues know about your desire to take on new challenges and your willingness to expand your role. Volunteer for interesting projects and tasks. Seek out additional training or development opportunities. This enables you to feel more engaged and invested in your work—which further enhances its evident purpose.
- **Build relationships with colleagues**. Having positive relationships with colleagues can make the workplace a more enjoyable and fulfilling environment for you. Take the time to get to know your colleagues on a personal level. Don't be afraid to share your own experiences and interests with your peers. Be a team player, and offer to help your teammates when they need it. Participate in work-sponsored social activities, such as team-building events or after-work gatherings to build relationships and develop a sense of camaraderie.

Think carefully about the ways in which your specific job makes the world better, and ask yourself how you can lean into that purpose in your day-to-day work. Embrace the challenges and opportunities that each day brings in your quest to fulfill the purpose, and trust that you have the skills and abilities to make a real impact.

Your work is a reflection of who you are and what you stand for, so make it count.

# Being Open to Others' Ideas

> "I like your plan, except it sucks. So let me do the plan and that way, it might be really good."
> *Star Lord to Iron Man in* Avengers: Infinity War

When you work for a living, you're likely required to work with other people. Lone wolves—rugged individualists who walk and work alone—aren't always interested in others' thoughts, opinions or ideas. They're not going to ask how to be more open and accepting.

**Good for them—and good riddance.**

People who don't have an open mind to others are hard to work for and with. It's a fact of the workplace that peers will have ideas they want to share. As their coworker or teammate, you need to listen to, thoroughly consider and evaluate their ideas. This means having an open mind, and that's an invaluable and essential skill to have at work. Being open minded means you're more likely to be adaptable, flexible and creative.

Even if you happen to be an impressively smart, funny, good-looking and hard-working person full of great ideas, that doesn't mean you're perfection incarnate; infallible and incapable of error. Not all your ideas will be great, and others may have better ideas than you.

If it's not natural to you to be immediately open and accepting of other peoples' ideas, don't worry. It's not a natural skill for a lot of people. I'm here to help you learn how to become more open to them.

## Why Does It Matter?

A lot of what we do at work is about solving problems and getting things accomplished. Because time is money, we look for the most efficient avenue—which tends to be the default "we've always done it this way". Believe me when I tell you that this kind of thinking can cripple productivity, stifle creativity and discourage openness to others.

When you choose to be open to new ideas, you can consider different perspectives, values, opinions and beliefs. Furthermore, the open-minded find themselves less prone to biases. They interpret and weigh information without being unduly influenced by their own opinions or expectations. In turn, this helps you learn new ways of solving old problems and making better, more informed decisions.

From a purely practical standpoint, being open also lets you work better with others—especially the ones who subscribe to different schools of thought or who have had different experiences than you. That difference brings diversity of ideas to work. Some of those ideas are going to be great, some just okay and some downright awful. Being open to them means you can combine many ideas with your own to come up with the best possible solution. This is where progress and innovation come from: pooling different ideas together and building on them. It's how you go from being good to being great!

Finally, it's not surprising that most people prefer to work with others who pay attention and take them seriously. If you're committed to becoming a better professional and advancing in your career, it's time to discover if you only consider yourself open-minded or if you really can "walk the walk".

## Action Steps

This is an opportunity to use your newfound conscientiousness to reflect on and test your openness.

1. **Consider a controversial topic you're passionate about**, even though you're aware that others hold differing views.
2. **Make two lists**. One should contain arguments in favor of your viewpoint; the other will argue against it. Remember, you don't have to agree with the arguments—but you do

have to be fair in listing them. Take your time and give it some thought.
3. **Count the arguments in the second list.** Did you have trouble coming up with arguments against your personal view and instead found favoring evidence in support of your beliefs?

If you didn't struggle with this exercise, congratulations! You may be more naturally open-minded than most. If you did struggle to come up with other arguments, you should consider why. Even if you think the other viewpoint is wrong, you need to think about *why* you believe it's wrong. What are its flaws?

Regardless of how you performed on this simple test, everyone can benefit from practicing open mindedness. This starts with making yourself think about things from a different perspective.

Take the example you used to test yourself. How might an eighteen-year-old think about it? What about an eighty-year-old? Would an entry-level employee, regardless of age, think the same as you? What about a veteran or C-Suite executive? How about someone from another country?

The viewpoints are endless, but the main idea is to encourage curiosity and empathy. It's impossible to fully put yourself into others' positions, but with a little imagination, you can understand why they might logically think, feel or act differently than you do.

These are your teammates. You need to take them seriously. Sometimes it serves everyone's best interest to hold your tongue, listen to each other, think and then build cooperatively.

# Collaborating With Others for Success

*"Talent wins games, but teamwork and intelligence
win championships."*
*Michael Jordan*

Collaborating well with others leads to improved problem-solving, increased productivity and greater team interconnectedness. That means that a person who is collaborative is *team* focused, not *silo* focused.

People who work in silos are hesitant to share information while collaborators share it freely and willingly. Collaborators think in terms of "we" rather than "I", and they focus on the group's goals rather than their own personal agendas. They lend their expertise and pitch in without being asked. Collaborative team members seek to understand an issue, asking questions and digging deeply into problems to get to root causes.

Great collaborators also open themselves up to build closer relationships. They earn and maintain the trust of their team, freely admitting what they don't know. In the same vein, they respect alternative views—a callback to the open mindedness we discussed in the previous chapter.

They build trust consistently through their actions and model the behavior they want others to follow. No matter whose success a victory was, they share the spotlight, give credit to others and celebrate as a team. Good collaborators take commitments seriously and hold themselves and others accountable.

Conflict is inevitable in a team setting, but collaborators have the diplomacy skills to manage and quell issues. They look for opportunities to compromise and work toward solutions that consider the views of teammates. And collaborators get involved. They come to their teammates prepared with their questions and ideas. They're problem-solvers, not problem-makers.

The skills involved in successful *teamwork* are important to successful *collaboration*. The characteristics you must embody as a good collaborator include:

- ✓ Helpful
- ✓ Curious
- ✓ Willing to share information
- ✓ A good listener
- ✓ Trustworthy
- ✓ Reliable
- ✓ Humble
- ✓ Respectful
- ✓ Diplomatic

## Why Does It Matter?

Today's workplace requires fluidity and flexibility. To compete and succeed, you must be able to collaborate in a variety of settings, often with very little ramp-up time.

Organizations look for employees with the skills to jump into a new team and quickly become a productive team member. This is the concept of rapid *teaming*, which helps organizations respond to opportunities, challenges and to innovate.

When a temporary, short-term collaborative group forms, its members must work effectively together—often without knowing one another. Having collaboration skills enables you to focus on both the relationships between team members and the dynamics within short-term groups.

## Action Steps

Achieving successful collaboration isn't easy. First, you need to identify your own approach to work and understand the working styles of fellow team members. There are four working styles based on how people commonly interact:

- **Innovators**, who cherish potential. They take risks and enjoy igniting their team members with energy and imagination. Individuals with this work style tend to make quick, spontaneous decisions and embrace risk.
- **Custodians**, who appreciate stability, order and predictability. They're practical, detail-oriented and avoid risk. Guardians are careful and think deeply about everything. They don't make snap decisions and are slower to adopt new things.
- **Achievers**, who thrive on challenges. They thrive on results, are goal-oriented and enthusiastically take on problems.
- **Harmonizers**, who prefer unity, agreement and consensus. They are empathetic and glue a team together.

Understanding the workstyles of your teammates allows you to make accommodations with those team members who have a different style. This is known as *flexing* or recognizing what you need to do to be a successful collaborator.

Flexing is the ability to navigate between different working styles. It allows you to relate, respect and value what other members bring to the team.

Once you clearly identify your preferred work style, the types of working styles your team members have and how those dynamics can work together, you're able to make decisions and interact with each other at a peak collaboration level.

# Being a Good Team Player

"If you're playing a solo game you'll always lose out to a team."
*Reid Hoffman*

What is a business but a large, professional team? We've already talked about working on ourselves to become better teammates in several capacities, so here's the most important one: simply choosing to be happy on a team.

## Why Does It Matter?

Most people in business work with others on teams to achieve the organization's goals. Learning how to be a good teammate will go a long way toward ensuring professional success. Think about your own preferences. Do you like working with someone who seems bored or uninterested in working with you?

No.

Conscientiousness, open-mindedness and collaboration create the perfect team player—you! There are specific practices you can adopt in order to ensure you're being the best team player you can be.

## Action Steps

Here are nine tips for how to be a good team player in the workplace.

1. **Understand your team's mission**. Outstanding teams start with a clearly-defined mission statement that all team members resonate with and know how to accomplish. Decisions and plans should always relate back to it.
2. **Deliver on your responsibilities and meet deadlines**. Your teammates depend on you, just as you rely on them. Follow

team processes to fulfill your individual objectives in support of the team's overall work. Continue to hold yourself accountable.
3. **Resolve team conflicts in the open**. If you have a disagreement with a team member, work to bring it out into the open so it can be resolved quickly. Don't let conflict stew and resentment build. Work with others or a mediator to diffuse it calmly.
4. **Freely share information with your teammates**. There is no place on a team for secrecy and/or information hoarding. Make sure that you remain transparent and honest, which encourages respect and an open highway of information.
5. **Focus on solutions**. It's easy to point out problems but good teammates focus on solutions. If you have made a mistake, accept responsibility and work on a corrective action plan.
6. **Prioritize the team's goals**. Avoid getting into battles over turf or who gets the most credit for work completed or whose skillset is best suited to a certain task. Work together with your amalgamation of strengths and weaknesses to produce the best results.
7. **Celebrate successes** when they happen, and urge yourself and your team to learn from failures.
8. **Demonstrate loyalty**. Similar to sharing information and prioritizing goals, look out for your fellow team members' best interests rather than step on them to achieve personal gain.
9. **Encourage and empower your teammates**. When everyone does their best work, the team gets closer to accomplishing their goal. Help them whenever you can by using your strengths, talents and capabilities to propel everyone—not just yourself—forward.

Being a standout team player isn't just nice. It's a necessity. In today's collaborative world, your ability to mesh and synergize with teammates is the secret ingredient for workplace success.

# Becoming a Proactive Networker

"Your network is your net worth."
*Porter Gale*

Your ability to get things done at work is tightly associated with your network. While for some people the word networking has negative or even manipulative connotations, having a robust network of relationships is one of the best tools you can possess. Think of networking as relationship building, talking with people, getting to know the people in your organization better and learning about the work of other departments and functions.

## Why Does It Matter?

According to numerous career surveys, 85 percent of jobs are filled through networking. Networking is all about maximizing the people in your corner to propel you in your career—and vice versa. It can help you secure a promotion, clinch a coveted assignment, switch companies or industries more easily or find out about a class or program to learn a new skill.

The benefits of a robust network are boundless, provided you nurture that network through mutually beneficial and harmonious relationships.

## Action Steps

Activating your current network and expanding it are easier than you might think. These thirteen tips will help you to become a more proactive networker.

1. Go out to lunch or for coffee with different people on a regular basis.

2. When you meet with someone, make the effort to get to know the other person as an individual, not just as a helpful professional resource.
3. Keep a network log. Record your contact's name, communication preferences and any personal information that will jog your memory about your personal connection with him.
4. If confidential information is shared with you, **keep it confidential**. People in your network need to be able to trust you.
5. Listen carefully and show consideration for any advice you receive. Even if you don't plan to follow the advice, showing gratitude is a sign of respect.
6. Cast a wide net. Join all relevant associations, trade groups, professional societies and other organizations to expand your network beyond your company.
7. Volunteer for committees, project teams or formal information groups that give you access to people outside of your department, functional area or division.
8. Don't let too much time lapse between discussions. Keep in touch with people periodically. If you lose touch, you should reconnect with your most valuable contacts.
9. Walk a fine line of present and proactive, but don't pester people!
10. Avoid making assumptions about who can or can't help your cause. You won't know unless you find out, so make the effort because you never know . . .
11. Make networking a weekly habit. Set numerical goals such as establishing one new contact outside your company per week, two networking lunches a month or one coffee meet-up per week and then hold yourself accountable for achieving those goals.

12. Don't make networking one-sided. If you treat your network as a cache of people you can use for your own gain, your contacts will see through your behavior and be less committed to your success. Networking needs to be a two-way street. When the opportunity presents itself, you should also offer information and support and help to those in your network.
13. Don't underestimate the power of the "weak" network. Not all networks need to be filled with executives or senior decision makers. Someone who may not be in a direct position to help you may have a lot of influence with someone who can.

It might sound cliché but your network *really is* your net worth. Invest in it. And keep it strong.

## Section 2

# Amplifying Your Game

Ready to amplify your game? Let's unpack the next set of competencies needed to elevate your professional success. Each of the eleven chapters in this section reveals a facet of what it takes to truly shine at work.

When examining attributes such as learning from failure and owning your mistakes, self-awareness and accountability are paramount. These traits exemplify your ability to acknowledge shortcomings, take corrective action and emerge stronger. Handling disappointing news with grace showcases your ability to manage work situations without letting emotions cloud your judgment or reactions.

Professionalism is exhibited through getting to the root of a problem and making sound decisions. These attributes underscore the significance of problem-solving and critical thinking in the modern workplace. Responding to questions in a thoughtful manner, speaking up in meetings and owning the details all highlight the importance of effective communication and attention to detail. They showcase the value of contributing actively in team environments and ensuring the integrity of your work through meticulous oversight.

Lastly, taking initiative and demonstrating charisma are integral to being a leader. Initiative signals proactive thinking, a drive to move forward without always waiting for others to tell you what to do. Charisma is about influencing and inspiring those around you, establishing connections and demonstrating confidence and empathy. These qualities contribute to a well-rounded person, equipped to navigate the complexities of professional environments with skill and grace.

Got it? Let's roll.

# How To Face Uncertainty at Work

*"Nothing in life is sure."*
Mrs. Patmore in Downton Abbey

Most humans are wired from birth to fear the unknown. Will you be laid off? Will your project succeed? Will you get a new manager? Will you be transferred overseas? The list goes on. Even though uncertainty is a constant in the modern workplace it remains an anxiety-inducing, draining and paralyzing part of the professional world.

While you may not like uncertainty, it does offer benefits. Uncertainty may blur your perception of reality, but it can also bring clarity to the truth. It can magnify your worries, while highlighting what truly holds significance. Uncertainty also has a way of revealing what truly matters to you and what you are capable of. It pushes you to take stock of all the positive things while giving you permission to let go of petty and irrelevant things.

Because you're guaranteed to face at least some degree of uncertainty at work, it's important to learn how to embrace it and thrive despite it.

## Why Does It Matter?

The ability to adapt to changing circumstances and uncertainty is a valuable skill in today's work environment. New opportunities and possibilities are only accessible through the path of the unfamiliar and uncertain. To unlock your potential, you must be willing to step outside of your comfort zones and embrace the unknown, opening yourself to new experiences and perspectives. To succeed despite uncertainty, you need to take control of your fears and become proactive in your approach.

## Action Steps

Here are four pieces of advice to help you deal with uncertainty at work.

*Make a move*
Taking action is an important step when facing uncertainty. Each step you take allows you to learn from the experience and adjust your approach. Making a move can mean collecting additional data, talking to a colleague, learning a skill or updating your resume. If you are uncertain if your company will be acquired and how that might affect your job, you can stay up-to-date with industry news, trends and developments at your company. If you fear your workload will increase because a colleague just resigned, you can establish a better system for keeping track of your tasks, deadlines and priorities.

*Ground yourself in the present*
Focusing too much on potential outcomes can lead to rumination and a detrimental spiral of anxiety. Instead of getting caught up in *hypotheticals*, focus on what you are doing *now* to reduce the uncertainty. No one can predict the future—so obsessing about what-ifs isn't productive.

*Reduce uncertainty elsewhere*
Establish routines in your personal life to regain some control. When you establish a sense of stability in your personal life, it can increase your ability to handle uncertain situations in your work life. By creating a sense of control in one area, you may feel better equipped to deal with ambiguity and unpredictability in other areas.

*Ask yourself two questions*
When you are faced with uncertainty ask yourself *"Will everything in my life be impacted by this if it doesn't go my way?"* and *"How can I*

*contribute to a better outcome drawing on my previous successes in navigating uncertainty?"*

Chances are you have a lot to be grateful for regardless of how things turn out. You can get through great uncertainty by holding on tightly to what really matters. Then, reflect on your past experiences of dealing with uncertain situations and consider how your skills and expertise might be applied to improve the current situation, even if it's just by a small margin.

Now ask yourself, What did you do? What lessons can you apply to this situation?

Uncertainty isn't going away, but your attitude toward it can improve significantly—which will shrink the anxiety that uncertainty can induce in your life.

An uncertain situation can be an external shock to your system. However, it is possible to live in a manner that enables you to embrace unforeseeable circumstances as they arise, advance toward the future and establish new possibilities for yourself.

Rather than being held back by uncertainty, embrace it as a chance to take risks and seize opportunities that might otherwise be unavailable. In doing so, you'll gain the confidence needed to move forward with purpose and achieve your goals. Remember that uncertainty offers a gateway to possibility and growth.

# How To Handle Disappointing News With Grace

"Expect disappointment and you'll never be disappointed."
MJ Jones-Watson

Sometimes it can feel like disaster and disappointment are always on the horizon, tainting even good moments with an undercurrent of dread. Why should work be any different?

- *"The fourth quarter numbers were lower than projected. We may be looking at layoffs."*
- *"We're sorry, but we're freezing wages for the foreseeable future. No raise for you."*
- *"That promotion you wanted? We've decided to go in a different direction."*
- *"Your performance has been poor. We may have to look at other options moving forward."*

Your job is probably not all doom and gloom. Work can be satisfying and even fulfilling. We take pride in work well done. We have work friends. We get a paycheck. But even those with the most charmed work lives are going to face the hardship of disappointment and bad news now and again. And no matter how much you prepare or anticipate it, it hits hard and it's tough to get through. But you *can* get through it.

## Why Does It Matter?

Disappointments at work come in all shapes and sizes. Some will simply annoy you. Some might change the course of your life. Whatever the case, how you deal with disappointment on the job has the potential to make you a better employee and a stronger person.

Of course, some bad news is devastating—you can't do much about getting laid off. However, you can take positive action. Update your résumé. Reach out to your friends and coworkers. Let your network know you're looking for a new (and hopefully better) job. Write that killer cover letter. Layoffs are not an indication you're a failure. It may sound hollow, but something better might be out there waiting for you.

Dealing effectively with disappointing news by taking action enables you to maintain your composure, reassess your approach and pivot strategically, transforming disappointing news into an opportunity for growth and learning.

## Action Steps

First, take time to step back, reflect, and consider your options. It can be *hard* to hear bad news, and chances are you're going to be either really sad or really mad. While you might be able to explode into tears or expletives at home, you have to avoid doing that at work.

Talk over the situation with someone you trust and make sure you understand all aspects of the news and its impact. How does it fully affect you? Is your job at risk or just your pride? How important is it to you? Is it worth making a fuss about it? Will making a fuss have the potential to do you any good? What are your options?

Second, unless you've decided to live with disappointment, talk to your boss. Explain that you're disappointed and why. You don't have to share all of what you're feeling but do show your boss that you care about the job and your work.

It's not going to be an easy conversation. You'll need to stay in total control of yourself while also being willing to advocate for yourself. If your boss can't or won't do anything about it, it's up to you to decide how you'll act beyond that conversation. Transparency is important, though, so it's good to let him know your feelings and how those feelings affect your attitude about your job moving forward.

Third, use it as a learning opportunity. Part of your earlier reflection is recognizing your own role in the disappointment. Maybe there really was nothing you could have done that would change things. You don't control anything but your *own* work—and if the company is struggling to stay afloat, it's hardly your fault.

But if you didn't get that promotion or work assignment you wanted, look at why. What did your boss say about it? Ask them what you can do to get that raise next time. Then decide if you're willing to do it.

Finally, reevaluate your work situation and take positive action. Some jobs really are a dead-end. Maybe you need to take steps to move on to another one. On the other hand, maybe the disappointment is something you can ultimately live with. If that's the case, then don't dwell on it, accept it and move on. Every job has its fair share of frustrations. Sometimes the best way to handle it is to simply put it behind you.

Recognize that disappointments on the job are a fact of life. By following these simple steps—taking a moment to assess the situation, seeking constructive feedback, engaging in self-reflection and devising an action plan—you can move past them and turn setbacks into stepping stones.

# How To Learn From Failure at Work

> "I am very lucky if I get through a day without something I did wrong, something I said wrong, gestured wrong. You talk of a lifetime? Good God. Practically everything."
> *William S. Burroughs, on mistakes and regrets*

Your presentation crashed and burned. Your inventory forecast resulted in stock-outs. Your report contained numerical errors. You lost the largest account.

Yes, it's disappointing. Of course it's frustrating. No one would judge you for feeling like an idiot. Welcome to the human race. More accurately, welcome to the world of work.

Mistakes and failures are regular occurrences. Everybody makes them, even those annoying coworkers who deny it. We all fail once in a while. The secret is to *learn* from failure so we fail a little less often. Here's how to start that learning process.

## Why Does It Matter?

Mistakes don't happen in a vacuum. They happen within the flow of how you approach and do your job. Is there something in the way you go about your work that might make you susceptible to more than your fair share of failure? If so, you need to know about it.

Failure isn't just an unfortunate outcome; it's a rich educational experience that provides invaluable insights into your capabilities and the effectiveness of your approaches. By dissecting your failures, you uncover not only what went wrong but how you can correct your mistakes. This iterative process sharpens your problem-solving skills and enhances your ability to adapt. In the modern workplace which prizes innovation and agility, learning from failure isn't just beneficial—it's essential.

Here's how to learn from failure.

## Action Steps

Figure out what happened and why. This means reflecting. Ask yourself the tough questions. It can be painful, but it's necessary.

- Were you not paying enough attention?
- Did you try to work too quickly and cut corners?
- Did you trust someone you shouldn't have?
- Do you lack the skills or knowledge to do the job properly?
- Do you need more training or information?
- Did you take a calculated risk that didn't pay off?
- Did you misjudge a process?
- Did you delegate to someone you thought was experienced?
- Did you seem to do everything right, but still something went wrong?
- Was it one step that went wrong or the entire situation?

Unless the cause of your failure is unambiguous, you may not fully understand what went wrong. Ask for feedback from your boss, teammates and coworkers. Get their ideas and input. Let them share their perspectives on what went wrong. They, too, will have stories of failure and what they learned.

Once you know what and why, look for patterns in your work that might indicate a blind spot or tendency to fall into the same types of mistakes.

- Do you rush through your work late in the day?
- Are you inattentive in the morning?
- Do you jump to conclusions without gathering all the facts?
- Do you ignore a coworker's ideas because you think he's against you?
- Are you so focused on trying to please the boss that you don't push back when a task is too complex?

Here's the obvious lesson: don't do the same thing again. To err is human, they say. But that doesn't excuse making the same mistakes over and over.

This is the practical definition of learning from failure: Not repeating the failure.

It doesn't mean not taking risks again. It doesn't mean not stretching yourself or trying to improve your skills. It doesn't mean crawling back to your cubicle or hiding under your desk. It *does* mean paying attention so you don't fall into the same behaviors and thought patterns that created *this* failure.

Don't be too hard on yourself as you go through these action steps. For example, it only takes one code error in a database to create an issue. But it takes countless correct steps to build the database in the first place. The error in the database might have resulted in a customer complaint, but *you* created a powerful database. Don't forget the good parts. Give yourself credit for your successes and what went according to plan. And then do your best not to make that same error again next time by putting additional quality control measures in place.

Failure is the greatest teacher you'll ever have, providing the lessons necessary to grow, improve and achieve greater success. Learn to embrace failure as the teacher that it is.

# How To Own Your Mistakes at Work

"One of the basic rules of the universe is that nothing is perfect. Perfection simply doesn't exist.... Without imperfection, neither you nor I would exist."
*Stephen Hawking*

Everyone makes mistakes. This is ground zero for being human. It's natural that you may experience self-doubt and some hesitation after making a mistake, especially a significant one. But you should also recognize that by working through the consequences of your error, you've learned and grown. You'll never be perfect, but if you're paying attention, you won't make the same mistake again.

## Why Does It Matter?

What makes professionals more or less proficient than others in the same field is in how they handle their mistakes. A lot of people like to pretend they don't make mistakes. They ignore them, deny them or blame others. Some people acknowledge mistakes, but come up with excuses and rationalizations for having made them. Then there are the martyrs; the people who go out of their way to blame themselves endlessly for every little miscue. *"Blame me,"* they say sorrowfully, *"I'm just awful."* They try to make *you* feel sorry for their mistakes.

Organizations aren't in the business of hiring these types for their workforce. They want someone who tries their best to not make a mistake but when it does happen, they accept responsibility and move on.

## Action Steps

You want to be able to own your mistakes and then move past them. Here's a handy checklist of how you can.

**Avoid freaking out**. Even if you realize that everyone makes mistakes, you still may overreact to making your own. Step back and give yourself space to process your emotions. It's okay to think you're an idiot as long as you banish the thought. You are *not* an idiot. Brooding and dwelling on how badly you messed up is counterproductive and risks taking ill-considered actions that could worsen the situation. You made a mistake. You wish you hadn't. Fine. Now what?

**Admit the error**. This is the part where it's easy to deflect the blame or spin an elaborate excuse. Don't do those things. Be calm, straightforward, honest and humble. You messed up and now you have to admit it. An apology would be nice too.

If the mistake makes your coworkers mad, hurt or frustrated, sit calmly and let them be mad, hurt and frustrated. Let them vent. Don't be defensive. Don't yell back. Use your active listening skills. Remember, it's your mistake and you're owning it.

**Take action to make it right**. Offer a practical way to correct or minimize the mistake and its effects on those involved. If a redo will fix it, then redo it as soon as possible. If it created more work for others, then help shoulder that load. If the mistake created a complex problem, then you need to take the time and effort to formulate a plan for fixing it.

**Take a long look at why the mistake happened and plan so it won't happen again**. Using self-reflection, consider how and why the mistake happened. Were you not paying proper attention? Were you in a rush to meet a deadline? Was it a judgment error? Was the task beyond your skill set?

Feedback helps here. Talk with your boss and your coworkers. Your mistake may be a common one; something others have made or dealt with before. Making mistakes is understandable, but making the same mistakes over and over isn't.

**Let it go and move on**. You have to get past your mistake. If you've taken the other steps, acknowledged and apologized for the mistake, worked to make it right and taken action to make sure it doesn't happen again, then you're done with it. You need to make peace with yourself and your self-confidence.

No matter who is looking in the mirror, they're seeing someone who makes mistakes. And the world won't end if you mess up—even if it feels like it might. Try to remind yourself that it is not the stumble but rather the rebound that defines your journey.

# How To Get to the Root of a Problem

> "We cannot solve our problems with the same level of thinking that created them."
> *Albert Einstein*

We all have to solve problems at work. Most of us have daily problems to solve. So how do you begin solving a problem?

Even if you think something can be fixed quickly and easily, always take the time to examine the issue to check for its root cause. If you want to get at the root cause of a problem it all comes down to asking the right questions. Using the Five Whys analysis can help you get to the root cause of any problem.

To do a Five Whys analysis ask the question *"Why?"* at least five times. Repeatedly asking "why" lets you drill down far enough to get to the root cause of a problem so that you can decide what you should do about it.

Don't be afraid to be curious when asking why questions. It may take five questions to get at the root, but it could take as many as fifteen or as few as three. Overall, be open and willing to explore all possibilities to avoid applying a quick fix to an issue that might just crop up again unless you've addressed it at its root.

## Why Does It Matter?

Problems crop up everywhere in the workplace. Often people immediately try to fix problems without taking the time to dig a little deeper. There's nothing wrong with wanting to solve a problem right away, but without getting to the root cause of the problem—the *real* source—the problem will likely recur.

Learning how to get to the root cause of a problem is *key* to being an effective problem solver in the workplace. And *everyone* appreciates a problem solver.

## Action Steps

If you're not a natural problem solver, don't worry. By following these action steps, you can get better at it.

Involve all relevant stakeholders when you engage in the "Five Whys" questioning process. A stakeholder is any individual who is affected by the problem. When you ask for stakeholders' input, you acknowledge the importance of their roles, ideas, opinions and contributions. It also allows you to see the big picture—the whole problem—not just what you can see from your own perspective.

Probe the problem further with stakeholders by asking questions about what is and isn't working:

- *"What's going wrong?"*
- *"What's your biggest headache?"*
- *"If you were to start over, what would you change?"*
- *"What would things look like in a perfect world?"*

Even if ideas seem unrealistic at first, you may find that quite a few of them can be implemented later. Always ask, *"What else?"*

When listening, show people that you genuinely understand where they're coming from and that you respect their opinions. Say things such as, *"I can see how you'd feel that way."* Validate the other person's view and encourage them to be honest and open with their input. Reward their honesty and make sure they understand that the goal is to get to the root of the problem, *not* to place blame.

Once you've gathered the relevant information from stakeholders it can be helpful to lay out what you've learned in a visual diagram. For example, you can create a fishbone diagram. Fishbone diagrams can help you take a systemic look at the effects of a problem and then sort contributing factors into helpful categories.

Place the problem at the head of the diagram. Then draw a horizontal line stretching to the left from the head. This is the spine of your effect-cause analysis, and it connects the causes you identify. Categories of causes you've identified sit on vertical lines extending from the backbone and specific causes extend from those vertical lines. (See the diagram below.)

Once you have a completed diagram, you should clearly see which categories of causes contribute the most to the problem. The fishbone diagram allows you to consider all the possibilities. This way, you'll be more likely to uncover the right solution. Problems are opportunities with thorns on them so approach them with care but don't shy away from grasping them to uncover the value hidden within.

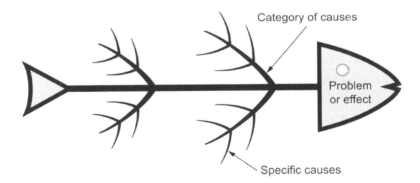

# How To Make Sound Decisions at Work

"The most difficult thing is your decision to act."
*Amelia Earhart*

All of us are expected to make decisions every day in the workplace. There are different categories of decisions and some decisions are more consequential than others. Strategic decisions deal with broad, long-term goals and are likely to have long-term consequences for the company. Tactical decisions deal with short to medium-term goals. They may involve budget, people, allocation of resources or schedules. Operational decisions deal with day-to-day systems and procedures. They tend to be more routine and pre-programmed to support tactical decisions. The outcomes of operational decisions are mostly short-term, with lower risks.

Regardless of the nature of the decision you need to make, whether strategic, tactical or operational, it's important to follow a sound process when making it.

## Why Does It Matter?

A good decision-making process can help you make more effective and well-informed decisions. By honing a well-structured approach to decision-making early in your career, you not only enhance your own capability to navigate complex situations at work but also establish yourself as an invaluable asset to any team you join.

The ability to make consistently sound decisions comes with practice and a systematic approach. Don't know how to go about it? What follows is a handy step-by-step guide so you can learn how to make sound decisions regardless of the nature of the decision.

## Action Steps

Here are seven steps you can follow to make sure your decision-making process is sound.

1. **Define the desired outcome of your decision.** Rather than getting stuck in the details, step back and carefully consider and openly state the desired outcome of the decision.
2. **Acquire the necessary information.** Collect all the *relevant* information you need to make a decision, and analyze it carefully to understand the options and their potential consequences. Be sure to seek input from others who may have different perspectives or expertise on the issue. Getting a second, third or fourth opinion can be very informative.
3. **Put on the six thinking hats*.** Take turns "wearing" each of the six hats and consider the decision from every perspective. This can help you gather a more complete and well-rounded understanding of the issue.
4. **Consider the alternatives.** Once you have listed a few possible solutions, you should evaluate each solution's positive and negative consequences in a structured fashion.
5. **Match each alternative with your goal.** Ensure that your decision-making process has short-term goals which are aligned with the company's long-term goals.
6. **Finalize and implement your decision.** After you have ensured that you have the necessary evidence and support for your decision, make sure that everyone involved is informed. Remember to clearly explain everything to your team. This includes the reasons behind your decision, its expected benefits and possible inconvenience or adjustments that may be necessary.
7. **Review the outcome of your decision.** Put your decision into action and monitor the results to ensure that it is effective and meets your goals.

During **Step 5**, it may be useful to construct a decision tree. To create a decision tree list all potential options and the outcomes of each option. These outcomes can be represented by branches on the tree. If you can, try to estimate the probability of occurrence for each outcome, and then (if you can) assign a value to each outcome to help you weigh the potential benefits and costs. Then you can calculate the expected value as illustrated below. This can help you to make more informed and strategic decisions by examining how each branch of the decision tree stacks up against your goals.

Consider this simplified example. Let's say you need to make a decision about whether to launch a new product. The goal of the product launch is to generate more profit for the company.

## Decision Branch 1: Launch Product

- **Probability** of Success: 70 percent or 0.70
    - Expected **Outcome**: $100,000 profit
- **Probability** of Failure: 30 percent or 0.30
    - Expected **Outcome**: $20,000 loss

## Decision Branch 2: Don't Launch Product

- Expected **Outcome**: $0 (no profit, no loss)

Expected value = (Probability of Success * Expected Profit from Success) + (Probability of Failure * Expected Loss from Failure)

So, in our example above, we can calculate the expected value of launching the product:

= (0.70 * $100,000) + (0.30 * -$20,000) which equals $64,000

Comparing it to the goal, the company is clearly better off making a profit of $64,000 than $0. We should make the decision to launch the product.

Finally, keep an open mind and be willing to revisit your decision if and when new information becomes available or if circumstances change.

By following these action steps when you face a decision at work you can turn challenges into triumphs that elevate both you and your team.

## *The Six Thinking Hats

The six thinking hats technique uses different points of view to consider a decision from multiple perspectives. This helps the decider gain a more holistic and well-rounded understanding of the issue to make better-informed decisions.

- **The white hat** represents the need for information and objective analysis. When wearing the white hat, you focus on gathering and analyzing data and consider the facts and figures relevant to the decision.
- **The red hat** represents emotions and intuition. When wearing the red hat, you allow yourself to think creatively and consider your gut feelings about the issue.
- **The black hat** represents caution and critical thinking. When wearing the black hat, you look for problems, risks and potential drawbacks to the options under consideration.
- **The yellow hat** represents optimism and positive thinking. When wearing the yellow hat, you look for the benefits of the options under consideration.
- **The green hat** represents creativity and innovation. When wearing the green hat, you allow yourself to think outside the box and consider new and unconventional approaches.

- **The blue hat** represents process control and organization. When wearing the blue hat, you consider how to best structure and manage your decision-making process.

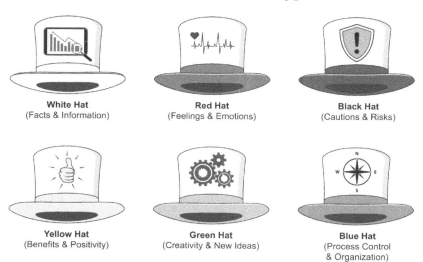

# How To Take Initiative at Work

"This is the space age, and we are here to go."
*William S. Burroughs*

Maybe you're young and in a hurry. Maybe you're stagnating. Maybe you're bored. Maybe you're stuck in a dead-end job. Maybe your boss doesn't care. Or maybe you're stuck in *their* rut, and they see you as something they've already defined; a suitable peg in the right hole. And they're happy to let you stay there.

Your job and your career don't have to depend on your boss. Grab the reins, mix your own metaphors and take matters into your own hands.

Show some initiative. Figure out what *you* really want!

What's your goal? Do you want a new, different and better job? Do you want to build your skillset for your current job? Are you looking for new challenges? Are you building a career or just bored with what you're currently doing?

## Why Does It Matter?

Nobody gets anywhere by standing still . . . which is fine for those who are satisfied with where they are and what they're doing. If you're not, you have the power to do something about it. Just don't do it rashly and without thinking carefully about where you want to go.

Initiative means taking responsibility for your own growth and development. It means *you* get to define **you**.

The changes you want to make, and the things you want to take on will affect others. When you take initiative, consider how your actions will affect the rest of the team. Are you thinking of something that you'd really like to do and will make you look good, but will make others' lives more difficult? Does your proposed idea or project align with the company's goals and strategies?

## Action Steps

How you ask for more work or responsibility and what you specifically ask for depends on *why* you're asking. Nobody's path is a straight line, but as you consider taking on more tasks, you should have some purpose in mind, even if it's short-term.

When deciding to take initiative, keep the following in mind:

- Taking initiative, being proactive, means possible rewards *and* potential risks. Without complete information or experience, you might initiate an action that is not well-received or effective. Maybe you misread a situation, misunderstood a problem or underestimated challenges. Just know that there are risks. There is also the risk that taking initiative on a new project or task might divert attention from other essential responsibilities, leading to potential neglect or mishandling of those tasks.
- You may bite off more than you can chew. Without proper time management you may find yourself stressed, overburdened and overworked. By taking initiative in a particular situation, you might inadvertently set a precedent for future expectations. Others might come to expect similar actions or results every time a similar situation arises.
- You can fuel resentment and jealousy in colleagues who think you're trying to show them up or trying to be the boss's pet.

Unless you're already in a position to approve your own projects and assignments, you must convince whoever delegates tasks to you that giving you more responsibility is good for the team and the company. Tell them how and why it's in *their* interest, too.

Once you get the go ahead, follow through and give it your best effort. The adage *"half-hearted efforts yield no results"* is a universal truth that applies here.

Only by taking whole-hearted actions can we hope to see meaningful progress and growth. If it's worth doing, commit to it. You might fail. That's always a risk. But if you do, make sure you fail having applied your best effort. Failure is only complete if you don't learn anything from it.

The flip side of taking initiative is also knowing when *not* to take initiative. Stepping up is great, but some things really are above your pay grade. Some things will be seen as overstepping your role which can cause tension with your boss. Others you may not have the right skill set to handle. And there will be certain tasks where you simply don't have the altitude to see the whole picture. Make sure that any initiative you take on is well-suited to your skillset and the situation.

Taking initiative at work demonstrates proactivity and a willingness to go above and beyond your assigned tasks. When you take initiative, you also show potential for leadership roles within the organization.

# How To Respond to Questions at Work

*"Every answer begins with a question."*
*T.A. Uner*

How did you get that number? What is the competitive response likely to be? What are the risks of changing the process? Why does the new software you're recommending cost so much?

Some people find it frustrating or annoying to be asked questions at work because they feel as if they are being interrupted. Or, they may find it difficult to answer certain questions because they do not have the necessary information or knowledge to respond. Perhaps they feel certain questions are beneath them.

Other people may feel as if they are being put on the spot or judged based on their answers to questions. These factors can contribute to a feeling of dislike, fear or resentment of being asked questions at work.

You may not always like being asked questions, but how you respond, especially to difficult ones, is important.

## Why Does It Matter?

Asking and answering questions is a means of gathering information. It also stimulates thought and creativity. You will be approached with questions at work on a regular basis. Listening carefully and attentively is always the most important action you can take. Similarly, answering questions can help you share your expertise. You contribute to the success of your team or organization when you increase others' knowledge.

Additionally, answering questions thoughtfully demonstrates your competence and confidence and helps you build trust and credibility with others.

## Action Steps

By following four principles you can navigate the interactions with someone who asks you a question at work.

*Make sure you understand the question you are being asked.*
The question you are asked always deserves your complete attention because you want to give an appropriate and comprehensive answer. If you don't understand the question, asking for clarification helps both parties—you get the information you need, and they realize how they can communicate better.

Think about the question and try to understand it *fully* before responding. Consider rewording it and asking it back by saying something such as, *"What you're asking is…"* or *"Based on my understanding, you want to know…"*

*Respond in a way that matches the nature of the question being asked.*
Your answer should match the nature of the question. General questions relate to the big picture, global issues so you should answer them in equally all-encompassing terms. Specific questions are focused and analytical that need detailed, data-driven answers.

By paying attention to words, tone and body language, you can better understand the emotional context and provide a more appropriate response. Phrases such as, *"I hear what you're saying…"* or *"I see your point of view…"* show not only appreciation for the question but for the requestor's act of coming to you for an answer. Always be respectful and professional in your response.

*Understand intent.*
You may have the answer to the question—but it may be prudent to not give immediately it. This happens a lot with interpersonal questions. You might say, *"Why do you ask?"* or *"Can you tell me more about why you are asking?"* Avoid being confrontational or aggressive in how you ask follow-up questions so you can detect the need that lies beneath the question.

*It's okay to say, "I don't know."*
In a genuine desire to appear helpful and in control, people tend to feel compelled to answer any question they are asked—even if they don't have the answer. It is important to be honest and direct if you don't know an answer. After all, you don't want to provide an answer that is incorrect. Still, try to provide as much information as possible to help the person who is asking the question. You may be able to provide access to resources, such as research or data or you could suggest someone else who might know the answer.

If it's your boss asking you the question, keep your answer as honest and helpful as possible. You can absolutely respond with *"Let me get back to you about that"* or *"I need to do some research before I can answer your question."* That way, he knows he'll get an answer, you'll build your credibility and you'll have the opportunity to learn something new.

# How To Speak Up in Meetings

*"Speak up. Believe in yourself. Take risks."*
*Sheryl Sandberg*

Early on in my career a mentor told me, *"If you aren't speaking up in meetings, you're losing market share."*

I never forgot his admonition. Meetings present opportunities for you to shine. Capitalize on the opportunities.

## Why Does It Matter?

Active participation in meetings does more than just get your name out there or your voice heard. It demonstrates your skill, it provides you with a chance to engage and it shows how invested you are in the collaborative work done on your team. The more people hear you speak, the more they will seek your opinions.

Also remember that asking a question can be just as impactful as making a statement—so nothing is off the table when it comes to involving yourself in a meeting discussion.

## Action Steps

If you are in a meeting where you are expected to be both seen and heard—or if you realize that you need to speak up more in meetings because everyone else at your level is doing it—these seven suggestions can help you.

- **Deliver your point with clarity and confidence**. In some meetings, especially larger ones, you may have only a single opportunity to speak up, and you'll want to make it count. Deliver your message as clearly and confidently as possible.

- **Be strategic about timing your comments.** Consider how best to enter the discussion. The earlier you speak, the sooner you establish your presence and the more sway you can have over the direction of the conversation, but your point might be forgotten when it comes time to make a final decision. The later you speak, the more sway you may have in the final decision, but you risk letting the discussion drift in a direction you might not agree with. You will want to carefully time your comment within the discussion to achieve your objective.
- **Find a hook.** There are any number of hooks you can use to enter the discussion. Contribute a relevant experience, comparison or data point. Point out an implication, contradiction, limitation, counterargument or exception. Introduce a framework to organize or summarize others' ideas or structure the question at hand. Steer the group back to the main topic, to a prior decision or to a decision on next steps.
- **Don't wait until you have a brilliant comment to speak up.** Whatever you say should move the conversation forward but it doesn't need to be groundbreaking. Don't agonize over or overthink the relative value of your comment. Even a question, for example, is often a good way to move things forward and won't be perceived as wasting the group's time.
- **Use chat functionality.** In the age of Zoom calls, making yourself heard over video conferences is a different beast. While not everyone pays attention to what's being said, many people generally read and respond to what's written in a chat window.
- **Recruit a coworker to be your meeting ally.** If a manager or mentor encourages you to speak more often in meetings, ask a coworker to call on you. Share a topic that you'd like to talk about with your coworker in advance so that you are

both prepared or request that you have some dedicated time to speak at an upcoming meeting on a selected topic.
- **Bring new information.** If you read an article, listened to a podcast, watched a video or otherwise learned something that can help the group make a more informed decision, mention it. The most interesting comments in a meeting often come from people who bring up relevant news or examples of what others are doing.

Don't be afraid to seize the mic in meetings. Your voice might just spark the collective genius that turns ordinary into extraordinary.

# How To Own the Details

> *"It's the little details that are vital.
> Little things make big things happen."*
> *John Wooden*

Attention to detail is not just a skill you throw on your resume because it sounds like a keyword for resume screener bots. It's an important capability that can make the difference between life or death in certain jobs, such as an airline pilot or a surgeon. Even if it doesn't make the difference between life and death, you need to pay attention to the details.

## Why Does It Matter?

No reasonable employer expects perfection from its employees, but all employers expect reliability and accuracy. If you're unable to meet that minimum, it could damage your reputation and limit your chances to be given more responsibility.

When you consistently demonstrate that you have excellent attention to detail, you show others they can trust your work. And trust is key in the workplace. Detail-oriented people are also more likely to spot mistakes and prevent costly errors.

## Action Steps

There are five foundational skills that foster attention to detail.

- Organizational skills
- Time management skills
- Active listening
- Observational skills
- Analytical skills

By improving your habits in these five skill areas, you can increase your attention to detail.

To improve your **organization skills**, begin by organizing your workspace. The act of decluttering your desk or organizing the files on your computer actually helps declutter your mind. You expend less mental energy trying to find things. You can also avoid wasting mental energy by establishing a routine. This structure makes you less likely to get distracted or procrastinate because of your clear plan of action. Keeping a to-do list is another great organizational tool. Being more organized sets you up to be more detail-oriented.

You can improve your **time management skills** by breaking up your day into intervals of work and rest periods, typically twenty-five minutes of work and five minutes of rest. By allowing time for rest, you improve the quality of your work and reduce mental exhaustion. Try spending less time on social media, too. Notifications are designed to grab your attention, and the more you are distracted, the greater the chance of errors in your work. In the same vein, multitasking causes you to divide your attention and your time across multiple tasks, which increases your error rate and reduces efficiency.

When it comes to **active listening skills**, learn to listen well. Maintain eye contact, give the speaker your full attention and ask follow-up questions to ensure you fully understand their message. Taking notes forces you to increase your attention to detail and determine the pertinent information that you need to record. The act of writing can help you retain the information better, and it provides a handy reference if you need to go back to it to make sure you didn't miss any details.

Your **observational skills** can be improved by being present, noticing social cues such as body language and facial expressions and observing your environment. Engage as many senses as you can, as each one provides you with a different set of details to focus on. See if you can find any patterns in behaviors or try to predict what may happen based on previous observations.

Improve your **analytical skills** by reading more books, playing brain games and asking more questions. When you get clarification or new information from others, you can compare your understanding to what you found out and it may lead you in a different direction. This is the basis of problem-solving and hones your ability to think analytically.

Being detail-oriented isn't a mere checkbox; it's the golden ticket that transforms how your work is perceived. Attention to detail elevates your credibility, showcases your commitment to excellence and sets the stage for trust and confidence in every task you take on.

# How To Demonstrate Charisma at Work

> "Charisma is a sparkle in people that money can't buy."
> *Marianne Williamson*

Charismatic people naturally attract and influence other people. Martin Luther King, Jr., Ronald Reagan, Barack Obama, Bill Clinton, Mohandas Gandhi and Oprah Winfrey are examples of famous leaders widely considered to have charisma.

Every time charismatic people interact with others, they try to evoke positive feelings. As Maya Angelou once said, *"I've learned that people will forget what you said, people will forget what you did, but people will never forget how you made them feel."*

While charisma is sometimes described as a mysterious quality that someone either has or doesn't, the qualities and skills of charismatic people can be learned and cultivated.

## Why Does It Matter?

Several large-scale studies have shown that charisma can be an invaluable asset and secret weapon in any work context. We all admire people who seem to be naturally charismatic. By developing and nurturing the following seven qualities, you can become the person who lights up the room and makes others feel valued.

## Action Steps

*Always maintain a positive attitude.*
It doesn't matter if you're having a bad day. Nobody wants to work with a negative person, so project optimism and enthusiasm.

*Be likable.*
Likable people are friendly, sincere and happy; they actively seek to build rapport with others by showing an interest in them. Asking simple questions such as, *"How did you enjoy the sales meeting last week?"* or making statements such as, *"I really liked the presentation you gave yesterday,"* can build rapport with others. Charismatic people don't mind taking a back seat and focusing on what others have to say.

*Project confidence.*
Body gestures, facial expressions and vocal tone all demonstrate a level of passion that leaves a more memorable impression of charisma on others. Make sure your voice is powerful and controlled. Your posture and stance should be relaxed and open and your body language should be animated by using gestures and facial expressions.

When your voice is too soft, your posture is slouched and your body language is meek, it is harder to project confidence.

*Use stories, anecdotes, metaphors and contrasts.*
Personal stories and anecdotes can be used to great effect, especially stories of struggles and challenges and how you overcame them. Metaphors simplify and stir people's emotions and imagination. *Contrasts* combine reason and passion. Think of John F. Kennedy's *"Ask not what your country can do for you—ask what you can do for your country"* speech.

*Demonstrate both emotional expressiveness and emotional sensitivity.*
Charismatic people express their feelings spontaneously and genuinely. Combined with emotional sensitivity or the ability to read others' emotions, you can make another person feel as if they're the only person in the room.

*Maintain emotional self-control.*
Charismatic people are not emotionally reactive or impulsive. Instead, they balance spontaneity and measured emotions as circumstances require.

*Be playful.*
Playfulness is an often-overlooked quality of charisma. Even when you are at a business event, people want to enjoy themselves. Instead of being another random person, be the person who is fun to talk to. Using humor or irony (when appropriate) and being able to laugh at yourself can be endearing. Humor, levity and a little bit of self-deprecation disarms people and can forge a bond.

With charisma in your toolkit, you're not just another face in the crowd; you're the unforgettable spark. Charisma can be your superpower for turning everyday interactions into golden opportunities. You just need to lean into it.

## Section 3

# Unleashing Your Inner Titan: Breaking Barriers Within

The themes in this section take your newfound ability to recognize your shortcomings and build on your strengths and emphasize a journey of overcoming habits, behaviors, mindsets and thought processes that may hold you back from reaching your full potential. This section is about conquering self-imposed limits, vanquishing bad habits and ditching mindsets that tether you from soaring higher. Is it lack of confidence? Is it pesky negative thoughts? No matter what's stopping you, you need to tackle them head-on.

Perception isn't just about looking in the mirror. It's about reshaping outside perspectives and confronting your own reflections. Understanding perception is pivotal. Inviting feedback, sidelining self-doubt and being confident in yourself and your choices demand a mature understanding and management of perceptions. They underscore the need to harness external viewpoints constructively, while firmly grounding your self-worth and identity internally.

This section addresses gaining mastery over your mind. Eliminating negative thought patterns, maintaining composure, and accepting less than perfection are all mental battles. It's about reorienting the mindset to be more solution-focused and forward-looking, setting aside debilitating thoughts, and embracing an attitude of optimism and continual learning.

So, gear up and dive deep as we navigate perceptions, master our minds, and champion resilience.

# Eliminating Negative Thought Patterns at Work

*"I have had a lot of worries in my life,
most of which never happened."*
*Mark Twain*

Everyone expresses negative thoughts now and again, but habitual or irrational negative thought patterns can have adverse consequences. Cognitive distortions are often at the root of excessive negativity so it's helpful to understand the main distortions in thinking.

*Cognitive distortion 1: All or nothing thinking*
If an outcome isn't flawless, it's seen as an utter failure. For instance, someone with an all-or-nothing mindset might perceive a project that's slightly behind schedule as a total disaster. But minor setbacks shouldn't overshadow the positive aspects or progress made.

*Cognitive distortion 2: Overgeneralizing*
When someone overgeneralizes, even a single event is seen as "always" or "never". For example, someone might say *"I can never do anything right."*

*Cognitive distortion 3: Mental filters*
A person with this thought pattern filters out everything that is positive and supportive and focuses only on negative statements. Even if their manager praised them for achieving six goals successfully, but was critical of performance in one area, the person will focus only on the negative feedback. Instead, find the balance between what you have done right and what you need to improve. Don't just focus on the negative.

### Cognitive distortion 4: Discounting the positives
This thought pattern magnifies a person's negatives and fails to consider that others might have a positive view of her character, skills and abilities.

### Cognitive distortion 5: Jumping to conclusions
A person who adopts this thought pattern may not even try to address a problem. They simply jump to negative conclusions.

### Cognitive distortion 6: Emotional reasoning
This reasoning is emotional, but it is *not* rational. You might tell yourself *"I am a bad person and I am worthless. They would be justified in firing me. I don't deserve to keep this job so I should prepare to be fired."*

### Cognitive distortion 7: Labeling
You might label yourself a failure after making a small mistake, or you decide that the CEO of your company is an idiot because you disagree with one decision she made.

### Cognitive distortion 8: Personalizing
This behavior focuses on a single culprit and fails to see other people's responsibilities and contributions.

### Cognitive distortion 9: Wishful thinking
This kind of thought pattern causes guilt, fear and anxiety. If you always think you "should" be doing something, you may end up feeling like you're always failing.

### Cognitive distortion 10: The grass is greener
These feelings lead the person to focus on other people's success, rather than their own chances of success. They may also feel that

they would be more successful elsewhere, so they do not devote energy to their current role. Oftentimes, a person may be better off than they think.

## Why Does It Matter?
Negativity in the workplace can cause significant adverse consequences. Distorted perceptions of reality may cause feelings of anxiety and depression in yourself and those around you. Excessive negativity compromises interpersonal rapport, decreases motivation and hurts productivity. For these reasons it is important to take action to address negative thinking patterns so you can view situations in a more realistic, positive light.

## Action Steps
By understanding the most common negative cognitive distortions, along with their corresponding negative thought patterns, you can put into practice effective solutions to address them.

*Cognitive distortion 1: All or nothing thinking*
The negative thought pattern: *"Everything is either black or white."*

A more positive approach considers the shades of gray. The project may be delayed, but you have still accomplished a lot because it is 70 percent complete. By adopting a positive approach, you tell yourself, *"Let's see how I can make further progress. A small setback may delay my timeline, but I'll get there in the end."*

*Cognitive distortion 2: Overgeneralizing*
The negative thought pattern: *"I can't do anything right."*

A more positive approach is to analyze the situation on its own terms rather than applying it universally to every situation. Tell yourself, *"I was successful in the past doing similar tasks. I can handle this one too."*

### Cognitive distortion 3: Mental filters
The negative thought pattern: *"My manager considers me an underperformer."*

The positive approach is to tell yourself: *"You have done a lot of good work. There is one area that you can continue to work on in order to grow."*

### Cognitive distortion 4: Discounting the positives
Like mental filtering, a person who discounts the positive actively rejects any positive recognition.

A more positive approach is to be less self-critical and reframe how you view your own contributions. Your success, your positive outcome, was *not* an accident. Your competency, skills and effort all played an important role in achieving a successful outcome.

### Cognitive distortion 5: Jumping to conclusions
The negative thought pattern associated with this distortion is "mind reading" when a negative reaction is predicted and "fortune telling" when a negative outcome is predicted. For example, you notice that your supervisor didn't greet you with her usual enthusiasm in the morning. Based on this observation, you assume that she is upset with you, even though you have no concrete evidence to support this belief. You resort to "fortune telling" by predicting that because of this perceived slight, you won't get the promotion you've been working towards. In reality, your supervisor might simply have had a stressful morning or been preoccupied with another matter.

A more productive approach is to ask questions and obtain accurate information so that you can jump to the **likely-case** scenario, not the worst-case scenario. You might tell yourself *"Let's do some fact checking."*

### Cognitive distortion 6: Emotional reasoning
The negative thought pattern associated with this distortion is allowing emotions to get the best of you.

A positive approach is to separate your current feelings and emotions from the reality of the situation. If you look at the facts objectively, they do not justify the strong emotions you are experiencing. Your feelings are certainly real, but they may not be rational. Knowing the difference is key.

*Cognitive distortion 7: Labeling*
The negative thought pattern associated with this distortion is using labels to explain away a problem or issue.

A more positive approach is to rip off the labels. Acknowledge your mistakes and commit to doing better. You are free to disagree with a decision that the CEO made but that doesn't make him an idiot. A one-time event or behavior does not define you or anyone else.

*Cognitive distortion 8: Personalizing*
The negative thought associated with this distortion is blaming yourself or someone else for everything that has gone wrong. You might say *"It's all my fault!"* or *"It's all his fault!"*

A more positive approach is to reattribute responsibility beyond yourself to everyone involved. Focus on understanding the problem and the roles that different parties played in the situation. Don't automatically just blame yourself.

*Cognitive distortion 9: Wishful thinking*
The negative thought pattern associated with this distortion is *"I should have done this"* or *"I shouldn't have done that!"*

A more positive approach is to practice self-compassion. Keep doing what you can, and break away from wishful thinking. It isn't about what you should, could or would do. It is about what you actually did. Accept it and move forward.

*Cognitive distortion 10: The grass is greener*
The negative thought pattern associated with this distortion is *"Someone else is better than me"* or *"Somewhere else is better for me than here."*

A more positive approach is to avoid excessively comparing yourself to others. Your grass may not be the greenest, but you're in charge of the color and condition. It's your job to keep it as green as you can, to cut it and to maintain it. The other grass may only look greener from afar.

# Overcoming Self-Doubt at Work

> "It's funny how doubt hides itself. It follows behind you.
> It waits in every corner. You never see it coming.
> But you feel it, on the inside."
> *Iris Chapman* in the movie *Clockwatchers*

You can picture the scenario. You emailed your boss a first draft of the client presentation three days ago and you still haven't received a response. The self-doubt starts to creep in in the form of ugly, negative self-talk.

*"She probably thinks I did a terrible job."*
*"I bet she's been rewriting the deck I emailed her."*
*"I'll probably get fired because she can't delegate important tasks to me."*

Here you go again doubting yourself and imagining the worst. We all have a lot of voices in our heads. For some people, many of those voices are negative.

The trick is to recognize that those negative voices are not inevitable truths. Decide if you are going to listen to the voice of self-doubt or overrule it with a voice of greater reason and confidence.

## Why Does It Matter?
When you ruminate excessively about the possibility of negative events and start to doubt yourself, your own thinking patterns can become self-destructive. In addition, negativity bias can lead to feeling overly self-critical.

If you accidentally sent the wrong email to the head of the department, that doesn't mean that your life is over. You obviously wish you hadn't sent the email but it's not going to lead to a series of events which will end in a complete disaster

Instead of telling yourself *"I'll never be able to put together a compelling client presentation,"* figure out how you can improve. Tell yourself *"Okay. This wasn't my best work, but I know I'll do better next time."*

## Action Steps

The good news is that there are four practical steps you can take to challenge your self-doubt and refocus your mind on more productive thinking patterns.

1. **Manage the three Ps: personalization, pervasiveness and permanence.**
   Instead of thinking *"My boss thinks I'm an idiot and that's why she's ignored my email for three days,"* explore more objective possibilities. Maybe your boss hasn't reviewed the presentation yet because she is traveling or has more urgent tasks to attend to. To manage pervasiveness, remind yourself to maintain perspective. Finally, ignore the pull to believe you are going to feel the way you currently feel forever.
2. **Distinguish between the "withins" and the "beyonds".**
   Events that cause self-doubt usually fall into one of two categories: either what happened is within your control and you can do something about it—or it's beyond your control and you can't. Instead of spending time doubting yourself, focus on taking concrete steps to do something about the event in the "within" bucket. Conversely, recognize and accept what you cannot control. If you don't let go of the "beyonds" and you always feel responsible for them, you will never feel like you have done enough.
3. **Stay in the present.**
   Research shows that a wandering mind is usually an unhappy mind. People are better off focusing on the present, not obsessing about past events or worrying about future outcomes.

When you find yourself ruminating over what happened in the past or anxiously anticipating what might happen in the future, remind yourself that the present is *right here, right now*. When it starts to wander in reverse or forward, bring it back.

4. **Celebrate successes.**

    Research suggests that people tend to focus more on their failures or perceived shortcomings than on their successes or positive qualities. So, build your confidence by acknowledging and celebrating wins, both small and large. Use positive self-talk to reinforce your sense of achievement. Take a moment to reflect on your achievement and recognize the effort you put in. Tell yourself, *"Look what I was able to do!"*

Ditch the doubt and dance with confidence.

# Accepting Less Than Perfection at Work

*"Strive for continuous improvement, instead of perfection."*
*Kim Collins*

People who are considered "perfectionists" have many desirable qualities such as punctuality, orderliness, attention to detail, thoroughness and high performance standards. However, when the "perfectionist" feels the need to achieve almost impossible goals problems may arise.

Many perfectionists are afraid of failure, worry constantly about the possibility of making mistakes and are overly preoccupied with thoughts that others might disapprove of them. They often feel dissatisfied even when they achieve success.

## Why Does It Matter?

If perfectionists are successful at work, it is actually *despite* their perfectionism, not because of it. Being a habitual perfectionist can make it more difficult for you to manage stress, optimize your productivity and develop positive relationships at work.

Excessive perfectionism can harm not only the perfectionist, but also their friends, colleagues and subordinates. At work, excessive supervision and micromanaging can cause unnecessary delays, inhibit the growth of others, and actually reduce productivity. Their intolerance of mistakes inhibits the innovation and creativity that comes from calculated risk-taking and experimentation. Perfectionists also have a tendency to be hypercritical, impatient and quick to show anger when others fail to meet their performance expectations.

You don't want your perfectionist behavior to limit your career. The first step is to recognize it and then take the steps to change it.

## Action Steps

Do any of the qualities in the previous section apply to you? If so, there are a few things that you can do to manage your perfectionist tendencies.

*Design the right goals for yourself and others.*
Make sure that you design attainable, yet challenging, goals. It's good to shoot for high standards, but don't set goals that go way beyond what is required because you want to fulfill your own desire for perfection. Work requires compromise and tradeoffs, and it's key to identify what matters most.

Ask yourself questions such as, *"Is there a simpler way to achieve our goal?"* or *"What is the opportunity cost of spending so much time on this part of the project?"* Learn to separate your personal desires from what is actually *required* to do your job well.

*Check yourself for perfectionistic thoughts.*
Challenge yourself to learn to recognize and reject the unreasonable demands you place on yourself. Avoid framing everything in black and white terms. There is a range of possible outcomes, not just perfection or failure. Oftentimes, 97 percent achievement of an outcome may be an excellent result— so ask yourself why you are focusing obsessively on that last 3 percent.

*Don't obsess about and overanalyze the negative aspects of past failures.*
Focus on the learning that happened. Failures and mistakes are common and expected aspects of the work process. Accept yourself as an imperfect human being, like every other person on the planet.

*Use positive self-talk and personal mantras to overcome hypercritical thoughts.*
Laugh off the worst-case scenario you are telling yourself. For example, *"Do I really think that if I don't deliver a perfect presentation this*

*afternoon I will be fired and never find another good job again?!"* Try to shine a light on your unreasonable catastrophizing. Repeat positive mantras such as, *"You don't have to be perfect to be great at your job!"* or *"Strive for excellence not perfection!"*

Don't let the pursuit of perfection overshadow the richness of the journey itself.

# Letting Go of What Other People Think About You

"I will not let anyone walk through my mind with their dirty feet."
*Mahatma Gandhi*

Close your eyes for a minute and think back to your middle school days. If you enjoyed it, you may have fond memories of being part of a championship sports team—or really wowing the audience in the school talent show. But for many of us, the memories that come flooding back still generate a visceral reaction. Long-ago embarrassments, humiliations or insecurities remain crystal-clear memories, including exactly how we felt. Sometimes, you can even smell the scents or taste the flavors related to those memories. That's how strong they are.

Why is it that those memories still hold so much power over us in our adult lives?

Caring about what other people think of us is a vestige of our evolution as humans. Being part of a group or tribe is vital to survival. For primitive people, being part of the tribe meant safety, food and shelter. The tribe's approval and acceptance were a matter of life or death.

Our evolutionary social nature still compels us to tie our value to the opinions and acceptance of others. And there are times when those opinions may help you understand that you need to change your behavior to preserve an important relationship. But when you worry too much about what others think, you allow insecurity and vulnerability to determine your self-worth.

## Why Does It Matter?

While we no longer need to be part of a group in order to survive, we still rely on other people for intellectual stimulation and emotional support. Releasing the weight of others' opinions frees you to soar on the wings of authenticity and self-trust. By doing so, you cultivate a life more aligned with your own truths rather than external validations.

## Action Steps

Here are some techniques you can use to retrain your primitive brain and care less about what others think of you.

*Recalibrate your sensitivity to what others think.*

- When you're worried about what other people think of you, what do you think they're thinking about?
- Do you imagine they're wondering how you got your job after you made that ridiculous comment in yesterday's meeting?
- Are they pondering how anyone could tolerate working with someone as annoying as you?

When you place too much emphasis on being well-liked by everyone, you set a very high bar for yourself. It's inevitable that you're going to encounter people who think you're not all you're cracked up to be. If you let their singular opinion hold power over you, then you're more likely to defer to their wishes and set aside your own. That's too high a price to pay to try to change one measly person's opinion.

*Stop being your own worst critic.*

Often, the things we tell ourselves about ourselves are far more critical than the comments of others. When you're already nurturing a deep dislike of yourself or a hearty skepticism of your own abilities, then the harsh opinions of others may validate your own negative thoughts.

Rather than letting that inner critic have free rein, practice self-reflection instead. Ask yourself questions such as, "*Who am I?*" "*What do I enjoy?*" "*What are the things I care about?*"

Those questions can give you insight into your core values and provide the foundation for your sense of self-worth. When you know who you are, you're able to filter comments made by others. You're also able to recognize useful feedback and what to reject as untrue.

*Mind your own judgment of others.*
Each time you form an instant opinion of someone with no idea about who they really are, you're perpetuating the idea that it's okay to judge people—and you legitimize others' judgments of you.

You can't change what other people do, but you can change your own behavior and become more open and accepting of others. By reducing your critical attitude and embracing a more generous spirit, you'll worry less about being judged by others.

*Dial down the haters and build up the supporters.*
Given all the ways we connect to people these days, you're likely leaving yourself wide open to the opinions and judgments of hundreds or even thousands of people. Judgmental friends and family can have a particularly negative effect on your mental health.

If your social media feeds leave you feeling bad about yourself rather than happy for others, consider taking a break from virtual judgment. Try abstaining for at least a week if you can, and while you're enjoying the judgment-free zone, think about who you really want to let into your day-to-day life.

Whether online or in your daily life, nurture the relationships with the people who embrace the real you and don't make you feel judged.

Don't let a bunch of random people be in charge of your daily moods or how you feel about yourself.

# Being Receptive to Feedback

*"Feedback is the breakfast of champions."*
*Ken Blanchard*

I never forgot a corny phrase a mentor once told me: "Feedback is the breakfast of champions; dine on it daily!" While the phrase might be cheesy, the advice is solid. Feedback at work can come from a range of sources: from managers guiding your professional growth, colleagues with whom you collaborate, subordinates who count on your leadership, to customers who interact with the end results of your efforts. To maximize the benefits of feedback from any of these sources, it's essential to approach it with an open mind.

## Why Does It Matter?

Receiving feedback, whether it is positive or negative, is fundamental to ongoing professional improvement. That's why it is so important to seek out feedback on a regular basis. Soliciting feedback from anyone willing to provide it helps you proactively identify opportunities to better yourself.

## Action Steps

Adopting the right attitude and approach when you receive feedback is the only way to effectively learn from it. If you struggle with being receptive to feedback from bosses or anyone else, follow these four tips to get more comfortable with receiving and implementing feedback.

*Ask for complete honesty.*
Welcome honest feedback from multiple sources; especially people that you know will be 100% honest with you—even if you don't like what they are telling you.

Don't let others say: *"You're doing fine."*
Ask: *"What could I do even better?"*

The feedback should be specific, with examples, if possible. Feedback is not helpful if it is too generic or not actionable.

Don't let others say: *"There is room for improvement."*
Ask: *"What specific areas or skills of mine need improvement?"*

*Maintain an open mind.*
Another mentor once told me that feedback–whether positive or negative–is a gift. They went on to say that if someone doesn't care enough to give you feedback, that's when you should be worried. Next time someone gives you feedback, remind yourself, *this is a gift and I'm going to receive it as such.*

Above all, do not adopt a defensive or closed mindset when you receive negative feedback. It's not about defending yourself from accusations. Also, avoid the temptation to blame others. Correct any inaccuracies in the feedback, yet understand that it might also reflect others' perceptions of you. Whether perception-based or factual, positive or negative, formal or informal, evaluative or developmental, the key is to maintain an open mind and try to learn what you can from every piece of feedback you receive.

*Take notes.*
The process of taking notes when someone gives you feedback sends important messages. Taking notes demonstrates that you are taking the feedback seriously. You will also be able to refer back to your notes at a later date to remind yourself of the details.

*Make an action plan.*
Summarizing feedback shows that you value the process and that you take the feedback seriously. If the feedback comes from your manager

and requires immediate action, you should express your commitment to improve by explaining what steps you will take to act on the feedback. If you don't know what steps to take talk with your peers, mentor or your manager to identify them.

After taking action to improve, note any positive consequences, then keep those who provided the feedback informed of positive progress. Your next feedback session will go more smoothly and you will be better prepared.

People who take the time to give you feedback most likely care about your performance. They want you to learn and grow. When you receive feedback with an open and positive mindset you set yourself up for greater success.

# Overcoming the Fear of Trying New Things on the Job

"Avoiding danger is no safer in the long run than outright exposure.
The fearful are caught as often as the bold."
*Helen Keller*

During a routine team catch-up over coffee, your boss casually mentions, *"I was talking to the board about our international expansion plans. You remember the discussions about a European hub, right? Well, it's happening! We're setting up in Barcelona, Spain. And here's the exciting part: they're keen on having someone with your expertise lead the project on the ground. Think sun, paella, and a well-deserved promotion!"* How would you respond?

If you're like most people, you'd probably have instant anxiety. It's overwhelming to absorb the idea of taking on so many new experiences all at once—a new team, a new boss, a new office, living in a foreign country.

It's okay to be afraid to try something new, but examine how that feeling of fear shows up. Your heart beats a little faster. Your hands get sweaty. Your stomach has butterflies. Fear presents itself that way, but you know what else does? Excitement. And the only difference between whether you're feeling afraid or you're feeling excited is the story you tell yourself.

## Why Does It Matter?

For those who have a fear of trying new things, even the idea of learning how to use the latest project management software or switching to a new process can feel just as overwhelming and scary as relocating to a different country. The common denominator when it comes to learning new things is that unless you uncover some previously unknown talent, you're going to feel awkward and uncomfortable for a while until you get up the learning curve.

To conquer a fear of venturing into the unknown, you must embrace the challenge and navigate through it head-on. Here are some actions you can take that will help.

## Action Steps

Consider trying this approach. First, don't let the fear of trying new things derail you. Fear serves a purpose when you find yourself in a potentially dangerous or threatening situation. Your primitive brain kicks in your fight-or-flight response, which is exactly what should happen. So, if you accept that fear in those circumstances makes sense, you can look at your fear response a little more critically.

Next, go in with the right attitude. Learning requires a level of humility and accepting that you'll make mistakes allows more room for enjoyment as you try. However, setting the bar too high and assuming you'll master it will likely cause you to feel frustrated and embarrassed.

Your attitude is shaped by your perspective on the new situation. If your friends suggest meeting at a local rock-climbing facility just for the fun of trying it out, what's your perspective? Do you go into it thinking *I want to learn this* or do you think *I'm going to master this?*

There's a difference between those mindsets. Saying *I want to learn this* is acknowledging that you don't yet know everything about how to do something, and you'll probably make mistakes, but that's the process of learning. Saying *I want to master this* is focusing more on knowing everything, being the best and showing other people what you can do. The prior mindset is more conducive to achieving success.

Third, give yourself time to succeed. Learning new things is hard and it takes time to get good at most things. The vulnerability that comes with learning new things kicks up feelings of anxiousness and inadequacy. However, once the "newness" wears off, your anxiety drops and you can begin to find ways to enjoy your new situation. Keep yourself focused on the present and resist worrying about what could go wrong. The best way to maintain focus is to tackle your new situation in incremental steps, or by creating small goals, so you have a way to mark your progress.

Finally, try to build up your tolerance for discomfort by being open to new things in your personal life. Try unfamiliar foods. Complete a challenging puzzle or play a new game. Sign up for a strenuous exercise class that pushes you hard. Your brain will be as exercised as your body, as you create new connections and thinking patterns. Once you make it a regular practice to step outside your comfort zone, you can diminish those initial fears and anxieties that set in when you think about trying something new at work. Who knows—you may actually start to seek out new activities and experiences just for the thrill they provide.

# Changing Behaviors That Hold You Back at Work

*"All our knowledge has its origins in our perceptions."*
*Leonardo da Vinci*

What is perception and what is reality?

We all may hold very different views of the same exact situation or behavior. What one person views as being persuasive someone else might view as being manipulative. What you view as indecisive behavior someone else might view as being careful.

The way we formulate opinions is influenced by our individual cultural background, knowledge, experiences and values. Despite wanting others to see us in a certain way, if our behavior does not align with that perception, it's unlikely that we will be able to change their opinion.

If we hope to influence how others perceive us, we need to be intentional about our behaviors and make sure that they reflect the image we want to project.

## Why Does It Matter?

Managing how others perceive our behaviors at work is not just about our reputation or career advancement; it's about creating a positive and productive work environment for everyone. When we are intentional about how we present ourselves through our behaviors, we have the power to positively shape the dynamics of our workplace.

When it comes to interacting with others, our personality, social skills, preferred communication channels and overall approach all have the power to influence our relationships. At work, in addition to objective metrics such as productivity, it is increasingly important to understand and help shape how others perceive our behavior.

How our behavior is perceived affects our ability to work with others, to be productive, and ultimately to be successful.

Perceived negative behaviors can become obstacles that hold you back professionally. An attitude of complete indifference to others' perceptions of you is typically not conducive to professional advancement in the workplace. Even small missteps can have serious consequences and damage your reputation.

## Action Steps

There are concrete steps you can follow to change your behaviors so that you can influence others' perceptions of you in a positive direction.

*Practice self-awareness.*
Developing self-awareness is not something that happens automatically for everyone. It requires a strong commitment and a willingness to be courageous in examining yourself.

Regular self-reflection can help you gain insight into almost any aspect of your behavior, like how you respond to stress, how you handle bad news and whether you give credit to others for their contributions. Seeking honest feedback from those around you, including your boss, peers, subordinates and customers remains invaluable in helping you see yourself more objectively—you may be surprised by what you learn!

Maybe you consider yourself to be stoic while others see you as insensitive. You pride yourself on being assertive but others perceive you as arrogant. What you think of as diligence others perceive as micromanaging.

Remember that people may be hesitant to provide criticism, especially to their leaders, so be sure to listen carefully for any subtle or indirect feedback. Don't forget that people in your personal life can also offer valuable insights into how you come across and interact with others.

*Develop your strategy for changing behaviors.*
Change may involve engaging in new behaviors or disengaging from old behaviors. If your colleagues perceive you as too reticent because you tend not to speak up in meetings, commit to speaking up once in each meeting you attend for the next month. Use email to communicate thoughts on key issues or convey your feedback through others. If you frequently interrupt others during meetings and are perceived as disruptive and attention-seeking, spend more time taking notes and asking others questions about their ideas.

These changes may make you uncomfortable at first, but the more you practice, the more natural they will feel and the more likely they will become ingrained habits.

However, let me be clear. This is *not* about acting like the person you never were and never will be. This is all about developing the ability to regulate your behavior in specific circumstances. Gaining a better understanding of your own tendencies and triggers and learning techniques for managing your responses in a more productive and effective manner allows you to maintain greater control over your actions and reactions without compromising your core identity or values.

Start by making small changes. At the end of the day, it's a process of trial and error with each iteration bringing you closer to your desired outcome of changing the perception.

*Gain support for your behavioral change effort.*
Take the initiative to talk to your manager about your desire to change specific behaviors. Ask your manager for his honest feedback and advice, and be open to constructive criticism. Work with your manager to further develop your plan including specific steps and timelines. This can help to keep you accountable and ensure that you are making progress. Update your manager at least once a month on your progress.

*Evaluate your progress.*

To stay committed and on track with your journey toward changing behaviors, regularly assess your progress. New behaviors may come more naturally to you over time—or you may notice a more positive response from others when engaging in new behaviors.

# Developing New Work Habits

> "A habit cannot be tossed out the window; it must be coaxed down the stairs a step at a time."
> *Mark Twain*

Much of what we do in life is routine, but forming new habits can be challenging. Developing new habits requires you to get to a place where you can rely on muscle memory instead of willpower.

Motivation is what gets you started with a new behavior but *habit* is what ensures you consistently engage in that behavior. Lasting habits form when behaviors are repeated until they become natural and routine.

## Why Does It Matter?

As I've mentioned before, no one is the all-knowing, infallible professional that makes zero mistakes. Inevitably there are at least a few things you could do better or optimize at work—whether it's how you perform an existing process or how you interact with the person who reports to you. We all need to create new habits, but success can be elusive.

People who have the self-discipline to define, create and carry out a new habit show the proclivity for growth and sustainable scaling within the company.

## Action Steps

While some habits are easier to form than others, here are five tips that can help regardless of the specific habit you are trying to develop.

1. **Concretely define your new habit.** Being specific helps you figure out exactly what you need to do and why you need to do it and ensures that the "what" is actionable. Put your goal

into the form of a concrete, manageable and measurable action such as "Walk every single day for at least thirty minutes at lunch to increase my afternoon energy level" or "Attend company-sponsored learning events at least three times per month to expand my cross-functional contacts."

2. **Begin with small steps.** Trying to take large strides too quickly may result in failure because it's hard to form new habits if you cannot repeat them easily and consistently. It is easier to run for fifteen minutes consistently every single day than to set a goal to run for two hours without stopping on Sunday. Forming lasting habits is not about how much you accomplish in any given time frame. Instead, it's about how long you can *sustain* those habits.

3. **Experiment to find the approach that works best.** It takes most people several attempts before they successfully form lasting habits—and before they are able to break bad habits. A study by researchers in the UK found that is takes an average of 66 days to form a new habit when it is performed daily. (A rule of thumb is two to three months on average.) To form a new habit the brain needs to cycle through a state of order, disorder and then reorder. You should not label your initial unsuccessful attempts at establishing new habits as failures. Instead, think of habit formation as an experimentation process with the end goal of helping you find the right solution to your problem. As you experiment you may find that you have better luck if you can simplify the process and repeat it often.

4. **Consistently monitor success metrics.** Habits are formed when behaviors feel intrinsically rewarding, not forced, so that you are repeating the habit with nearly 100 percent reliability. One way to make a habit rewarding is to measure your progress and watch yourself reach milestones.

5. **Use checklists**. An effective checklist helps you specify critical moves by forcing you to create a list of items or criteria that are very clear, measurable and important. Checklists are also mindless reminders that reduce decision fatigue. They tell you the very least you should do when you are distracted, fatigued or demotivated. You can easily tweak checklists to experiment with different solutions until they work optimally to achieve your goal.

By putting new habits into play, you revamp your routine and redefine your results.

# Finding a Sense of Purpose in Your Job

> "To see the world, things dangerous to come to,
> to see behind walls, to draw closer,
> to find each other and to feel.
> That is the purpose of life."
> *Walter Mitty*

We would all like to feel completely fulfilled by our jobs, but what do you do if you no longer feel fulfilled by your work and your motivation is seriously lacking? There are many reasons why you might feel this way. Maybe your work has become too routine, you don't feel that leaders in your organization know you or care about you or your professional growth, or maybe you question the fundamental meaning of the work you perform.

## Why Does It Matter?

Sometimes we lose a sense of purpose in our work. You are not alone in feeling this way. A 2021 Gallup study found that only 36 percent of Americans feel engaged at work.

Having a sense of purpose is important. Without a guiding purpose, tasks can become haphazard, bonds with colleagues might fray and excitement for new assignments often decreases. Rather than considering the broader impact of your work, you might merely complete tasks with minimal or even no effort. As a result, your productivity plummets.

When you lose a sense of purpose in your job, it's important to adopt strategies that can help you rediscover your motivation and re-engage with the work you do.

## Action Steps

Whatever the reason for your sense of purposelessness, there are strategies you can adopt when you feel this way.

*Make tweaks to your current job to increase your sense of fulfillment and satisfaction.*
Identify the type of work which motivates you, and try to do more of it in your current job. For example, if you are feeling lonely and need more interaction with colleagues, request to work on projects which allow you to increase your interaction with others. If you like creative work, find ways to incorporate more creativity into your current job.

*Invest in passions outside of work.*
Not everyone wants a high-powered career. If your work is not your calling, find an outlet for your passion outside of work. The energy and motivation you derive from your external passions can have positive spill-over effects on your work.

*Find the purpose in your work and focus on it.*
Connecting your job to those who benefit from your work can make doing your job more purposeful. While admittedly it might be easier to do this if you are a teacher or a doctor, *everyone's* work is in service to someone. Focusing on who you serve in your work can provide the additional motivation you need.

*Take pride in mastering your craft.*
Focus on molding yourself into a master craftsman. Treating your work as a craft and dedicating yourself to perfecting certain skills required in your craft can give you a greater sense of fulfillment in your job.

*Invest in positive relationships with others.*
Who we work with can be very important to our overall sense of fulfillment and satisfaction in a job. Find ways to develop positive relationships with your colleagues at work. Those relationships can give work greater meaning.

*Remember who you are working for.*
When you are dealing with long hours, monotonous work and menial tasks, think about who you are working hard for at the end of the day. Often people work hard to provide for those they care about in life—whether it is their children, other family members, pets or charities. Remind yourself that your work is an *act of service* to those you provide for. Doing so can give you a daily sense of deeper purpose, regardless of the nature of your job.

# Becoming More Confident at Work

> "Your success will be determined by
> your own confidence and fortitude."
> *Michelle Obama*

When you are confident, you have trust in your abilities, qualities and skills. Confidence in the workplace is important because it allows individuals to communicate effectively, make decisions and take initiative.

Confidence is not something that you either have or don't have. It's something that you build within yourself, day by day, with every step you take. It might sound easier said than done, but believe in yourself and your abilities, and trust that you have what it takes to achieve your goals.

## Why Does It Matter?

Confident employees are more likely to speak up and share their ideas, which can lead to more creative solutions and improved teamwork. Additionally, confident employees are more likely to take on new challenges and responsibilities, which can lead to personal and professional growth.

Confidence can also help employees navigate difficult situations and conflicts, and can improve their ability to handle stress and pressure.

## Action Steps

There are three steps you can take today to achieve and display greater confidence at work.

*Identify and challenge negative self-talk.*
Recognize when negative self-talk is happening and challenge it with positive thoughts.

If you find yourself engaging in negative self-talk, give your detrimental thoughts labels such as "self-doubt" or "negativity". Labeling your negative thoughts can help you see them as something separate from yourself. Once you've identified and labeled your negative thoughts, reframe them in a more positive light by using positive affirmations.

For example, instead of thinking *I can't do this,* try thinking *I can do this; it might be challenging, but I am capable.*

Repeat positive affirmations and positive mantras to yourself, such as:

- I am capable.
- I am worthy.
- I am constantly improving and growing.
- I trust in my abilities and believe in myself.

It can also help to revisit memories of successful past achievements. Reflect on moments that made you especially proud of yourself and times when your skills were recognized, celebrated and rewarded. Remind yourself of obstacles and challenges you overcame. It's normal to have negative, self-critical thoughts from time to time, the important thing is to not let them take over. You need to keep challenging them.

### Make the effort to look confident.

Even if you don't always *feel* confident, make an effort to look the part. Use body language to send a message of self-confidence by sitting upright, standing tall and making sure your neck and shoulders are relaxed. Look others directly in the eye, use natural gestures, be engaging and exude optimism.

Avoid slumping in your chair, frowning, crossing your arms, putting your hands in your pockets, raising your voice or talking too fast.

Dress in a way that makes you feel good about yourself and that is appropriate for the occasion. It's always a good idea to dress not just for the position you currently have, but for the position you aspire to reach.

*Surround yourself with positive and supportive friends and family members.*
Seek out people in your personal and professional networks who are positive, supportive and encouraging. They can help lift your spirits and boost your confidence.

Look for individuals whose confidence inspires you and who you would like to emulate. Observe how they interact with others and how they approach challenges and try to incorporate those techniques into your own behavior.

Confidence comes from taking action. Keep working on building your confidence and soon you'll see that the sky's the limit for you.

# Keeping Your Word on Work Commitments

*"Your word is everything.
Keep it and good things will happen to you."
Thomas "Tip" O'Neill*

It can be hard to say *no* when you are asked to do things at work. However, if you say *yes* to an assignment and then you don't deliver, the outcome is worse than if you had just said *no* in the first place.

## Why Does It Matter?
Professional integrity is important to your job success.

Some people believe that overpromising is always a career-advancing strategy. Think again. While having a "can-do" attitude and taking initiative are important, you need to be able to deliver on your commitments. We all occasionally struggle to fulfill our work commitments—but doing so repeatedly can harm others' perceptions of you. Neglecting your work commitments not only can tarnish your reputation but it can cast a shadow of doubt, making others hesitant to place their trust in you. Keeping your word regarding work obligations is key to maintaining professional integrity.

## Action Steps
There are five rules to adopt to keep your word regarding fulfilling work commitments.

1. **Be careful about the promises you make.** Avoid making rushed and rash decisions regarding work commitments. If you need more time to fully evaluate whether you are prepared and able to take on a new assignment, say so, and promise to get back to the individual making the request.

2. **Make specific, not general promises.** Don't commit to doing something without having a *detailed* understanding of what you are committing yourself to do. Double-check to make sure that your understanding is consistent with that of the individual making the request. Confirm your understanding in writing if necessary.
3. **Make your promises closed-ended, not open-ended.** You need to understand the exact timeframe you've committed to when promising to undertake a new assignment. If you require additional resources to fulfill the commitment, make sure that the resource requirements are clearly understood and agreed to upfront.
4. **Underpromise but overdeliver.** Most people overpromise and underdeliver. You want to do the opposite. Take a conservative stance with respect to what you promise and you will put yourself in a solid position to overdeliver.
5. **Be proactive if you commit and then find that you cannot deliver.** Sometimes you will find yourself in a position where you cannot keep your word on commitments you've made. When this happens and the situation is beyond your control, be proactive. Tell the people you've committed to that you won't be able to fulfill your obligations. Simply clarify what you can accomplish and then make sure that you deliver on that.

Promise made, promise kept—that's the signature of a standout professional.

# Maintaining Your Composure at Work

"Without accepting the fact that everything changes,
we cannot find perfect composure."
*Shunryu Suzuki*

Maybe you're one of those people who takes everything in stride and nothing throws you off your game. You're perpetually calm, cool and collected. Congratulations if you are—because most of us are not!

Everybody gets stressed. Everybody gets angry. By the time we reach adulthood most of us have learned to choose our battles and pick our spots. However, many people can still have a meltdown under the right conditions.

For a lot of us, the workplace can provide the right conditions for a meltdown. You're under pressure to get things done. Somebody else makes the important decisions and you have to accept them. You work with different types of people, some of whom drive you crazy. It can feel like a powder keg at times.

## Why Does It Matter?

Put simply, you can't let yourself blow up at work. You need your job, and you need to maintain positive relationships with your boss and your coworkers. Throwing things around the room and calling them all a bunch of idiots is not the way to do that. Instead, you need to learn how to maintain your composure when work gets tumultuous.

## Action Steps

Here are some suggestions for how you can do that.

**Know your triggers**. If you're old enough to hold a job, you're old enough to become self-aware. Think about what gets you worked up and sets you off. By being self-aware, you can learn to anticipate situations that might set you on fire and prepare for them.

**Practice calming yourself**. Think about what you can do when you start to get angry or upset. Maybe it's stepping away, taking deep breaths or counting to ten. Maybe it's doodling, tapping your foot or silently repeating a calming word or phrase. As long as you learn to call on your go-to practice when you feel yourself losing your composure—and it doesn't hurt anyone—it's good. Make it a part of your routine so it's ready when you really need it.

**Vent, but only with someone you really trust**. Everybody, even your dog, needs to blow off steam now and then. You do too, but only when it's safe. Practice self-preservation along with self-awareness. As you cool off and get past it, remember: don't take it personally, even when it feels personal. Your credit-stealing coworker isn't singling you out. He'll try to take credit for *anybody's* work. And hey, even if it is personal, who cares? It's not worth risking your reputation, your good working relationships or your job.

**Look for the laughs**. As Mark Twain said *"The human race has one really effective weapon, and that is laughter."* Humor reduces stress. It calms you and defuses tense situations. It's free. Think about how absurd and silly it is to throw a tantrum because of something somebody else did.

You know your credit-stealing colleague is foolish and pathetic. So does everybody else who's worked with him. It's better to laugh inside and shake your head at the foolishness than to go on a useless rant. Smile and laugh, if only internally. It will let you keep your composure and get you through to a better part of your day.

# Being More Patient With Others at Work

*"He that can have patience can have what he will."*
*Benjamin Franklin*

We've all been impatient at one time or another. Especially with partners, kids, and pets, many of us wish we were more patient. As hard as it is to develop or find it within ourselves, patience is more than just a sought-after trait for hiring managers; it's a foundational soft skill.

As a professional, it's important to recognize that your impatience can have negative impacts on both your own productivity and the productivity of those around you. By learning to manage your impatience, you can create a more positive and productive work environment for yourself and everyone around you.

## Why Does It Matter?

While impatient people might argue they are efficient or get things done quickly, the reality is that impatient team members are hard to work with and be around on a day-to-day basis. They exhibit a range of behaviors that can negatively impact their own productivity and the productivity of others.

Impatient peers may try to:

- Rush or pressure others to work faster which can lead to mistakes or poor-quality work.
- Interrupt others when they are speaking or working which can disrupt the flow of communication.
- Do too many things at once which can lead to scattered attention and decreased efficiency.

- Become easily frustrated when things don't go as planned or when progress is slow, which can negatively impact their interactions and relationships with others.

As the old adage goes: patience is a virtue. It's cultivated, not granted as a gift.

## Action Steps

There are a few steps you can follow to become more patient at work. Here's a handy checklist to guide you through exercising greater patience.

- **Acknowledge your impatience.**
  Recognize when you're starting to feel triggered. Evaluate how factors such as deadlines, meetings, assignments and interactions with others affect your responses. Paying attention to how stressors affect you physically and emotionally allows you to improve your ability to notice when you're starting to become impatient. This can help you be more aware of your own emotions and reactions in order to respond with greater patience.
- **Keep a log of what triggers you.**
  Keep a journal or a log of what triggers you to feel impatient with others. Are you irritated that a coworker ignored your suggestion? Are you frustrated that the printer jammed? Are you embarrassed that your idea was shot down in the meeting? Are you anxious that you might have to work overtime? Regularly review your trigger log. Look for any patterns that emerge with certain people, places or situations that cause you to feel impatient. Try to work on one trigger at a time by being more conscious of your reaction in those situations.

- **Reframe the situation within the bigger picture.**
  Seek out alternative explanations for what is happening and why. Instead of jumping to the first conclusion that comes to mind, try to come up with other possible explanations for the situation. If a person is causing you to be impatient, look at the situation from his perspective. Remind yourself that putting up with whatever delay or frustration you're facing will ultimately help you get to where you want to go. By staying focused on the bigger picture, you become less frustrated with minor situations.
- **Set realistic expectations.**
  Make sure that you and the person you're setting expectations with are on the same page, but be open to compromise. You may need to adjust your expectations based on the resources or constraints that are in place. If you're unsure if your expectations are realistic or if you're feeling frustrated with the progress being made, communicate openly and honestly. This can help resolve any misunderstandings so you can find a way to move forward.
- **Reflect on the outcome.**
  When you are tempted to react impatiently, pause and reflect on the consequences of allowing your emotions to take over. Avoid acting impulsively by reflecting on what could happen if you show impatience.

Patience isn't just a nice-to-have virtue; it's the silent maestro orchestrating harmony, understanding and progress in the workplace.

# Succeeding at Work as an Introvert

*"Quiet people have the loudest minds."*
*Stephen Hawking*

Do any of the following phrases ring a bell?

- I just wish I could email my comments to my boss instead of saying them aloud in the meeting.
- We're only one hour into the sales conference and I'm already exhausted.
- The team wants to brainstorm but I do my best creative work on my own when I can really reflect.
- It's not that I don't like people. I just prefer working alone.

If you're an introvert, you can probably relate to some or all of these statements—and you're in good company. Research suggests that between 25 percent and 40 percent of people in the workplace are introverted.

The concept of introversion and extroversion is not a new one. It was actually first developed in the early 1900s by the renowned Swiss psychiatrist Carl Jung, the founder of analytical psychology.

As Jung described it, introverts prefer to be in a minimally stimulating environment and tend to go inward to recharge, while extroverts need interactions with others to re-energize.

Although the COVID-19 pandemic expanded remote work and increased virtual interactions—a welcomed change by most introverts' standards—the need to establish relationships and communicate effectively in the workplace remains unchanged.

## Why Does It Matter?

Your effectiveness in personal and professional relationships is based on your adaptability, attentive listening, insightful comprehension and the quality of your connections with those around you

Striking a balance between personal ease and professional demeanor will empower you to thrive as an introvert in the workplace. Many introverts believe the extroverts are the ones with the most workplace success—because they're always talking about it. Extroverts like the limelight, and they can have it. Introverts don't need the limelight to do great work, but they do need to set limits and boundaries for themselves so their work environment is conducive to productivity instead of draining their energy.

## Action Steps

Here are some tips you can use to succeed as an introvert at work regardless of whether you work in an office or remotely.

- **Set physical boundaries**. If you find yourself in a noisy, busy or loud workspace or you are asked to sit through too many meetings that don't help your work, you need to find your quiet place. If your work situation does not provide you with access to a private office, find a quiet spot and use noise-canceling headphones.
- **Schedule regular downtime**. Develop a schedule that allows you to take breaks at regular intervals. Use the break to engage in an activity that recharges you. Take a walk, read a book, meditate away from sensory input.
- **Speak up when needed**. Actively listen to others and think about what you are learning. Then, process it, integrate it and make your valuable contribution. Don't let other people who like to talk and be noticed more than you do prevent

you from making a contribution. It is important for you to contribute to the conversation.
- **Leverage your strengths**. Introverts tend to be very good listeners, thinkers, and problem-solvers. As your colleagues learn to appreciate your work habits and performance, you should showcase your strengths. Your colleagues and boss will appreciate you for it.
- **Build relationships**. It may not be easy or come naturally, but you still need to build relationships with your colleagues. Make an effort to introduce yourself and interact. As an introvert, your communication style may be more deliberate, and you may be less vocal than your extroverted counterparts. That's absolutely fine. Leverage your innate ability to connect with others on an emotional level as a means to establish meaningful interaction.
- **Communicate effectively**. Use emails, texts, memos and other methods to share information. If you don't want to speak up during a large gathering to express an idea, take time afterward to write an email to the presenter to tell them what you thought of a point they made or share the report/article you think they might enjoy. Do make an effort, though, to speak up regularly in smaller gatherings and meetings where you feel more at ease.

Being an introvert is a strength, not a weakness. Many successful people in business are introverts. So embrace your qualities and your skills. Your personality is not a flaw or a weakness.

# Changing Others' Perceptions of You

> "People seldom change. Only their masks do. It is only our perception of them and the perception they have of themselves that actually change."
> *Shannon L. Alder*

No matter how you intend your actions and words to come across to others, you can't change your peers' perception of how that manifests in the world. Once you speak, act or share your thoughts, they're out there for others to interpret as they want. And another person's perception may be very different from what you believe to be correct. That doesn't make their perception wrong—it's right from *their* perspective.

That's why it's so important to understand the many meanings of what you say and how you may come across to others.

## Why Does It Matter?

Other peoples' perceptions of you in the workplace matter—as such, you should take them seriously.

If others perceive you as a bully, they may avoid you and refrain from including you in team activities. If you are perceived as being "meek" you may be passed over for a leadership position.

Regardless of who you believe you are, it's who others believe you are that counts too. So, how do you create the "you" who you want others to see?

## Action Steps

Follow these suggestions to change the perceptions that others have of you.

- **Increase your self-awareness.** To manage the perceptions that others have of you, gain a clear understanding of yourself and the current reality of their perceptions. Look for patterns in the feedback you receive. What are the consistent themes? You may not be aware of the behavior patterns that are creating the perceptions that you want to change. Avoid the temptation to dismiss feedback that does not align with your own perception of your behavior.
- **Encourage unbiased feedback.** Get informal feedback from anyone willing to provide it, such as your manager, coworkers, friends and family. Suggest that they consciously pay closer attention to your behavior patterns. Give them enough time to observe you before they offer their input.
- **Make others aware of your intent.** Communicate your intentions by letting others know why you're behaving the way you are. If you don't proactively communicate your intent, people can passively misinterpret your behavior and develop perceptions of you that may be unfair or inaccurate.
- **Be mindful of the nonverbal signals you send.** The receiver is more likely to trust nonverbal signals if the speaker says one thing but sends a contradictory message through nonverbal signals. For example, if you avoid making eye contact, people may perceive you to be unsure of yourself or believe that you lack self-confidence. You might be very self-confident, but if your body language suggests otherwise people can form inaccurate perceptions of you.
- **Take steps to change your behavior.** Once you understand the perceptions you need to change, take meaningful steps to modify your behavior patterns. Keep in mind that if you want to alter perceptions more rapidly, you might need to make a big splash.

- **Be consistent and patient**. Changing perceptions can be a heavy undertaking and it takes time and consistency. Perceptions will only change if you consistently apply changed behaviors. If you stick with it long enough your efforts at behavioral change will work and perceptions of you will begin to change.
- **Accept that you won't be able to change everyone's perceptions**. No matter how hard you try, not everyone will see you the way you want to be seen. You can try everything to be seen in a certain way, but you won't necessarily be successful at changing *everyone's* perceptions of you. Make peace with that reality, but stay positive and focused on changing the perceptions of most.

Changing others' perceptions of you can be a heavy undertaking, but it could make all the difference in your career. Following these recommendations can increase the odds that you'll be successful in your efforts.

Section 4

# Synching With the Squad: Navigating Coworker Dynamics

Human interaction is the heart of any workplace. Interpersonal dynamics often prove to be the most challenging and, consequently, the most critical to navigate. The intricate dance of personalities, backgrounds, ambitions and emotions brings opportunities for collaboration but they also bring the potential for conflict.

It's almost inevitable that you'll work alongside others throughout your professional journey. This is the premise for the fourth and most extensive section of this book. The length and depth of this twenty chapter section underscore the importance of understanding and effectively handling coworker relationships.

Why all this emphasis? Because the most intricate puzzles in a professional setting are about human interactions. The way we communicate, empathize and collaborate with our peers and coworkers can significantly influence our job satisfaction, productivity and overall career trajectory. This section delves into the multifaceted world of coworker relationships, offering insights and advice to help you navigate workplace dynamics with confidence and skill. Whether it's repairing damaged coworker relationships or expanding your network, understanding human interactions is paramount to a fulfilling career.

Just as with any community, the workplace thrives on strong bonds, mutual understanding and clear communication. Coworker relationships, once established, need nurturing and regular check-ins to ensure that everyone is on the same page. However, as with all human interactions, challenges inevitably arise. From the minor irritations such as a colleague who talks excessively, to the more profound issues such as dealing with outright conflict or a coworker's undermining behavior, a gamut of situations requires tact and strategy. These kinds of situations can even escalate to more toxic scenarios, where negativity, gossip or jealousy come into play. If not addressed promptly and effectively, strained peer relationships can threaten the cohesive fabric of a team.

The intricacies of workplace dynamics don't stop there. There are unique situations, such as dating a coworker or transitioning from a peer to a leadership role, that introduce additional layers of complexity. These scenarios necessitate careful consideration and boundary-setting to maintain professionalism.

The ultimate goal remains consistent: fostering healthy, productive and mutually respectful relationships. Whether you're mending a strained bond, countering negativity or deepening an existing peer connection, every action and interaction contributes to the broader goal of creating a cohesive and harmonious workplace for you and everyone around you.

Buckle up because we're going in deep.

# Building Relationships With Peers

*"Even the Lone Ranger didn't do it alone."*
*Harvey MacKay*

Did you know that Americans are more likely to make friends at work than any other place? It's not particularly surprising when you consider that on average, a person spends 81,396 hours at work. That's equivalent to over nine years! And 30 percent of employees say that their best friend is a work peer. Research shows that people who have a best friend at work are seven times more likely to be present and engaged in their jobs, which produces higher quality work.

## Why Does It Matter?
Given how much time you spend at work and the value that having good relationships with work peers can add to your engagement at work and the quality of your work, it's helpful to know how you can develop stronger relationships with your coworkers.

Forming positive relationships can make all the hours you spend at work more enjoyable and more productive. Relationships with peers can also provide valuable support when you need it the most.

## Action Steps
If you'd like the chance to build better relationships at work with your peers, consider trying one of the five helpful strategies I've found useful in my career.

*Go the extra mile to be friendly.*
Smile at your coworkers, wave to them when you come into the office and make a point of greeting them. Just saying *"Have a good trip!"* or *"Have a great weekend!"* can go a long way toward building a bond with

a peer. Kindness and warmth are the top two characteristics people seek in friendships. Beyond gestures and greetings, show appreciation and respect for your coworkers. Here are a few things you might say:

- *Thanks for always being willing to lend me a hand.*
- *I really enjoy working with you.*
- *Having you on the team makes a huge difference.*
- *I learn so much from you. Thanks for always sharing your perspective in team meetings.*

### Communicate frequently and consistently.
Effort and consistency are the most important keys to success if you want to solidify relationships with peers—but always be genuine in your approach. When conversations feel transactional, they don't have the same impact.

Find opportunities to listen to others. Ask your colleagues what they did over the weekend. If you know that you share a particular interest, reference it. *"Can you believe that touchdown in the last fifteen seconds of the Giants game?"* Or use the opportunity to ask your peer for a time when you can connect more deeply. *"Let's grab fifteen minutes to chat next week over coffee."* Remember, though, that close relationships form over time and cannot be rushed.

### Attend company-sponsored events.
There are likely going to be events, activities, initiatives and programs that your company sponsors to foster social connections, camaraderie and team building and bonding. They provide great opportunities for you to make new connections and deepen existing ones. Make sure you participate whenever possible.

### Suggest activities outside of work.
Get together socially with peers to create fun memories and shared experiences. Whether it manifests as Thursday drinks after work,

Wednesday lunches, Tuesday evening runs or Friday virtual meet-ups, routine social gatherings foster deeper connections. When planning, though, be sure you respect and manage boundaries if someone declines your offer.

*Build trust.*
When others trust you, they are more likely to want to form a stronger relationship with you. To establish greater trust among your peers, admit when you are wrong and correct your mistakes. In the same vein, people who say *"I don't know"* are viewed as more trustworthy than people who pretend to know everything.

Follow through on your commitments and don't miss deadlines. Assume positive intent and give people the benefit of the doubt. Avoid passing judgment and spreading gossip. People are unlikely to want to share information with you if you are judgmental or known to be a gossip.

When you develop and foster bonds with coworkers, you not only enrich your daily work experience, but you also create a stronger foundation for professional growth.

# How To Deepen Your Workplace Relationships

> "Our rewards in life will always be in exact proportion to the amount of consideration we show toward others."
> *Earl Nightingale*

Valuable relationships are not built from singular conversations with people. It takes some effort to deepen them. Stronger connections grow from a multitude of interactions over weeks and months and years. Once you've had a conversation or two with someone with whom you'd like to develop a stronger relationship, it's up to *you* to keep it alive.

## Why Does It Matter?

Professional success doesn't just boil down to hard work or intelligence. It's a mixture of many factors—including the relationships you build with coworkers. You're only as solid as your strongest connections.

## Action Steps

Here are seven tactics to use to deepen your relationships with others at work.

1. **Greet the person next time you see them**. It's surprising how many people neglect to greet a person they've met before. If you don't remember someone's name, say *"I'm so sorry that I have forgotten your name. Would you mind reminding me?"* Ask how things are going. A simple question such as *"How did your presentation go?"* or *"How was your trip to Seattle?"* can signal that you were paying attention during your last conversation and that you care about the other person.

2. **Share relevant news.** Did you find an article, video, podcast or book that's relevant to someone? If so, forward the link with a comment such as *"You may already know about this, but it reminded me of our conversation."* It's an easy way to signal that you're still thinking of the person and are eager to be helpful.
3. **Offer an introduction.** If you come across anyone who has similar interests or who might be helpful to the person you met, ask if he'd like you to make an introduction. Then reach out to your contact to see if he'd be interested and, if so, become the broker.
4. **Show gratitude.** If someone gave you advice or help, send a thank-you email shortly after your meeting. Not doing so, especially if you requested the initial conversation, can be interpreted as a lack of gratitude. Consider also updating and thanking the person who made the introduction.
5. **Mention you'd like to work together.** When you're talking to someone who works on a team or project that you'd like to join, try saying, *"If you could use some help, please keep me in mind."* You'll never receive what you don't ask for, so offer to contribute your talents and capabilities when it makes sense.
6. **Ask to grab lunch or coffee or schedule a follow-up call.** This approach can also work if you want a longer conversation, such as if you're interested in learning more about someone's experiences working on a specific project or with a certain team. Meetings can be burdensome, so make sure you have an agenda and that you respect the other person's time.
7. **Consider connecting on social media.** Establishing connections with peers on social media sites such as LinkedIn, Facebook and Instagram can pave the way for stronger relationships, acting as a catalyst to foster trust. Social media connections can also provide conversation starters, enriching

everyday interactions and deepening camaraderie. They also offer colleagues a glimpse into the multifaceted nature of your personality and interests outside the office setting.

On the flip side, connecting with colleagues on social media sites create some challenges. Your peers might gain insight into facets of your personal life that you'd prefer remained private. Before connecting with work peers on social media, ask yourself two questions. What facets of my life become accessible via my online profile? And am I at ease with colleagues delving this deep into my personal life?

Remind yourself that nurturing coworker connections fuels collaborative success. It's worth making the effort.

# Maintaining Professional Relationships With Personal Friends at Work

> "The challenge of leadership is to be strong, but not rude;
> be kind, but not weak; be bold, but not bully;
> be thoughtful, but not lazy; be humble, but not timid;
> be proud, but not arrogant; have humor, but without folly."
> *Jim Rohn*

When work has you completely stressed out, sometimes the only thing that makes you feel like showing up are the friendships you've built with coworkers. These are the people you spend the most time with, so it's easy to form bonds that can feel like a work family.

As colleagues working side by side, it's great to be able to unload your frustration about management or worries about job security with someone you know and trust.

## Why Does It Matter?

It happens. Your boss gets promoted, and then you get promoted to be the new boss. You're pumped about the salary increase and also worried about your new responsibilities, but, hey, you're going to be with your friends. They'll still be on your side, right?

If you do things properly, there is no reason your friends can't stay your friends even when you're the new manager. You, and they, just need to make some slight adjustments so you can be the boss *and* remain the friend.

## Action Steps

Here are six strategies that will help you balance your responsibilities as manager and friend.

1. **Keep your roles straight.** It's perfectly fine to be a friend and a manager in the workplace, as long as you keep in mind the distinctions between your two roles. Maintaining professionalism during discussions may require some self-discipline, so keep that in mind when interacting with employees who are your close friends.
2. **Set clear boundaries.** An effective way to compartmentalize you as "manager in the office" and you as "friend and confidante after work" is to put some boundaries on your behavior.
   - Don't talk about work when you're interacting socially, and don't talk about deeply personal matters at work.
   - Agree that whatever corrective feedback you have to provide at work does not carry over into your personal friendship.
   - Don't gossip about coworkers or speculate on the state of the business.

   You should show friendship and kindness to everyone on your team *equally*. You can and should be politely interested in their lives, their challenges and celebrate their successes, whether work-related or personal. Good managers remain open to listening to their team members with patience and empathy.
3. **Define your workplace friendship.** When you're at work, remember that your primary responsibility is to provide the support your team needs to perform their jobs to the best of their ability. When you're outside working hours, then all formality of work should disappear and you can dissolve into the comfortable friendship you've always shared.
4. **Prioritize business responsibilities.** The expectation is that you focus on your team or department goals and the corporate goals. When you let your personal friendships consume your focus, you endanger business objectives and potentially

your career. A good way to keep yourself and your team on track is to set up one-on-one meetings with your team members and talk about their career goals.

5. **Remain professional with your words and actions.** You can still enjoy yourself, but keep it to a level where you're able to clearly recall it the next morning without embarrassment. If you're just hanging out with your work friends at dinner or on the weekend, be cautious if someone starts ranting about the leadership team or work in general.

6. **Don't let anyone exploit the situation.** Watch for indications that someone you counted as a friend might be trying to exploit you by frequently asking for small favors, taking credit for work you know they didn't do or asking you to move some of their work onto somebody else's plate. Ignoring that behavior can create a toxic work environment and negatively impact your career. Whether someone's a friend or not, you're still responsible to maintain a safe and collaborative workplace, so you must shut down any attempts by others to exploit you.

By always maintaining a professional demeanor and not allowing anyone to take advantage of you, you can help your team function effectively and ensure that your career is moving in the right direction.

# Getting on the Same Page With Your Coworker

> "It is not the absence of conflict that defines a successful team,
> but the ability to navigate through it and
> come out stronger on the other side."
> *Brian Scudamore*

There will always be conflicts and disagreements among coworkers. The key is to not avoid them, but to learn how to resolve them effectively.

While conflict at work may seem like an unwelcome hurdle, it's important to remember that everyone's diverse backgrounds and distinct experiences can lead to differences in perspectives. Try to see the positive side of conflict. Do you really want to work with a bunch of carbon copies of yourself?

Conflicts demonstrate the existence of different ideas, opinions and approaches. Innovation and opportunity emerge from uniqueness. The process of resolving conflict can teach you about your own thinking process.

## Why Does It Matter?

Working through disagreements with coworkers can lead to better decision-making, improved productivity and a more positive work environment. When teams consider different perspectives and ideas, it can result in more innovative and effective solutions.

Additionally, addressing and resolving conflicts can help build trust and respect among team members, leading to better communication and collaboration.

## Action Steps

There are five steps you can take to resolve a conflict with a peer.

*Identify the conflict type.*
As the saying goes, *"Know thy enemy and know thyself"*. The enemy in this case is the conflict, *not your coworker*. There are generally four types of workplace conflicts: disagreement about who is responsible for completing a task, disagreements about what exactly needs to be done to complete a task, disagreements about the best approach or process for executing the task and personal feelings that one peer may have toward another. You first need to understand the nature of the conflict you are dealing with before you can appropriately set the stage for cooperation in resolving the conflict.

*Look inward first.*
When we face a disagreement with a coworker, most of us think we are viewing the situation clearly and objectively. We believe that anyone with an opinion that differs from ours must be misinformed, unreasonable or biased. It's critical to acknowledge and suppress this instinctive response. Ask yourself questions such as, *"How can I be certain that my beliefs are accurate?" "What if I'm mistaken in my view?" "How would I alter my actions?" "What presumptions did I make?"* to remind yourself that these are *your* views, not necessarily the whole truth.

*Get into the right emotional state.*
Once you have examined your thoughts and resolved to maintain an open mind, it's time to get yourself into the right emotional state to resolve the conflict. Remaining calm not only helps you solidify your reputation as a professional who can control his emotions—it can also keep your coworker from becoming defensive or aggressive. Adopt the mindset that you will make an effort to empathize with your peers. You need to understand why they might be frustrated and acknowledge their emotions.

*Identify areas of common ground and confirm joint goals.*
Each side should be given the opportunity to openly voice points of view. There is likely to be at least some common ground between you and your coworker. While addressing areas of disagreement, remind your coworker that you are both on the same side. You both want the project to succeed. You are both passionate about creating more value for yourselves, the team, the department and the organization. Your objective is not to win the argument, but to complete the task at hand. To do so, jointly make a list of common objectives.

*Find a solution through compromise.*
If areas of disagreement remain, find a solution together. Compromise is often necessary for problem solving. Offer a plan that you believe will work while leaving room for the other person's ideas and opinions. Constantly ask your coworker questions such as, *"What do you think?" "How can we make this better?" "What would you change?"*

In the end, if the plan works out well, you should celebrate with your coworker and emphasize that it was a team effort. If the plan doesn't work, repeat the process to find a new solution. If you simply cannot find a mutually agreeable solution, as a last resort, it might be necessary to involve your manager or others who can help you achieve resolution.

# Engaging in Challenging Conversations at Work

*"Communication works for those who work at it."*
*John Powell*

Rarely, if ever, do challenging conversations at work have a comedic twist like in an episode of *The Office* when Jim threatens Dwight with a "full disadulation".

Engaging in difficult conversations at work is not always easy, but it's an opportunity to build stronger and more effective relationships with your colleagues. By being open and honest and by approaching conflicts with empathy and understanding, you can turn difficult conversations into opportunities for growth and positive change.

## Why Does It Matter?

In contrast to a sitcom, difficult conversations at work often involve sensitive or uncomfortable topics such as conflicts, mistakes, performance issues or disagreements. They can be emotionally taxing on both parties. Unfortunately, if a problematic conversation is not handled well, it can ripple into a strained relationship.

Many people avoid tough conversations because they simply don't want to confront the other person. However, by taking the right approach, engaging in a difficult conversation can ensure that your message is heard and lead to better collaboration, teamwork and goal attainment.

## Action Steps

There are seven recommendations to keep in mind when engaging in a challenging conversation at work.

- **Address the problem as early as you can, but do not catch the other person off guard.** It is important to ask for permission before you intend to speak with someone. Doing this allows them time to prepare for the discussion. Failure to do so might result in the other person feeling ambushed and getting defensive in the conversation.
- **Come prepared.** Outline your points before addressing the person in a meeting. Explain how the problem affects you and the organization. Substantiate your claims with facts and data. Anticipate the other person's reaction and response.
- **Be clear, direct and specific.** The clearer and more specific you can be when giving feedback, the more effective you will be at addressing the issue. Clear content facilitates comprehension for the listener and simplifies the process of processing information, rather than complicating it.
- **Adopt a neutral tone.** It can take effort to deliver tough messages in a neutral manner, but starting with a neutral tone is the optimal approach. Avoid getting defensive or raising your voice. Always stay calm and composed.
- **Use measured language.** Use language that is not harsh or extreme, but rather balanced and measured in its tone and delivery. For example, instead of saying, *"Stop mishandling our customers in the intake process!"* you can say, *"Can we work on improving the customer experience during the intake process?"* This phrase is more polite and less confrontational. It focuses on the desired outcome (improvement) rather than on the negative behavior (mishandling), and it frames the request as a collaborative effort to achieve a common goal.
- **Use the passive voice.** Employing the passive voice can be extremely useful since it draws attention away from the person and places it squarely on the subject matter. For example,

instead of *"You did not meet the client's expectations,"* you can say, *"The client's expectations were not met."*
- **Make sure it is a two-sided conversation**. Give feedback in a way that allows for a response. It is possible someone may have a good reason for what he's doing. There is a greater chance of reaching a mutually-satisfactory solution when both parties feel heard.

There are three things you should <u>avoid</u> doing when engaged in a challenging conversation.

- **<u>Don't</u> sugarcoat or sandwich your statements**. While preferred by many, these methods can downplay the importance of the intended message. Also avoid using euphemisms, repeating yourself or delaying making your point. In most cases, you are better off being direct and just telling the person the truth.
- **<u>Don't</u> have the conversation in front of others**. Don't publicly embarrass the other person. Choose the right time and place to have the conversation, and avoid having difficult conversations in public or in front of other people.
- **<u>Don't</u> focus on the person**. Always provide feedback based on the issue, *not the person*. The other person should not feel targeted or attacked. Remember, creating unnecessary hostility in the workplace is the opposite of your goal.

Don't shy away from challenging conversations at work; tackle them head-on so everyone can productively move forward.

# Creating Boundaries for Chatty Colleagues

*"In this age of media and Internet access,
we are much more talkative than ever before."*
*David Duchovny*

Workplaces have increasingly offered more flexibility to work remotely over the last few years, but for many businesses the office is open and full of employees. And office chatter is as prominent as it ever was.

Yes, it's great . . . except when you're trying to concentrate on your work and you hear office chit-chat buzzing all around you. You put in your earbuds and listen to something soothing, which probably helps until your chatty colleague stops by *your* desk. What starts as a simple question then morphs into a monologue about the latest show they're streaming and suddenly, fifteen minutes have passed.

## Why Does It Matter?

For some people, social interaction at work is the way they deal with other problems in their life, such as loneliness and anxiety. And when you've worked hard to build good relationships with your coworkers, you don't want to become known as the "rude one" who cuts people off or the "no-fun one" who stops conversations cold by reminding everyone that it's time to get back to work.

It's important to find ways you can tactfully set boundaries so that you can get back to work *and* preserve your relationships with your chatty chums.

## Action Steps

When you know you don't have time for long conversations, greet your incoming colleague and immediately state your time limit. You can say, *"Hey, there! I have to join a virtual meeting in about five minutes. What's up?"*

By making it clear you have limited time before the conversation even starts, you don't come off as rudely as you might have if you'd interrupted your chattering friend to announce there's a clock on the conversation. When you're close to the time limit, make good on your claim by saying, *"Okay, I have to join this meeting. Maybe we can catch up later!"*

Some other options for controlling the chatty Cathies in your office include:

- Suggest sharing lunch or a break together so you can offer your full attention. You're still controlling the time while giving your friend the option of when to use it.
- When there are about ten minutes left in a planned conversation, summarize what's been discussed or agreed and what still needs to be covered.
- Invite your coworker to summarize their understanding of the discussion, which may give them the cue that they've wasted time and still didn't get what they need.
- Perfect your interruption skills. This strategy is useful in meetings where you're faced with people who monopolize the discussion. For instance, you might interject politely with, "Excuse me, John, I see your point and appreciate your insights. I'd like to build on that by sharing a different perspective."
- Use tactical interruption when a colleague stops by your desk for a quick question and then starts jabbering about non-work things. As soon as you can get a word in, take a quick glance at the nearest clock and say, *"Oh geez, look at the time. I'm supposed to get this email response out today. Catch you later, okay?"*

- Set up "office hours" in your calendar and make it generally known that you'll be free to answer questions, troubleshoot problems or catch up only during that time-boxed period.

When listening to coworkers, if you hear something that you believe could be considered harassment, have a word with the participants. Say that their conversation was more graphic than you'd like to hear and ask that they refrain from discussing potentially offensive, explicit or divisive topics.

If offensive conversations persist, let them know that the next time you have to listen to an inappropriate conversation, you'll go to HR to request help in resolving the situation in the interest of trying to maintain a good working relationship.

Don't forget to reflect on your own behavior and make sure you're not guilty of chattering on when you strike up a conversation. If you're setting boundaries for your colleagues, you'd better observe them yourself too.

# What To Do When a Coworker Annoys You

> "It is very humbling to see my own character defects in someone who annoys me. At the end of the day, I realize they have actually prompted positive change in me."
> *Auliq Ice*

We all have habits and some can be annoying to those we work with. At one point or another, most of us have had to deal with the annoying habits of coworkers.

Whether it's the colleague who can't stop bragging about their perfect children or the one who talks incessantly while you're trying to get your work done, it can be frustrating and draining to deal with. Even worse is the coworker who violates your personal space, eavesdrops on your conversations or spreads rumors about you. Or how about that person who has a habit of stealing your lunch from the breakroom refrigerator.

## Why Does It Matter?

The annoying habits of coworkers are a major source of stress in the workplace. According to several studies, nearly 60 percent of employees say that annoying habits of coworkers have negatively affected their work relationships and 40 percent of employees have even left a job because of a coworker's annoying habit.

Unfortunately, we can't always choose who we work with. We spend a significant amount of time in close proximity to our colleagues, often with nothing but a flimsy cubicle wall separating us. So it's no surprise that learning how to effectively deal with the annoying habits of colleagues can make a huge difference in our overall job satisfaction and productivity.

## Action Steps

Developing avenues to handle annoying coworkers will depend on the specific situation. These best practices will help you choose the right method.

- **Pick your battles.** You need to decide if a coworker's annoying habit is really something you want to challenge. Habits such as gum popping or loud chewing are annoying, but they don't decrease your productivity, threaten your safety or interfere with your ability to be effective on the job. If no one else is annoyed by the behavior, maybe you need to just let it go.
- **Experiment with coping mechanisms.** Figure out if there is anything you can do to help yourself adjust to or deal with the annoying habit so that you don't have to make an issue out of it. One universal hack you can try is to focus on your colleagues' positive contributions and concentrate on those rather than on their annoying habits.
- **Self-reflect.** Before you talk to your coworker, clarify exactly what is bothering you and ask yourself whether this is something that she can change or if it is beyond her control. If it's the latter, talking about it won't help. Understanding the root of the issue will enable you to have a more productive conversation and increase the likelihood of a positive outcome.
- **Approach your colleague in a non-confrontational manner.** If you decide to confront your colleague about his annoying habit, approach the situation with a positive mindset. Don't assume malicious intent on the part of your coworker. Also, enter the conversation in the right frame of mind—calm and collected.
- **Work together to find a solution.** Ask the person if she would be willing to change her behavior or if there's anything you can do to help. Be flexible and willing to compromise.

- **Acknowledge progress**. Recognize and appreciate your coworker's efforts if she's made strides to improve the behavior. It's not always easy to make changes, so if she's taken steps to address the behavior, acknowledge it. Recognizing efforts can help foster a positive work relationship and encourage her to continue making progress.
- **Don't gossip about coworkers' habits**. Gossip can have negative consequences. Take the high road and don't gossip or spread rumors about your coworkers and their habits.

If the behavior continues or escalates and it continues to negatively impact your productivity and morale, you might need to take the issue to a supervisor. But make sure that before you do, you've tried to resolve the situation on your own first.

Dealing with annoying coworkers can be a daily challenge. (I'm probably not alone in wishing that gum popping and loud chewing were outlawed in the workplace.) Although it may be impossible to eliminate all irritating habits, you can manage the situation and make your work environment more bearable.

# What To Do When Your Coworker Is the Slacker

"The dream is free. The hustle is sold separately."
*Unknown*

Most every workplace has at least one person who does the minimum amount of work possible and still manages to keep their job. We all probably know a few people like that.

The people who work with that slacker know the real deal. Your coworker strolls in late every day, sometimes ten minutes late and sometimes more like thirty minutes. You pass by them periodically, and they're scrolling through images on Instagram or browsing the internet instead of working on the spreadsheet that's due. As each day passes, you grow more resentful, and you fear one day you're going to lose it.

Does their laziness affect your job? There's no doubt that a slacker coworker is infuriating because they upset the balance of fairness on the team. If everyone else is coming in early and skipping lunches during a major push to complete a task, but the team's slacker isn't contributing their fair share, it creates friction. Before you take steps to confront the problem, ask yourself a few questions:

- Am I unable to be successful in my job because they aren't pulling their weight?
- Do I have to work harder or longer to pick up their slack?
- Does their behavior reflect negatively on me?
- Does their behavior affect the success of the team or the company?

If you've answered yes to one or more of those questions, take steps to address the situation. But if the answer is "no" across-the-board, then it's better to step back and let it go. In all likelihood, eventually the slacker's own failings will become evident to management.

## Why Does It Matter?
Dealing with a slacker coworker requires taking a cautious approach, because if you just start complaining, especially in front of others, you're going to look like a whiner or a grouch. Still, you may not feel like you're doing your part in taking care of the team (*or yourself!*) if you let a slacker's lack of contribution fly under the radar.

## Action Steps
By following these steps, you can preserve your own reputation while you work toward a resolution.

*Start a conversation.*
Approach your coworker when you're composed and in control, and work hard to maintain a professional demeanor throughout the conversation. Keep the focus on how their late work or weak contribution is directly affecting your work performance. Say something to the effect of *"You didn't reach out to the media team to make sure the videos were finished, and I had to reschedule the client presentation so we lost the deal."* Once your coworker is faced with the fallout from their failing performance, they might amend their slacker ways.

*Give them the chance to explain.*
If you happen to have a congenial relationship with your slacking coworker, you can demonstrate compassion by gently inquiring if there's anything going on in their life that's affecting their ability to complete their work on time. It's possible that what you see as intentional slacking is actually evidence of someone who is depleted and heading for burnout.

If you learn that their slacking behavior isn't intentional, then you can choose to build your relationship by offering support. However, be explicit about the extent of your help and for how long you're willing to provide it.

*Talk with others on the team.*
If having a conversation with your coworker has resulted in a dead end and their behavior doesn't change, then it's a good idea to widen the conversation to include others on your team—simply for you to check your perspective to make sure your observations are accurate.

Do they see the situation in the same way you do? Is their work being negatively affected too?

Leverage your network too. Getting some perspective about how your other connections have handled things and how the situation was ultimately resolved will help you maintain your professionalism.

*Speak with your manager.*
This step needs to be approached carefully. If you come across as complaining or whining, your manager may think you're just being childish and you risk undermining your credibility.

Adopt a fact-based approach and describe how you've tried to handle the situation on your own—but there's been no improvement. Avoid inserting your own feelings and speak primarily in terms of how the slacking behavior negatively impacts the success of the team and the organization.

You could say, *"I tried to talk to Pat, but the conversation hasn't changed the situation. I don't know what to do next and I was hoping you could give me some advice."* This approach makes it less of a complaint and more about seeking a solution.

Ultimately, it's your manager's responsibility to address poor performance among their direct reports. You've put them on notice that the behavior of your coworker is negatively affecting the performance of the company, so it's much more likely that they'll proactively deal with your slacker coworker.

# How To Deal With Coworkers Who Are Always Asking for Help

> *"As you grow older, you will discover that you have two hands, one for helping yourself, the other for helping others."*
> *Sam Levinson*

Many people would rather work nights and weekends than ask someone else to help them finish their work. That's not necessarily a healthy attitude, but the point is that people often resist asking for help. Perhaps you're one of those people.

The flipside of those nose-to-the-grindstone people are those who choose not to overwork themselves when there are other people who can do some or all of their work for them. They are usually attuned to notice who's highly capable and who's always willing to be helpful, and they take note of that and capitalize on it.

You can turn these people on their heads by assisting help-seeking coworkers to become problem-solvers. That way, you'll help them build a critical skill that not only benefits them on the job, but also enables them to make important decisions in all aspects of their lives.

## Why Does It Matter?

Helping other people once in a while demonstrates that you're capable, responsible and willing to do what it takes to ensure business goals are met. It provides you with a sense of accomplishment and personal pride that you were able to help make something happen when it didn't look like it would be possible. That's a satisfying feeling.

However, you need to make sure that your helpfulness is not taken advantage of. There are a few warning signs that can help you identify whether your helpful nature is being misused.

- It's happening on a regular basis.
- It makes you feel used instead of helpful.
- Your own work is suffering.
- It becomes an expectation, not a favor.

## Action Steps

If you're tired of being the go-to person for everyone who needs help, there are ways you can be a supportive colleague without taking on the work of others.

1. **Set clear boundaries for what you will or won't do.** This is important if you've conditioned yourself to just automatically say yes when asked to help. Instead of letting habit take over, find out what kind of help your colleague needs and let that information help guide your decision.
2. **You don't have to say yes to doing everything.** Instead, you can agree to provide help on one specific task, or you could offer to find someone else who could assist.
3. **Feel empowered to say no without any guilt.** Don't be afraid to communicate that you know your own limits and for the sake of your own well-being, you won't take on more than what you know you can handle.
4. **Encourage coworkers to develop self-reliance.** Some coworkers may be genuinely lazy but other coworkers may have real difficulty keeping up because they're weak in some essential skills. In that situation, talk with them about the basic skills they should have and encourage them to seek training for the skills they lack.
5. **Empower coworkers to become problem solvers.** Instead of providing solutions or taking over, ask questions that will guide your coworkers toward finding solutions on their own. You can also recommend resources, including other

colleagues, that can help them identify potential solutions and evaluate their effectiveness. Then you can offer to review their solutions and provide constructive feedback that focuses on their strengths and areas for improvement.

# What To Do When Coworkers Gossip About You at Work

*"Great minds discuss ideas; average minds discuss events; small minds discuss people."*
*Eleanor Roosevelt*

You're probably not a famous pop star who inspires years' worth of online gossip, but you may still be surrounded by haters. Or at least gossips. And unlike Taylor Swift, you may not be able to simply shake it off with one sick beat.

Workplace gossip serves different purposes and sometimes jealousy is at the root of it. People want to find a scapegoat for their professional and personal frustrations. It may be that the scapegoat ends up being *you*.

## Why Does It Matter?

Unchecked, malicious gossip can poison a workplace or relationships within a work team. It can cast doubt on someone's performance, skills and character. In those cases, it requires taking action. No one wants to be the center of prolonged, negative attention.

Malicious gossip can, indeed, run rampant and has the potential to undermine your peace of mind and your career. Understanding how to deal with it helps you to figure out a course of action in specific situations—depending on how slanderous the gossip is.

## Action Steps

There is no hard and fast rule here. Only you can decide if the talk about you is something you can shake off.

If it's something minor, your best option is likely to just ignore it. Let your actions speak for you. Go about your business, behave professionally, do good work and be a positive, supportive teammate.

Most minor gossip and sniping will often go away on its own while you rise above it.

Some things you just can't ignore. If the gossip is potentially harmful to your work, your working relationships or your reputation, you'll need to act. In these instances, address the gossip when you hear it. Once you decide it must be dealt with, do it immediately. Whether you hear it from others or directly from the source, don't put it off or let it spread further.

The important thing is to remain calm and professional. Being combative is counterproductive.

If you *have* done something that inadvertently offended the person, explain in professional terms that it would be better if he came to you directly with the issue. You don't have to apologize unless you've done something you're genuinely sorry for. Even then, he should talk to you and not behind your back.

If you aren't sorry, then address it the way politicians and celebrities do: you didn't mean to offend anyone.

If it's gossip about personal behavior, you don't have to defend yourself. Your private life is just that, private. If you are getting divorced or need to take time off to deal with a health challenge, it's not the whole team's or company's business.

Sometimes it's hard to take, but be the bigger person when gossip is slung your way. It will pay off in the long run.

It's rare that gossip ever gets to a heightened point. Far and away, most gossip stays small and can be countered with a calm, professional, private response. But if it does merit a response, then act decisively.

No one deserves to be subject to a hostile work environment. If your manager is the gossip, don't be afraid to confront her. If you do and the gossip doesn't stop, go over her head. Abuse and harassment are non-starters. You must take steps to protect yourself.

# Counteracting Coworkers' Negativity

*"Negativity is like a flat tire.
You can't go anywhere until you change it."*
*Unknown*

When I talk about coworkers' negativity, I'm not talking about toxic people or worse, a full-on toxic workplace where abuse, harassment and unethical behavior are rampant. Those environments are lethal and require a different level of response. Negativity is simply a significant, deep-seated grumpy gray cloud that doesn't seem to move away from over your coworkers' heads.

When dealing with negativity you first need to evaluate the situation. Everyone, occasionally, needs the chance, a safe space and a sympathetic ear to blow off steam. That's understood.

But people do like to complain. Some people love it. And others seem to really thrive on it.

Nothing is ever good enough. Nothing *ever* goes their way. All change is bad, but so is the status quo. Everyone else, especially the boss and everyone above their paygrade, is out to create trouble and make their life miserable. It is an endless, dissonant litany of negativity. It's both cacophony and drone.

## Why Does It Matter?

Let's face it: negativity at work is a drag. It drags down your mood. It drags down your motivation. It drags down your productivity. Some days, it can feel like it's dragging down everything in your life.

Chronic negativity can make your workday miserable. It wastes your time and saps your energy. And negative people have the potential to turn you into one of them because negativity is contagious.

But dealing with chronic negativity is still a serious, day-to-day issue that many of us face, and it must be dealt with if you're going to be a reasonably happy camper at work. Don't give in. Negativity is a bottomless pit. You have to fight it.

## Action Steps

If you love to complain and nothing is ever good enough for you, stop right now. You're the problem. You cannot always control others, but you can control yourself.

If you're not the problem, then you must determine how much negativity you can comfortably live with. Jennie, who occasionally erupts on particularly bad days, may be tolerable. Ryan, who whines non-stop about how unfair his supervisor is, may be another matter.

The best way to bust negativity is to stay upbeat and professional. You're in charge of *you*. Be the person people want to work with, not the one they try to avoid in the breakroom. Negativity can build up over years of dissatisfaction, so if you're struggling to feel positive or rise above your coworkers' negativity, work through this checklist.

- **Evaluate your options**. Confront the negativity. Are people complaining about a valid issue? Maybe you can put your heads together and offer a solution.
- **Talk directly with the complainers**. Tell them how their behavior affects you and likely others, too.
- **Excuse yourself from the conversation and walk away**. Steel your resolve and stay above the fray. Know that this may anger your negative coworkers. Misery loves company. But walk away anyway.
- **Be a positive example for those around you**. This doesn't mean you have to sow rainbows and pass out cookies, though even the most hardcore pessimist might struggle to turn down a gooey chocolate chip cookie. It *does* mean that you

can help alleviate the situation by modeling better, more positive responses to negativity.

Look for things to be positive about and share them. Surround yourself, as much as possible, with positive coworkers. Deflect negativity and, when possible, nip it in the bud. Replace it with what's going well. Share your coworkers' successes, highlight the upside potential in workplace developments and point out the positive qualities in others. Look for things to be happy about and champion them.

# Dealing With Conflict on the Job

*"You gotta know when to hold 'em, know when to fold 'em, know when to walk away . . . "*
*From the famous song, "The Gambler"*
*by Kenny Rogers*

In the workplace, just as in life, there are times when you must decide if you should confront another person about an issue. Size up the situation and ask, *"What are my chances of prevailing in the argument?" "Why might it be prudent to avoid an argument with this person?"* or *"Is the argument of vital importance to my organization?"*

Your reputation may benefit more from showing your ability to achieve conflict resolution rather than disrupting peace and productivity with an argument. A fight, with all its potential for disruption, should remain a last resort. Your goal should be to avoid conflict and resolve disputes peacefully.

## Why Does It Matter?

If you fight often, your reputation can be negatively affected. Unless necessary, arguments are seen as disruptive to productivity and workplace harmony. **There are some situations where you need to defend your position and doing so may result in an argument.**

- **Ethical concerns**: If you believe that a decision or action is ethically or morally wrong, standing up for your principles can be justified.
- **Safety and well-being**: If you've identified a threat to the safety or well-being of colleagues, customers, or the public, you should voice these concerns.

- **Legal and compliance issues**: If a proposed course of action might violate laws, regulations, or company policies, you have a responsibility to speak up.
- **Project or product integrity**: If you believe that a decision could jeopardize the quality, integrity, or success of a project or product, you might need to argue against it.
- **Resource allocation**: Disagreements can arise over how resources—including time, money, and personnel—are allocated. If you believe that resources are being wasted or misallocated, you are justified in voicing your concerns.
- **Workplace rights**: If you are being treated unfairly or are the victim of harassment or discrimination, it's essential to stand up for your rights.
- **Role and responsibility clarity**: If there's confusion or disagreement about job roles, responsibilities, or project ownership, it might be necessary to have a serious discussion to clarify things.

Your willingness to stand up for an important issue may be seen as a sign that you genuinely care about and are committed to your organization. The key is to choose your arguments wisely and not make engaging in arguments your "go to" approach.

## Action Steps

While you are considering if the issue is worth a fight, your goal should remain to resolve the problem at hand.

As with every important decision, before committing to an argument, you should assess your expected risk/benefit ratio. To do this, ask yourself four questions.

1. What's at stake?
2. How does it affect you?

3. How does it affect others?
4. How does it affect your boss?

There are always risks and there's sometimes a price to pay when engaging in an argument. The stake had better be worth the fight.

You may join in someone else's argument or he in yours. Either way, some of your colleagues may feel pressured to take sides and the argument can be uncomfortable for everyone involved. You want to be known as a problem solver, rather than a fighter. Try to engage in fruitful discussions about change, rather than arguments. And remember, never focus only on a single, short-term victory, because you may end up losing the war.

If after careful consideration you decide to engage in the argument, there are six general principles for arguing effectively.

1. **Argue about a principle**. Show how your idea, proposal, initiative or solution could benefit the organization, the team, the customer.
2. **Fight the problem, not the person**. Always focus on the issues at the heart of the argument, not on the person with whom you are arguing. Never attack the other person's character.
3. **Emotions are okay**. If you show strong, but controlled, emotions, it illustrates how deeply you care about the issue. That display may actually strengthen your argument for change. However, you must always remain in control and never lose your temper.
4. **Allow face-saving**. You want to prevail in the argument, not humiliate your opponent(s). After all, you may embrace some aspects of your opponent's point of view. Help the other person save face.

5. **Lose gracefully**. The argument may not end as you had hoped. Even if you don't agree with the verdict, you should maintain your dignity and commitment to moving forward, regardless of what you consider to be a sub-optimal outcome.
6. **Mend fences**. Preserve your professional rapport and ability to work together. Remember that your opponent in this argument may become your partner in the next. Don't let your relationship and reputation be adversely affected by one disagreement.

Remember that professionals who can balance what they perceive as a concern for their perspective with the concern for others in the organization are assets to any team.

# What To Do When a Coworker Dislikes You

"It's okay if some people dislike you. Not everyone has good taste."
*Anonymous*

You pride yourself on being an easygoing person. You have a few close friends at work and generally, you think they consider you likable.

And then a well-meaning friend tells you something that shakes you to your core. One of your coworkers dislikes you. Every doubt and insecurity you had about yourself in the past comes flooding back. You try to think about why this coworker might not like you. Did you inadvertently insult her somehow? Say something she misconstrued? Take her preferred parking space in the employee lot?

Then feelings of insecurity really accelerate. What if she turns *other* people against you? What might this do to your career?

## Why Does It Matter?

Dislike—and even hate—in the workplace is not as unusual as you might think. In 2017, Comparably conducted a survey of workers across the technology sector and the result found that one in three people were ready to leave their job because of a coworker they don't like.

It's more likely that a colleague who hates you isn't going to do it in an overt way, because that may put his own job at risk just as you fear it could jeopardize yours. Instead, he may reveal his dislike in subtle ways such as:

- Not smiling when you're around.
- Not maintaining eye contact with you.
- Avoiding you.
- Not acknowledging your presence.

- Using negative body language.
- Constantly disagreeing with you.
- Creating cliques that exclude you.

If your coworker sticks to subtle avoidance behaviors, then you can try techniques to build a better working relationship. However, if your coworker's behavior veers into bullying, tell him that it's not acceptable and you won't tolerate it.

## Action Steps

So what can you do when your existence bothers someone you must interact with on a daily basis? Here are six ways you can attempt to defuse the negativity from a coworker who clearly dislikes you.

1. **Don't obsess about it**. As much as you may want to pursue answers, consider taking some time to cool off. Feelings aren't logical, so even if you do discover the reason she doesn't like you, it may still not make sense or alleviate your hurt feelings.
2. **Address the situation**. If you can't ignore the situation any longer, then drag it into the open. Find an opportunity to speak to your coworker where it's difficult for him to ignore you. You could try saying something such as, *"I feel like there's some tension between us, and I would like to clear the air so we can both focus on doing our best work. Am I doing something that bothers you?"* You may not get an answer, or you may hear something you didn't expect. Either way, focus on trying to forge some sort of relationship that improves your work environment.
3. **Try appealing to their ego**. Flattery will get you everywhere. This might be hard to do but praise his successes. Show your appreciation for his efforts. Ask him to lend his expertise with a problem you're working on. These approaches can be especially tough if your hater really makes

you feel uncomfortable, but if you're able to humble yourself, you may serve up the opportunity for your relationship to move in a more positive direction.
4. **Recognize that dislike is a two-way street**. There is no rule that says everybody who works together must like each other. If you can admit that it's possible to dislike people and still do your job, then you have no excuse for not finding a way to work together without creating tension. Your focus should be on doing *your* best work, not on getting your coworker to change how she feels about you.
5. **Take the high road**. You have no control over the actions and feelings of other people. You can only control your own reaction. Stop spending your time trying to get them to like you and instead demonstrate integrity and respect in your interactions with them. Know that it may sting a little to be the bigger person, especially if your coworker persists in his dislike, but the sting will lessen over time. Being the bigger person doesn't mean you have to like him.
6. **Recognize when a boundary has been crossed**. Understand the difference between passive dislike and outright bullying. Bullying is behavior that's designed to cause hurt, harm or distress to someone else. It includes things such as intimidation, insults or humiliation. If the bullying doesn't stop, then it's reached a level that requires escalation to your manager or human resources. Don't forget that you're not just deserving, but entitled to a workplace that champions respect and is free from bullying.

You won't always like or be liked by all of your workplace colleagues, but you can do your best to correct any misunderstandings and try to find a way to peacefully coexist.

# Dealing With a Toxic Coworker

> "Let go of negative people. They only show up to share complaints, problems, disastrous stories, fear, judgment on others. If somebody is looking for a bin to throw all their trash into, make sure it's not in your mind."
>
> *Dalai Lama*

You've been working long hours on a project for several weeks, and you're finally ready to share your progress with the rest of the team. As you show off your work, you notice that one of your coworkers, Alex, seems really interested. You take this as a positive sign. It's just the boost in motivation you need to finish your work.

A few days later you present your work on the project to your manager but you are shocked to learn that Alex sent your boss an email two days before outlining some of the same ideas and suggestions you just presented. Your manager seems to think that Alex came up with those ideas and he praises Alex's creativity.

You're stunned and your stomach sinks as you realize exactly what's happened. You try to explain that these were your ideas and that you presented them to your colleagues, including Alex, but your manager seems skeptical. As you silently scream at the injustice of it all, you also mentally kick yourself for failing to see that this might happen. It's not like Alex hasn't done this before….

You can probably think of a few good names to call Alex in this situation, but the technical term to use is "toxic coworker". This is someone who consistently exhibits negative behavior that can range from overt and aggressive—criticizing, blaming or excluding—to passive and subtle actions such as manipulating, sabotaging, controlling or undermining.

## Why Does It Matter?

You don't have the authority to just go ahead and fire people who drive you crazy. Toxic coworkers engage in destructive tactics because they are often fearful of having their own incompetence known or they may be envious or resentful. But even just one toxic coworker can have a powerful impact on the people around them and seriously erode the overall work environment. They can decimate morale and drive great employees into the arms of other organizations if their actions go unchecked.

Imagine your workplace as a garden. When everything's in sync, it's a vibrant space where creativity blossoms and productivity soars. But throw in a toxic coworker? Suddenly, it's like there a stubborn weed in the garden, overshadowing the blooms and choking out everyone's potential, including yours. Addressing toxic coworkers isn't just about keeping the peace; it's about ensuring that everyone can shine, innovate and collaborate to their fullest. By tackling the issue head-on, you can make sure you and others have the space and potential to bloom.

## Action Steps

If you're dealing with a toxic coworker, follow these steps to reduce their impact on you:

### Don't bottle it up.

Annoyance and frustration are part of life in any society. The workplace, even when you're remote, is a society. But even though it's a part of life, ignoring, bottling up or burying your emotional responses is a lose-lose proposition. Swallowed emotions eventually leak out or even explode at inopportune times, at innocent people. Don't let your colleague's toxic behavior lead you to behave badly toward others. You're only going to make *them* upset, too. Suppressing your emotions won't make the situation better. So talk to someone, write down how you feel, take a break or do whatever helps you get your feelings and emotions about the situation out of your system.

### Stay focused on your own work
Toxic coworkers may act in disruptive ways because of a lack of self-confidence, personal problems or other issues. Your goal should be *your own* performance and *your* professional development.

Invest your energy in doing your own work well and promoting it. Resist the temptation to stoop to their level and engage in similar tactics just to "get back." That can backfire and make you look bad.

This includes not dragging others into it. You may feel the need to vent. That's natural. Vent if you must, but not to your other teammates. Chances are, some of them feel the same way you do, but your toxic teammate has friends and allies too.

This goes double for sending angry emails. It would be bad enough for your colleague's bad behavior to lead you to your own boorish response, but a paper trail is bound to lead to worse. Starting a war drags everybody down and the body count is sure to include some innocent civilians.

Your job is not an action movie. Vengeance is not best served cold; it's best tossed in the trash and taken to a dumpster. So don't do those things.

### Have a conversation
You can try a gentle approach, giving examples of ways your toxic coworker has bothered you and how it makes you feel. You may be surprised and get some insight into your toxic nemesis, and even if you don't influence their behavior, you might at least have a better understanding about it. A conversation may not change who they are, but you can at least point out that *you* see who they are.

## Protect and defend yourself

In addition to trying to take credit for your work, your toxic coworker may try to publicly discredit you. If this happens, immediately but calmly correct any inaccuracies.

Communicate that you won't let their behavior go unchecked. This can manifest by asking direct questions such as, *"Why did you present the work we did together as your own?"*

Asking direct questions shifts the burden of proof to your toxic teammate. They'll have to explain their actions. If appropriate, use humor to show your confidence. Humor is disarming to the troublemaker, yet engaging and memorable to your witnesses. Don't give your toxic coworker the satisfaction that they can upset you, even if they insult you. Use phrases such as, *"You must have misunderstood . . . "* or *"You are free to express your opinion, but the facts simply do not support it."*

Talk calmly in a spirit of cooperation. This person is, after all, your teammate. In theory, you and your teammate are allies. In theory, you want the same things: to get the job done and done well.

Unless your troublesome coworker is also extremely dense, they'll probably tone it down if you approach them calmly, in the spirit of providing constructive feedback. Be honest, but not brutally honest. Remind *them* that you're allies with the same goals. At the very least, they'll probably make some attempt to watch their behavior more around you, and that's the point. And it's fine if they need to think or act like better behavior was their idea. The point is to get them to change.

## Set the record straight

If you suspect someone is trying to steal your ideas, find ways to protect your work and the credit you deserve. Document what you're working on in emails and other forms of hard proof. Give frequent and timely updates and progress reports to your boss. A paper trail can stop toxic coworkers from undermining you.

*Make the toxic coworker owe you*
You might decide to change course in your approach and engage them in some form of collaboration. Suggest working on a project together, offer to brainstorm a solution to a problem, or provide information they'll find valuable. Most people are inclined to help those who have helped them. This way you turn a toxic coworker into a collaborator.

*Request their advice*
Seeking the coworker's advice—from how to deal with a sticky problem to how to negotiate a new contract—could help you earn their trust. If they know you value their opinion, they may begin to see you as an ally. The troublemaker may actually become somewhat invested in *your* success.

*Keep your boss informed*
While you might feel as if it's your manager's job to fix the problem of a toxic coworker, it's quite possible your manager may not realize there's even an issue. As part of their operating plan, toxic coworkers keep their behavior under the radar. Consider bringing their actions to your leader's attention if they negatively affect the team and everyone's productivity.

Your manager may know something you don't know about your toxic coworker. There might be a record of previous issues or important political or personal connections. Let your boss provide input and advice on how to deal with the actions of your toxic coworker.

Remember, though, when you involve your boss, you'll want to frame the issue from the perspective of what is best for the organization, rather than from the perspective of you needing a referee. You don't want your boss to think you can't solve your own problems. Stay calm and collected when talking to your boss. If you start ranting, *you* look like the problem. Approach it as a matter of team morale and productivity. When something or someone disrupts your team's ability to get work done, your boss will generally be willing to step in to help. Avoid getting personal. Thinking your exasperating teammate is a venomous puffer fish is one thing; calling him that out loud is another. Stay professional and focus not on your personal feelings, but instead on how his behavior negatively affects the team's work.

### Don't let them get to you and boost your coping skills

Finally, toxic people enjoy getting under your skin, so don't give them the satisfaction. Every complaint you make to your friends or family about how your coworker makes you feel bad about yourself implies that you're not in control of your own feelings. Instead, put your energy to better use by seeking out positive friends and fill your free time with activities that bring you happiness. To boost coping skills, try practicing meditation or yoga. You can also try artistic pursuits that awaken your creative side, like painting or playing an instrument. Enriching your life in other ways will make it easier to tune out the negativity when your toxic coworker is in your orbit. Taking these steps doesn't mean that everything will always smell of roses. But it does mean that in the big picture of your life and your job, your irksome teammate is just another irritant to learn to live with, like mosquitos and Ticketmaster fees.

# What To Do When You Are Jealous of a Coworker

*"As iron is eaten away by rust, so the envious are consumed by their own passion."*
*Antisthenes*

You've been working hard on a project for weeks, but your colleague Jack seems to have effortlessly completed a similar project in half the time. You're jealous of Jack's success and your resentment is growing. Your boss only seems to recognize Jack's work—not yours. Despite your efforts to suppress your jealousy, you find yourself becoming increasingly negative and competitive toward Jack.

There is a reason jealousy is referred to as the green-eyed monster. It's deeply rooted in our evolutionary history as a means of protecting important relationships and resources. Jealousy is often triggered by a sense of competition or comparison with others.

However, it's possible to prevent jealousy from sabotaging your success and relationships at work and instead focus on your personal growth and development.

### Why Does It Matter?

When we perceive someone else as a threat, it can trigger feelings of resentment and insecurity. These feelings can be intense and all-consuming, causing us to behave in irrational and self-destructive ways.

Jealousy is common in every workplace, especially when coworkers feel competitive with each other. No one is immune. While feeling jealous is natural, it can lead to self-sabotage, damaged relationships and decreased job satisfaction so it's best to address your envy head-on.

## Action Steps

If you find yourself jealous of a coworker, there are several steps you can take to address these feelings and prevent them from causing harm.

*Get to the bottom of what is making you jealous.*
It's essential to accept your feelings of jealousy. Trying to suppress or deny them will only make the situation worse. Instead, allow yourself to feel the emotions and try to understand what's triggering them. Envy is a natural human reaction that can provide valuable insight into what we value—it's a data point that can tell us what we aspire to achieve. Discover the meaning attached to the jealousy and see where this discovery leads you.

*Ask yourself "Why do I feel this way?"*
Write down your reasons . . . anything that comes to mind. Then, write what you can do about them.

For instance, if you envy someone for his ability to learn new skills quickly, earn a higher salary or receive praise from the boss, it's an indication of your own aspirations.

If you wish you had a specific certification, spend time to get it.

If you want your boss to praise you more, volunteer to work on a project your boss considers to be strategic.

*Don't focus on other people; focus on yourself.*
Maybe you've heard the sayings: *"Jealousy is the art of counting someone else's blessings instead of your own,"* or *"Comparison is the seed and jealousy is the fruit."*

It's natural to compare ourselves to others, especially when it comes to our accomplishments at work. In some cases, this can be a source of motivation, pushing us to strive for better outcomes and a higher level of success. But when we compare ourselves excessively with others, we feel inadequate, overlook our own progress and plummet our self-worth.

*Shift your focus from comparing yourself to others.*
Measure your current self against your past self. By tracking your progress over time and acknowledging your own accomplishments, you cultivate a sense of self-appreciation. Maybe Jack has five certifications while you have two, but that's two more than you had last year. Jack might have been selected to present at the sales conference, but for the first time *you'll* lead a session at the next executive update meeting. Congrats!

Recognize how far you've come and celebrate your own journey.

*Practice gratitude and affirm yourself.*
When we see someone else succeed, it's natural to experience a range of emotions. Among those emotions, remind yourself of your own achievements. Be grateful for what you have rather than dwell on what you lack. This shifts your focus from feeling threatened by others to feeling confident in yourself.

*Remember that success isn't a finite resource.*
Remember that someone else's success doesn't diminish your own accomplishments. There's enough success to go around. View others' success as motivation to strive for your own success. This can be a powerful mindset shift that helps you break out of a cycle of negative emotions and focus on your own growth.

# Mending Relationships at Work

"Sometimes good things fall apart so better things can fall together."
*Marilyn Monroe*

No matter how long and tight your relationships might be, there is always the potential they'll go sour. Relationships with friends, partners, loved ones or family—they're always susceptible to stress, strain and damage. That's why we cherish, treasure and take care to protect them. Working relationships are really no different.

I'm going to take a wild guess that you probably don't live with your coworkers. You aren't likely to plan futures together or share year-long histories of closeness and support. But you do spend eight or more hours a day in a confined space with one another working toward similar goals. In such close quarters and with the daily pressures inherent in the workplace, it's inevitable that relationships will sometimes fracture and when they do, in most cases you'll want to try your best to mend them.

## Why Does It Matter?

You don't have to like the people you work with. You don't even have to fully trust them on a personal level. You just have to make sure that you get things done together with them. And it's a lot easier—and more pleasant—to do that when you have solid working relationships.

Genuine and lasting friendships can come from working together. At a minimum, you and your coworkers form a team. That friendly cooperation and collaboration is important to accomplish tasks and achieve goals, and getting them done harmoniously can be easy to damage or break because it's a more superficial relationship than the deeper ones in your life. Something as simple as miscommunication or as complex as a breach of trust can bring ruin to a working relationship.

Unfortunately, fractured relationships can cast shadows over productivity and team morale. Of course, there are some situations in which one person doesn't want to mend the relationship. Unless you're the person who doesn't want to mend the relationship, it's always worth the effort to try—up until you would need to beg and plead.

## Action Steps

While anything can break a working relationship, it doesn't have to stay broken. If you sincerely want to mend it, there are ways to do it.

First, you need to be honest about what's gone wrong and your part in the breakdown. It doesn't always matter *what* happened. But, fixing it requires taking a good hard look at it and taking responsibility for your actions, even if your intentions were good.

Consider the other person's perspective. You may feel innocent of any wrongdoing but put yourself in her shoes and view the situation through her eyes.

Don't fixate on being right. The need to assign blame is one of the major causes of permanent relationship damage. When one person has to be right, the other person automatically becomes wrong. It's the easiest way to destroy a relationship of any kind, including a work relationship.

Relationships can sour even if no one did anything wrong. Relationships can suffer from too much attention and oversharing. Conversely, they can also fail from drifting apart, not getting enough attention.

And with that in mind, it's time to have a heart-to-heart. Is the damage the result of a specific incident? Talk it through, openly and honestly. Is it something that's been growing and festering? Get the issues out in the open. But do it calmly and in the spirit of getting past them. Nobody *has* to be at fault. You can both be right.

If it's your responsibility to apologize for something you did wrong, then do it humbly and mean it. If the other person apologizes, accept it graciously, without recrimination. Avoid *"I told you so"*.

Gloating is for middle school. You're adults—work together to fix something that matters to both of you.

The important thing to remember is that once damaged, relationships can take time to heal. All may be forgiven, but it takes a while to forget. By focusing on moving ahead, you can take steps to reestablish trust and reciprocate. When the other person does something thoughtful, kind or helpful, pay it back.

You don't need to keep an accounting of actions, but remember that healing is a two-way street. Give as much as you get.

Trust that broken limbs can heal. Hurt feelings can be soothed. Relationships can be mended. If it's important to you, put in the effort to make it right.

# How To Handle Dating a Coworker

> "Nobody knows our future, but it's not going to be decided by the company. It's not gonna be decided by anybody but us. What we are is up to you and me."
> *Holly to Michael in* The Office

If movies and television are to be believed, workplace romances are happening all around you. Some are unrequited, some are slow to happen, some involve sweet, happy endings and some ignite only to be quickly extinguished, usually with comical or heartwarming results.

Maybe you notice someone at work. Someone you find attractive. As you get to know him, you realize he's funny and smart, and you share interests. It's clear there's a mutual attraction. The trouble is, in real life, you don't know which ending you're headed for.

## Why Does It Matter?

It's not surprising that crushes between coworkers happen. After all, you spend more of your waking hours at work than anywhere else. Having your relationship play out in the workplace is complicated, though. While it may seem unromantic, it's best to think ahead and consider all of the implications associated with starting a relationship with a coworker.

## Action Steps

Let's explore five considerations when entering into a romantic relationship with a coworker.

*Identify and acknowledge the risks.*
A new relationship, especially a secret one, feels exciting. If it's going to be conducted in the workplace, it's a good idea to examine how

serious your feelings really are. If you're already thinking it's not going to last, then it's probably better to go no further and avoid the possible risks.

However, if you both believe it could last, you owe it to yourselves to talk about the "what ifs."

- What if you break up and you're forced to see each other every day with all of those hurt feelings you're carrying around? How will you handle it?
- What if your relationship creates potential conflicts of interest? Will colleagues see you as two independent individuals or will you automatically be considered a voting bloc?
- What if your relationships with colleagues are damaged? They may be suspicious of your motives, especially if one of you is in a more senior role.

*Know the rules and policies in your workplace.*
Some employers prohibit romantic relationships between managers and subordinates, and others may prohibit dating between colleagues, regardless of organizational rank.

Closely examine your workplace handbook for rules about dating and romantic relationships at your company. If there are rules against it and you're already well into your relationship, it's wise to immediately inform your manager so you can explore options. If you keep it a secret, remember that colleagues are keen observers and there's always a risk that someone will figure it out and report you.

*Consider making the relationship public.*
If there is no requirement at your workplace that you disclose your relationship, I advise you to strongly consider doing it anyway. By putting it out into the open, you eliminate the possibility that someone will misunderstand a look or a comment with your romantic partner

as inappropriate banter or even sexual harassment. Even if colleagues aren't thrilled to know you're dating a coworker, at least you've put it on the record and can manage potential fallout.

If you're both working for the same manager then you definitely need to inform your boss so she can decide whether she can manage you both fairly. If your manager is concerned, this creates the opportunity to discuss the situation and try to alleviate her concerns.

*Set boundaries with your partner for how work and your relationship intersect.*
Mutually agree upon boundaries that make you both feel safe and comfortable in the workplace. Maybe there's a rule about no display of physical affection or flirting on the job.

You should also talk about how your relationship might affect your individual relationships with other colleagues. Your workplace friends may start to distrust your friendship or question your loyalty if there's a situation where it looks like you're taking sides.

All relationships require time and attention, so make sure you're not sacrificing key workplace friendships for the sake of your personal relationship—and vice versa.

*Be prepared in the event of an unhappy ending.*
Whether one of you ends it or you both decide to, your workplace will find out sooner or later. It's best to take the initiative and let your manager know. You don't have to explain it all; keep it as simple and straightforward as possible, such as *"We're no longer together, and I hope you can understand that I'd rather not discuss it any further."* Don't speak badly about your ex, and don't accept others' disparaging comments, even if they think they're being supportive of you. Keep it professional.

If it becomes too painful or difficult to work alongside your ex, then you have to decide if you want a position elsewhere in the organization or if you need to find a new job. Although that may seem drastic, finding something new will end the drama and give you a fresh start.

As hard as a breakup can be with someone you work with, you *can* and will survive the breakup and keep your professional life on track.

# What To Look Out for When You Go From "Buddy" to "Boss"

*"Every boss started as a worker."*
*Rick Ross*

When you start out as a boss, your success depends on how well you are able to forge strong relationships with the people above you, with your peers and with your direct reports.

It's not easy to become a leader of former peers. You need to learn how to balance the humility needed to listen to and include your team with the courage to assert yourself in your role as leader.

## Why Does It Matter?

When your direct reports have previously been your peers, it can sometimes be difficult to move from just being one of the group to being in charge of it.

The role you play affects the way others relate to you, so your transition to a leadership role means that, even if you've known your direct reports for years, your relationship with them in the role of manager is brand new. You've got to re-introduce yourself and renegotiate terms with them if you're going to be successful.

## Action Steps

*Meet one-on-one with each member of your team.*
Having your first boss-subordinate conversation on an individual basis helps you personalize the message you want to deliver and be more candid. Spend a considerable amount of time listening to your new direct report. Ask specific questions such as:

- *Take me through your objectives and where things stand?*
- *Tell me about your development planning.*
- *Are there any specific areas where you would like my support?*

Listen carefully to his answers. Rephrase and summarize to make sure you have understood everything. This helps your reports realize that you are approachable in your new role.

*Explain how you would like to operate and what your rules are going to be.*
Distill your philosophies into two or three concise guiding principles. Be explicit about areas such as communication, role clarity and delegation of responsibilities and how you want them to deal with an issue. You can say *"I want all issues to be shared openly so that they can be resolved,"* or *"Please don't come to me with an issue before you've addressed it directly with one another first."* This helps you set important precedents from the get-go.

*Create a culture of inclusivity and inquiry.*
Your new status can create stress and uncertainty for your team. Talk about your concerns openly and honestly with them. Let them know you value their input. The key is to establish trust and to exercise influence by creating a culture of inclusivity and inquiry among former peers. The more power a supervisor is willing to share, the more influence she will command.

*Set boundaries and expectations.*
When you move up the career ladder and start leading people, you've got to adjust your behavior. Set new boundaries and expectations right from the start, and let your team know that your relationship has undergone a change. Think twice about the choices you make and how you conduct yourself when you are with your new reports, and refrain from gossiping.

As a new manager of former peers, there are a few challenges you may face, but there are effective ways of dealing with these challenges.

- **A decision is made without your knowledge.** If you learn that a decision you should have been part of has been made without involving you, talk with the person who made it and communicate your displeasure. Draw the line between the type of decision that your employees can make autonomously and when they need to loop you in.
- **An issue that has been closed is reopened.** Discourage this behavior by making it clear that dissent is welcome, but only before the decision is made. Use this moment to reinforce that you want the team to move efficiently and that your expectation is that once a decision is made, everyone is on board.
- **A team member resists your leadership.** Resistant team members often don't have the courage to challenge you directly. They'll show irreverence with subtle and sometimes not-so-subtle body language such as rolling eyes, turning away from you in meetings or disengaging from the conversation. When you notice this behavior, respond by sitting across from or directly beside the person in the next meeting. If resistance persists, confront the person one-on-one with direct feedback. You can say, *"I've noticed that you sit at the back of the room during meetings and only respond with one-word answers. I'm concerned that you're struggling to accept me in my new role as team leader. What are you willing to do differently to show you're on board?"*
- **A group of people gang up on you.** It is difficult enough to deal with one passive-aggressive team member. The stress is amplified when multiple people on your team question your leadership. If you face this challenge, meet with everyone individually and then address the issue in a team meeting.

Be direct, and don't be afraid to make people a little uncomfortable. If there are things you've been doing that may have contributed to the resistance, take responsibility for them. Use the team meeting to reinforce the ground rules you set at the beginning.

- **A team member wanted your role.** Identify team members who are having difficulty adjusting because they hoped to have your new role. Meet with them and acknowledge their feelings. Help them understand that you're committed to helping them succeed, but you're still the boss.

Transitioning from buddy to boss can involve some difficult navigation over rough seas, but with the right approach, you'll find smoother waters ahead.

# Meeting Colleagues Face-to-Face for the First Time

> "Not finance, not strategy. Not technology.
> It is teamwork that remains the ultimate competitive advantage, both because it is so powerful and rare."
> *Patrick Lencioni*

For virtual employees, when you're called upon to leave the house and go meet your peers in person, you may be in for some surprises. Out of their usual settings and context, you might not even instantly recognize them. And like running into a celebrity at the grocery store, you may not be certain it's really who you think it is at first.

And beyond that you may not know what they're like when the camera isn't on. And, of course, they have all the same anxieties about you.

## Why Does It Matter?

Remote work is so common now that many people know their colleagues only as little images on a screen. And depending upon the nature of your job and your team, you may not be able to gauge much about them beyond how they present themselves professionally. It can feel like you are attending a masked ball with everyone hiding behind a virtual mask.

Meeting your colleagues doesn't have to be scary. Even in the real world, this is still work. You're all there for the same reason and, at the very least, you all have that in common. So go break some ice.

## Action Steps

It's natural to be a little wary when meeting anyone face-to-face for the first time, so there are some things to keep in mind as you get ready to head to an office you've likely never visited, to interact with people you've never shared oxygen with.

- **Mind your wardrobe.** This can be tricky for those who've never gone into the office or attended a company function. At the very least, you want to look professional. This means clean and crisp. Check your closet and make sure you have something appropriate that fits and isn't wrinkled or stained. Shave, unless facial hair is your thing. Wash and brush your hair. Little details that don't show up on camera can come into clear focus in person. Use your mirror, full-length if you have one.
- **Mind your manners.** You don't have to say what you think all the time. If Shauna is much shorter than you thought, keep it to yourself. Same goes if Leon is a lot skinnier than he looks onscreen or Bryce is a lot heavier.
- **Avoid sidebars and gossip.** You may find Karen intolerable, but that doesn't mean Bryce does. Bryce and Karen sometimes remain on the meeting link after calls and talk hockey and have become good buddies. It would be wise to gather more information about your teammates' relationships to avoid unintentionally offending anyone.
- **Plan your transportation and commute ahead of time.** Whether you're going across town or across the country, know where you're going and how to get there. Being late may be fashionable, but it's not professional.
- **Relax and be the out-in-public version of you.** To a great extent, you really *do* know each other, even if it's within the parameters of team calls and meetings. These really are the same people. If your team vibe is loose and casual, it will reassert itself even when you're all in the same room.

First impressions are lasting, even more so when virtual ties turn tangible. Seizing that face-to-face moment sets the tone for fruitful future collaboration.

# Interfacing Virtually With Coworkers

*"In a digital age, connecting virtually bridges distances, making every corner of the world our office and every screen a window to collaboration."*
*Heide Abelli*

Being part of a virtual team can be difficult. Virtual team members often feel isolated and frustrated. For example, they sometimes suffer from a lack of personal contact with others or they can find it challenging to follow conversations as people talk over each other in meetings.

You can overcome many of the challenges of being in a virtual team by making an effort to connect with your colleagues and build trusting relationships. It also helps to know how to communicate effectively and be prepared to handle issues when they arise.

## Why Does It Matter?

In today's digitally-driven world, interfacing effectively with colleagues virtually has become a linchpin of successful collaboration. With remote work and global teams becoming increasingly commonplace, the ability to communicate and work together virtually is no longer just a luxury but a necessity. Failing to interface effectively can lead to misunderstandings, missed opportunities and a lack of cohesion in team efforts.

The nuances of virtual interactions, without the benefit of face-to-face cues, demand heightened clarity and intention in your communication. Building trust, fostering understanding and nurturing relationships in a virtual space can influence the overall productivity and morale of the team.

You and your team members must build trust with each other, even when working remotely. The easiest way team members can build credibility is by being conscientious, delivering against expectations and by being generous with their praise and gratitude for others.

## Action Steps

If you're a virtual team member, there are a few things you can do to help the situation.

- Get to know your colleagues better.
- Set boundaries when it comes to communications.
- Pick the right form of communication for everyone's needs.
- Freely share information.

Developing stronger relationships with your virtual colleagues helps to avoid misunderstandings and makes communication easier and less impersonal. Be persistent about making a personal connection with your colleagues, even if it's difficult at first. Look for any opportunity to connect and build rapport. Talking about non-work-related subjects builds professional relationships. Consider asking your coworkers about their hobbies.

Virtual collaboration requires that everyone be fully present and engaged—not multitasking during online team meetings. Being predictable involves scheduling routine, consistent communications and responding to communications in a dependable, reliable way. To respect virtual team members' time and personal schedules, block out specific times during the day when you'll attend to non-urgent messages. You also need to learn how to politely end instant message conversations that go on too long and remove yourself from discussions you don't need to participate in to avoid wasting time and becoming distracted.

Finally, for a virtual team to be successful, information must be freely shared and easily accessible to all members. Make sure you proactively share information that is needed by your teammates.

# Section 5

# Navigating Boss Issues

Now that you can deal with your coworkers' issues and balance them with your own, it's time to look at your boss. No relationship holds as much sway over your day-to-day experience as the one you have with your boss. It all starts with building that foundational rapport. Syncing with your boss can set the rhythm for your professional journey. By understanding his or her goals and aligning them with yours, you create a symbiotic working relationship. But, what if your plans go awry?

There are inevitable challenges to finding harmony–the unpredictability, the occasional lack of empathy or even the dissonance of feeling unheard. Some bosses may exhibit challenging behaviors, from being abrasive to gaslighting. It's not just about managing up, but also about handling emotions and expectations and ensuring mutual respect.

Yet, amid these challenges, there are moments of growth. Finding your voice, especially when drowned out, can lead to personal evolution. Learning to be comfortable around senior leaders and advocating for yourself when you don't feel backed up by your boss can be transformative. And while it might feel overwhelming when the boss's spotlight turns into jealousy, remember that this too is a testament to your growth and potential.

This section is full of advice on how to get along with your boss and how to cope with a boss who is, well, less than ideal. Think Miranda Priestly from "The Devil Wears Prada" or Michelle Darnelle in "The Boss"—every challenging boss has their nuances, but with the right strategies, you can still find your rhythm and jam well together. So, grab your drumsticks.

# Building Rapport With Your Boss

*"Don't think of me as your boss.
Think of me as a good friend who can fire you."*
*Anonymous, presumably intended as a joke*

"*You just have to work together, you don't have to like each other.*" Everyone's heard this saying and probably thought it multiple times over the course of their work lives. And it is true. But when it's your boss, it makes your life a lot more complicated. If Oscar in the accounting department doesn't like you, big deal. But if your boss doesn't like you, you've got a problem on your hands.

## Why Does It Matter?

You can certainly work with people you don't like. You can even hate your boss and wish they would just go away and leave you alone. You can sigh, shake your head and go about your business, ignoring your boss as much as possible.

But that's really no way to work. You spend a lot of time in a shared space with your boss. While you and your boss don't have to be best friends, the work day will go a lot more smoothly if the two of you develop a good working rapport. And it certainly can't hurt if you actually like working together.

Building rapport with your boss can be key to determining whether your job is just something you suffer through every day or an experience you can enjoy and grow with. The choice is yours.

## Action Steps

Fortunately, there is a checklist to help build rapport and strengthen your relationship with your boss.

- **Try to understand where your boss is coming from**. This helps foster better communication and minimizes misunderstandings. For instance, if your boss emphasizes punctuality, it might not just be because they're a stickler for being on time; perhaps they've seen how late starts can negatively affect the day's productivity.
- **Think about the challenges your boss faces every day**. Understanding this is important to building positive rapport. For example, they might have to balance competing priorities, such as when they're stuck between upper management's expectations and the well-being of their team.
- **Show your boss your value**. Demonstrating your value to your boss goes beyond just fulfilling your job description; it's about showcasing initiative. For example, if you notice a recurring issue in your workflow, proactively researching and suggesting a solution not only solves a problem but also displays your commitment to helping improve your boss's operation.
- **Make your boss look good**. Ensuring their decisions and leadership yield positive results strengthens their position and their team's reputation. For instance, if your boss proposes a new project, taking the initiative to execute it efficiently and effectively will showcase their sound judgment and leadership.
- **Solve problems for your boss**. Proactively solving problems for your boss alleviates their workload and demonstrates your initiative. For example, if you identify a bottleneck in a process that slows down productivity, address and streamline that process and make sure your boss knows about it.
- **Share your good ideas with your boss**. If you suggest implementing a new software program that could automate and expedite certain administrative tasks, it showcases your commitment to enhancing efficiency within your boss's operation.

- **Speak up when you see a way to improve things.** For instance, if you notice that team members often spend hours manually generating monthly reports, suggesting the integration of a data visualization tool might not only save time but also provide clearer insights, demonstrating your proactive approach to enhancing operational efficiency.
- **Be honest and have opinions, just be able to back them up.** For example, if you believe a proposed marketing campaign might not resonate with a target demographic based on recent market research, candidly presenting your insights can pivot the strategy.
- **Communicate clearly and regularly on their terms and preferred platform.** For example, if your boss prefers to receive weekly project updates via email rather than your twice-a-month impromptu office visits, consistently send concise, well-organized emails to keep them informed.
- **Ask your boss for input.** Asking for input shows respect for their expertise. For instance, before finalizing a presentation to a potential customer, seek your boss's feedback on the content and delivery.
- **Identify your boss's pet peeves.** Most bosses appreciate organization, punctuality, reliability and valuable input. Even if you consider them little things, they may be very annoying to your boss. They probably have a reason for that pet peeve, too. Is a messy desk a threat to finding important documents? Is being consistently late to meetings disrespectful toward others?
- **Consider getting to know your boss on a personal level.** To be clear, this is *not* about being their buddy and hanging out after work. It's about connecting on a basic, human level. Don't force it and don't pretend you care about things that you don't. But it can be helpful to find some common

ground. Liking the same rock music bands won't change your working relationship, but it might make it more pleasant for both of you because you've built a rapport that isn't dependent on work.

# Getting Off to a Good Start With a New Boss

*"The changes we dread most may contain our salvation."*
*Barbara Kingsolver*

Picture the scenario: Samantha has been with the company for years and had grown accustomed to her supervisor's management style. Her old boss suddenly left the company and the uncertainty of what type of new boss would be stepping in made her anxious. Would they be a micromanager or a hands-off type? Would they be friendly or strictly professional? The questions swirled in Samantha's mind. She could only hope for the best.

Love 'em or hate 'em, your old boss was the devil you knew. And now a new boss is coming along and who knows what they're like. Or what they'll want. Or how they'll behave toward you.

## Why Does It Matter?

Getting a new boss can be a significant source of anxiety and stress. Your boss plays a major role in how much you enjoy your job and what your day-to-day life will be like. A good new boss is a delight. A bad new boss is disheartening.

It's normal, natural and expected to be nervous about a new boss, but bear in mind, they're nervous, too. They don't know you either. They probably want to make a good impression, but they may also want to make their mark and feel the need to shake things up.

You probably didn't have any say in who got hired, but you do have some say in how well you get along and how effectively you work with them.

## Action Steps

Here are some ways to make it easier and set yourself up for a productive working relationship.

- **Onboard your new boss unofficially**. They may be the boss, but they're also the new kid in town. There's a lot they'll need to know and you might as well be their guide. While *their* boss will probably show off all the ritzy stores on Main Street, you can show them the great little shops and restaurants on the side streets. And the parts of town they might want to avoid.
- **Decide what you want your relationship to be**. Not in the BFF sense, but professionally. Do you want to be an indispensable right hand or simply a valued member of the team? What level of interaction do you envision? How do you see the balance between maintaining a strictly professional relationship with your boss versus having the occasional personal conversation?
- **Look for common ground to break the ice**. This will give a lot of insight into what your future relationship might evolve into. Let them talk about themselves. Listen closely and you'll get to know more than where they went to school or where they grew up. You'll also get a sense of how they approach work, their role at the organization, and their role as your manager.
- **Focus on what's going well *and* what could go better with the right attention**. Don't lie, but remember there's a big difference between *"we're experiencing some challenges in that particular area"* versus *"that part of the department is an unmitigated disaster."*
- **Check in and monitor your relationship on a regular basis**. You have the power to help shape this into a relationship that works for you. Use that power.

- **Remember that you don't have to like each other.** Focus on a relationship based on mutual respect, effective communication and working toward shared goals. That's all that matters.

# Getting Comfortable Around Senior Leaders

> "I think it's glorious to be nervous. Being nervous is great! Being slightly nervous means you care, and you're alive, and you're taking some kind of risk. Hooray for being nervous!"
> *Amy Poehler*

Almost everyone gets nervous when the boss is in the room. It's only natural. We're wired to constantly evaluate whether what's around us is a potential threat or possible reward. Senior leaders have a way of putting people on edge, even when they don't intend to. This is because social threats and rewards are strong conscious and subconscious motivators.

What happens to us if top executives decide our department isn't worth keeping around? How can we get comfortable around these shadowy people who seem to have our work lives in their hands?

## Why Does It Matter?

When it comes to senior leaders, it's no wonder most of us get nervous, because from a career standpoint they pose potential threats. They have higher status. They outrank us and their decisions have major impacts on our lives. They're the ultimate insiders. They guide the business to where it's going. All of this means that they can control our work destinies.

## Action Steps

There are six steps you can take that will go a long way toward letting you relax and be more comfortable around the senior leaders in your organization.

*Don't judge people ahead of time.*
Don't put too much weight on appearances and titles. The Chief Executive Bigshot in charge of All Important Things may just be an informal person with a great sense of humor who loves cat videos. Take a step back and observe. It's easier to relax when you know what someone's actually like.

*Learn what you can about senior leaders.*
Who you know is never as intimidating as who you don't. Senior leaders generally have all kinds of information about them publicly available. Look them up online or on the company intranet. Look at their social media posts and read their blogs or publications. Get familiar with what they have to say about the company and the industry.

*Practice.*
Think about and rehearse what you might want to say to them if and when you meet them. For the chance meetings in the hallway or the elevator, you don't have to try hard to appear brilliant or scramble to impress them. Just be calm, courteous and friendly. If you've read about them, talk or ask about what you've learned. Most conversations can't really be planned ahead of time, but just knowing a bit about them and being yourself can help put you at ease.

*Be a good employee.*
The senior vice president of your division may not know your name, but if they do, you want them to know that you're hardworking, dependable and a solid contributor to their division and the organization. For whatever is in your control, make sure what they've heard about you is positive.

*If you've made a mistake, fix it.*
If you made a mistake, admit it. No one likes the person at work who tries to blame others for their own mistakes. Share your regret and then move on to explain how you'll fix it. Show leadership that you're accountable and a problem solver.

*Remember that you and senior leadership are allies.*
Ultimately, you and the C-Suite have the same professional goal: you want the company to succeed.

You may always have some butterflies when the big bosses are around, but you are all on the same team and pulling for the same positive outcomes. Keep your eye on achieving the common goals and you might find your nerves calming down and your heart rate slowing to a normal pace.

# Bringing a Problem to Your Boss

*"Focus on the solution, not the problem."*
*Jim Rohn*

Problems are an inevitable part of business—but it's not always easy to tell your boss or team leader about a problem. Maybe the project you've been working on is 10 percent over budget or a key person on the team has just resigned. Problems remain a constant in the workplace, but choosing how to bring them to your boss can either help or hurt your career.

## Why Does It Matter?
None of us enjoys bringing a problem to our boss, but if done right it can be a useful way to develop a trusting relationship with your boss.

Regardless of the nature of the problem, a proactive response to problems can make all the difference. It shows you care about the organization, have compassion for your teammates and care more about finding a solution than focusing on the problem.

## Action Steps
There are eight steps to take when bringing a problem to your boss's attention.

1. **Alert your boss to a problem early.** The worst thing you can do is let your boss be blindsided or surprised by a problem that you haven't alerted them to. Tell your boss about problems, challenges and issues early enough so that there's still time to fix them.
2. **Be mindful about how you bring a problem to your boss's attention.** Schedule a meeting in advance and provide a short

description of the nature of the problem so that your boss will be more prepared for the discussion. This provides them with the space to think about helpful solutions and guidance.

3. **Describe the problem in detail**. When you meet with your boss, offer a few specific details about the problem and give examples for clarity. Provide enough background so that they understand the problem quickly, but you don't need to provide every last period and comma. Just give an overview of the problem and explain how it affects you and the organization.

4. **Describe your proposed solution in detail**. Recommend a solution when you present the problem. Explain what you have already done to try to solve the problem and what you have learned from your attempts.

5. **Explain the implications of your proposed solution**. Thoroughly consider the impact that your proposed solution will have on all stakeholders, resources and organizational goals.

6. **Discuss the benefits of your proposed solution**. Provide your boss with concrete examples of the benefits of your solution. Use facts and data to back up your statements.

7. **Accept responsibility for the outcome of your proposed solution**. Make sure your boss knows you are committed to ensuring success. Ask your boss for input on your proposed action plan and don't be afraid to ask for help if you need it.

8. **Stay positive and solution-oriented**. Once you begin implementing your solution, don't focus excessively on the problem. Stay focused on the solution. Being in an opportunity-based frame of mind will help you communicate professionally with your boss and come across as the leader you are.

# Fighting To Be Heard When Your Boss Doesn't Listen to You

> "Listening is an effect. Communication is the cause."
> *Meir Ezra*

There are various types of bad bosses, ranging from incompetent to irritable, but one of the most exasperating managers is the one who doesn't seem to listen when you talk. Whether it's your opinions, suggestions or ideas, it feels like everything you say falls on deaf ears.

If you feel that your boss doesn't listen to you, you can either do nothing and continue feeling invisible or take a look at your own communication approach and see what you might do differently to make your voice heard.

## Why Does It Matter?

Feeling like you're invisible can be psychologically draining. A 2020 survey conducted by the Society for Human Resource Management found that 84 percent of U.S. employees felt that poorly-trained managers cause excessive stress. And the skill that workers believe needs the most improvement is communication, including listening to team members. This is a common problem but there are steps you can take to address it.

## Action Steps

Here are five tips that can help *you* fix your boss's listening problem.

- **Self-reflect**. Is your boss not listening or just not listening to *you*? Talk to your coworkers and see if they're experiencing the same listening gap you are. If your coworkers have more

success, then take the opportunity to learn from them. Or talk directly to your boss. Be straightforward and say that you'd really like to bridge the communication gap, and ask what's the best way for you to relay your thoughts, ideas or concerns. Then take what you learn and put into practice.
- **Work on your timing.** Give due consideration to what's going on in the organization. Is it budget time? Performance review time? If your boss has a lot of managerial stuff to tackle, then it's best to schedule a meeting instead of showing up at their desk and saying *"Hey, got a minute?"* Once you have their attention, remember to communicate in the style that works best for them, and leave enough time for your boss to ask questions or provide guidance.
- **Start with an attention-getting statement.** When you have to meet with your boss about a problem, you want to immediately grab their attention. Say something such as, *"I want to talk to you about something important and I'd really like your guidance."* When you make a statement like that, any good manager will lean in to hear what comes next, because they know it's probably not good news.
- **Identify what you need them to do.** Keeping in mind that your manager has a lot going on, you can take some ownership of the "listening" they should be doing by telling them exactly what you need them to do for you. State it in specific terms and that you need a "deliverable" within a set timeframe. This is a really helpful tactic for your boss because they can choose where to prioritize your request among the other things they have to do.
- **If you have a problem, have a solution.** If you want to make your boss happy, then don't bring them a problem without also bringing at least one solution. You don't want to be known as the "problem child" who brings in bad news but

no solutions; you'll go right back to being invisible. However, if you show yourself to be capable of solving issues for your manager instead of just being the bearer of bad news, your manager will have more respect for you and will take the time to listen the next time you want to talk.

# Coping With an Unpredictable Boss

> "The best way to live life is to flow with it;
> accepting what is, making sincere efforts to repair
> whatever needs fixing and trusting the process . . . ."
> *Avis Viswanathan*

So, which one will it be today?

Coping with an unpredictable boss is exasperating. This morning your manager was all smiles and handshakes, encouraging and cheering you on. This afternoon they ranted and raved, tearing you down and ripping apart your work.

So what can you do when your boss is unpredictable? Do you just shrug, keep your head down and wait for the next "good boss" appearance? Do you keep working on project A and ignore the fuss about project B? Do you hide in the bathroom, scrolling through job openings on your phone?

## Why Does It Matter?

Your boss isn't unpredictable because of anything you did or didn't do. They didn't suddenly become volatile the day you got hired. Their behavior won't change after you're gone, whether that's in two weeks or two years. It's *their* issue, not yours. You're just trying to live through it.

Dealing with a challenging, temperamental, unstable and erratic boss can be a source of frustration, irritation, exasperation and discomfort. However, it is possible to manage this kind of behavior without resorting to bad behavior yourself. Adopting a strategy that allows you to maintain your self-respect and mental well-being is the key to handling your Dr. Jekyll and Mr. Hyde manager.

### Action Steps

The first thing you have to do is to decide whether the problem is truly toxic or just annoying. Does "bad boss's" behavior cross over into bullying and harassment or is it just frustrating? Does it have long-term effects, such as creating chaos with customers or negatively impacting your emotional well-being, or is it just temporarily confusing, like shifting priorities and petty reworking?

Above all, maintain your own integrity and stay professional. Do your work as best you can. Stay positive and reliable with your teammates and take pride in what you accomplish—individually and collectively.

To help you cope, look for patterns in their behavior. Is there something that triggers "bad boss"? The more you can understand what causes your manager's swings, the more you can at least try to be on the lookout and prepare yourself for them.

Do their swings seem to correspond to certain days, times of day or specific situations? The boss, good or bad, is human and may respond to different circumstances in their own way. If your boss is under pressure from their boss, they may take it out on you and your teammates. If the boss is having trouble at home, it's likely to make itself known at work, too.

This doesn't mean you should try to justify "Mr. Hyde" boss, but it can help you understand why "Dr. Jekyll" boss sometimes disappears without warning. And, frankly, being able to understand and potentially empathize with the boss may help smooth out some of the edges and make life a little calmer.

If the unpredictability shows itself as ever-shifting, ever-conflicting priorities, ask for clarification, a lot. Keep a paper trail every time priorities shift. You don't have to weaponize it, but at the least it will provide defense and let you refer back to prior communications when "bad boss" changes their mind again. You can consult it now and then to confirm you're not the crazy one. And if push comes to shove, you have a record to share with your supervisor's boss or HR.

Whether you ultimately decide stay or go, remain calm and focus on your own work and goals. Perhaps the worst thing you can do when dealing with an unpredictable boss is to let it get into your head. You can start questioning yourself, wondering if you're not sensitive enough or paying enough attention. Don't let it make you crazy.

Only you can decide what you will or won't put up with. If you must get up and get out, take a deep breath and weigh your options. Know your next move before you hand in your resignation.

# Handling a Boss Who Can't Show Empathy

> *"Empathy begins with understanding life from another person's perspective. Nobody has an objective experience of reality. It's all through our own individual prisms."*
> *Sterling K. Brown*

Did you know that 54 percent of American employees have left a previous job because their boss wasn't empathetic to their struggles at work? Or that 49 percent of American employees have left a job because their boss wasn't empathetic about struggles in their personal lives?

## Why Does It Matter?

Understanding and sharing the feelings, thoughts and experiences of others is called empathy. Your ability to be empathetic is at least partially inherited, and there are regions in your brain that influence your ability to share and understand the feelings of others.

We all have the capacity for empathy, but it doesn't exist equally among people, and while other factors such as family and social interaction might shape your empathetic reaction, some people simply lack empathy.

If you work for a manager who lacks empathy, there can be adverse consequences on your work experience:

- A lack of motivation because your boss doesn't understand your concerns or problems.
- Feeling unsupported and unappreciated because you don't get any guidance or feedback to improve in your role.
- An increased stress level because you feel like you can't approach your boss with concerns or issues.

## Action Steps

If you're dealing with a boss who lacks empathy, you can't change their nature, but you can use these six techniques to help you cope.

1. **Remember that it's not you, it's them.** Although it can be difficult not to take their actions personally, consciously setting aside your initial emotional reaction can help. By reminding yourself that they have difficulty connecting with others at a deeper level, you can rise above your own feelings. Some things are worth crying over, such as your best friend's wedding or the ending of *It's A Wonderful Life*. Your boss isn't worth it.
2. **Accept that you each react differently.** No matter how much you try, you can't force-feed empathy or insights into a non-empathetic person. As counterintuitive as this sounds, it's better to just accept that you're not going to get empathy from them and move on.
3. **Communicate with facts.** Seek common ground by focusing on the facts of a problem or situation and what you think about it, rather than what you feel about it. Depending on what's being discussed, it may be difficult to remain neutral, but you'll have a better chance of successfully working through the problem if you can keep emotions out of it.
4. **Look to coworkers for support.** Cheers to the coworkers who make each day better, especially when you have a boss who lacks empathy. Sharpen your observation skills and try to amass a group of empathy allies. It's always good to have people you can call on for help or guidance.
5. **Nurture your self-esteem.** Remember that the one person who has to believe in you is you. Periodically reflect on what you tell yourself about yourself and be aware if it's more negative than positive. Be gentle with yourself and avoid harsh

self-criticism. Focus on what you do well, and take pride in your achievements.
6. **Consult with HR or an outside professional**. While you can lean on personal relationships, your friends and family may not be able to provide the tools you'll need to get through a persistently challenging relationship with a boss who lacks empathy. A caring and empathetic therapist or life coach can provide you with valuable guidance.

It's normal to want to feel valued and appreciated at work. Even if you end up with a manager who isn't capable of giving that, you now have the tools to survive and thrive on your own.

# Handling a Boss Who Gaslights You

*"Gaslighting is mind control to make victims doubt their reality."*
*Tracy Malone*

The term "gaslighting" originated in a 1930s British play about a husband who tries to make his wife believe she's losing her sanity by secretly changing the intensity of the gas lamps in their apartment, knocking on walls and making household items disappear and then reappear later. She soon begins to doubt her memory and perception of reality.

The use of the term has grown in popularity in recent years as it seems to reflect a lot of the behavior that happens in politics and in social media. It's also rife in the business world with leaders and managers who don't have the competencies to do good work or own their mistakes.

## Why Does It Matter?

Managers who gaslight use many tactics to manipulate others. They stir up confusion, undermine self-confidence and try to interfere with people's sense of reality using underhanded and difficult-to-prove schemes.

A boss who uses these gaslighting tricks can quickly create a toxic environment, and if you are a victim, you may find yourself feeling paranoid, anxious and off balance.

## Action Steps

If you believe you're being manipulated by a gaslighter, here are six steps that can help you address this abuse.

1. **Gather your evidence**. Because gaslighters are so adept at warping reality, your first step is to start documenting every

bit of evidence that offers proof of what's happening. Keeping meticulous records serves a dual purpose. By writing it down, you may be able to regain clarity and written evidence, especially with corroborating witnesses, is much more difficult for a gaslighter to refute if you decide to go to HR.
2. **Guard your mental health**. Treat your situation as toxic, and do everything you can to protect yourself. Try to minimize the power of their words by seeing them as coming from someone who is clearly insecure and behaving childishly, much like a two-year-old throwing a tantrum. Once you're able to mentally separate from the toxicity of your gaslighter, then you can work on repairing and restoring your self-confidence.
3. **Seek the support of others**. Silence only isolates you, allowing the gaslighter to remain in control. Talk to others on your team, especially if you believe you're the only one being targeted. You may find that other people are also being victimized, which corroborates your experiences and removes your stigma. You could also seek additional support from a trained professional.
4. **Minimize interactions with your boss**. Do your best to avoid informal conversations or situations that would force you to interact. When you are required to meet, try to ensure at least one other person is part of the meeting. Work on building relationships with managers in other parts of the organization.
5. **Take a chance on improving the situation**. Instead of a confrontation, set up a conversation that's focused on finding common ground between you. Present it as an opportunity to work together and resolve your problematic relationship with the ultimate goal of helping the organization be more successful. Your boss's reaction will quickly tell you if your relationship can be fixed or not. Either your boss didn't realize

the damaging effect of their behavior and you get an apology or they really have a toxic personality and things are likely to get worse. It's a risky step, but doing nothing will ensure your relationship never improves.
 6. **Explore your options with HR.** If all of your efforts don't improve your situation, consider escalating the problem to HR. Unfortunately, it's often difficult to prove gaslighting because it's subtle and rarely violates company policies. The documentation you collected will help support your complaint, but unless there's a clear violation of a stated policy, you may not get any immediate improvement.

This is where any relationships you've built with other managers may be helpful. Gaslighting might spur you to transfer to a different team. If that's a possibility, you could reach out and ask if there are any potential openings on the teams of your contacts. They already know you and your skills, so that can give you an advantage over external applicants.

If there are no internal opportunities, then it may be time to look for a new job elsewhere. That may feel like a drastic step, but if you're still feeling miserable, preserving your mental and physical health should be your top priority. Sometimes with gaslighting there isn't a bucket big enough to bail out the shipwreck so you should just get out while you can.

# Managing an Abrasive Boss

> "You don't lead by hitting people over the head.
> That's assault, not leadership."
> *Dwight D. Eisenhower*

Have you ever heard this phrase?

*"I didn't ask for your opinion. Just do your job."*

Or maybe this one?

*"You can be replaced in a heartbeat, so just get it done."*

These phrases reflect a management style that is not exactly supportive or encouraging. Managers who use an abrasive leadership style may reflect a psychological attitude shaped by a general lack of trust in others with an emphasis on their own status and authority.

## Why Does It Matter?

Abrasive bosses may be technically competent, action-prone and achievement-driven. They may have reached their status because of their ability to execute and produce results. However, they may suffer from feelings of insecurity, uncertainty, low self-esteem and low self-confidence. An understanding of the root causes of such behavior can help you feel more empathetic toward an abrasive boss.

Having to deal with an abrasive boss is never easy and can have significant consequences on your personal and professional well-being. A rational and deliberate approach to handling the situation will help you achieve the best possible outcome.

## Action Steps

What can you do if you are managed by an abrasive boss? Here are five easy steps to guide you.

*Carefully analyze your situation.*
Start with some introspection. Carefully analyze your relationship with your boss and any criticisms your boss has offered. Have you met your boss's goals and performance standards? In what areas do you need to improve? Are other employees being treated the same way or are you the only one? You should carefully and clearly document your responses to these questions.

*Try to understand your boss and empathize.*
Maybe their management style is the only one they have ever known because they've only had abrasive bosses themselves. Maybe your boss has personal or family challenges. Trying to understand your boss and finding some empathy will enable you to be more relaxed and more confident when interacting with your boss which may help change your boss's behavior.

*Set clear goals and change your own approach.*
It's in your best interest to set goals and expectations that are aligned to your boss's goals. What aspects of your current behavior might irk your boss and cause them to be abrasive? Get some pointers on how you might do things differently. You might not be doing anything to make your boss act abrasively toward you, but if there is any opportunity to improve the situation by changing something you do, that can be easier than trying to change your boss's behavior.

### Meet with your boss.

Let your boss know that you want to find ways to improve your working relationship. Position the discussion as your desire to seek advice or mentoring from your boss. Express yourself in a factual and constructive manner. Keep your focus on your desire and your potential to be more productive, and let your boss know that you want to make sure you are doing everything you can to ensure that you help your boss be successful. Use practical examples of tasks and assignments. If your boss doesn't pick up on your signals, then you might need to be more direct and suggest that the two of you don't seem to interact well and that you'd like their suggestions regarding how to remedy the situation.

### Implement change.

Be patient because change can take time. However, over time you may feel that meetings with your boss do not result in less abrasive behavior. Lodging a formal complaint against your boss with their boss or with human resources should be a last resort. If you decide to go above your boss, you need to make a substantial business case for why your boss is a liability to the organization because their abrasive management style is causing the team's or organization's performance to suffer. Do you have records of how long the behavior has lasted? Was any action by your boss severe enough to constitute harassment or clear discrimination? The more people you can get to go on record with similar complaints and evidence, the harder it will be for the organization to ignore or deny the problem.

Sometimes you cannot continue to work for an abrasive boss. For example, when you are unable to change your relationship with your boss and despite your best efforts the organization is unwilling to make a change, or when the personal and professional costs are too high. The best course of action may be to look for a job elsewhere.

Remember that if you decide to leave the organization you may still need references from your old boss. If you can, avoid burning bridges as you seek a new opportunity.

# Handling a Rude Boss

*"Rudeness is the weak man's imitation of strength."*
*Eric Hoffer*

There's rude and then there's *Rude* with a capital R. There's full-on hostile behavior and there's somebody who gets a bit short because they're having a bad day. What we're looking at here is probably something in between.

## Why Does It Matter?

Of course, rudeness doesn't have to be a full-blown, long-term pattern to be a problem. Even once or twice can be enough to create an issue. While once or twice could just be bad days or simple aberrations, if your manager's rudeness seriously affects your job and your relationship with them, it's worth doing something about it. Nobody needs to be insulted and demeaned to do a good job. The bully boss went out with the rotary phone. You don't have to put up with one.

## Action Steps

So how do you deal with a rude boss? Try anything on this handy checklist to keep your sanity and avoid a blowup at work.

- Don't take it personally, even if you feel like you're being singled out.
- Don't respond in kind.
- Consider your timing if you do choose to respond.
- Plan out what you want to say and when you want to say it.
- Offer to take them out for coffee, or ask if they have some time to discuss something important this afternoon.

- Tell your boss how their behavior makes you feel: hurt, disrespected, angry, confused. You should be honest here.
- If the behavior continues despite your best attempts to resolve the issue on your own, write it all down, in detail and take the issue to HR. Dates, times and specific behaviors are harder to ignore or deflect.
- Don't necessarily count on your colleagues. Lots of people will recognize the poor behavior but very few will back you up when push comes to shove.

So, you may be standing alone when dealing with a rude boss, but if you're being treated badly and you're tired of it, it won't change unless you take action. The good news is that you probably won't need to involve HR. Most bosses really do want to have good relationships with their people. Talking it out will likely take care of it, even if an occasional slip requires a reminder.

# Feeling Supported If Your Boss Doesn't Back You Up

*"To add value to others, one must first value others."*
*John Maxwell*

If you work hard, your boss should have your back—even if you make an honest mistake once-in-a while.

A good boss will work to make sure you know that they have your back. But not every boss is a good boss. And even some *pretty* good bosses have holes in their game.

Working for a boss who doesn't support you is frustrating. But you can overcome it. You don't have to live with it. While your job and your career are ultimately in your own hands, you deserve to know that the person you report to has your back.

## Why Does It Matter?

It's nice to know you're acknowledged as an important part of the team. It also helps you get clarity on assignments and expectations. And it provides validation for your hard work, skills and judgment.

Having your boss's support is also important for doing your job properly. To do good work, you need to know that you'll have resources available to you when you need them. To make good decisions, you need to know that you aren't going to get thrown under the bus if something goes wrong. To feel secure and at your most productive, you need to know that your boss cares about your well-being and your professional future.

## Action Steps

So what can you do when you don't feel supported by your boss?

First, determine the kind of support you need.

- Do you need resources?
- Do you need clarity?
- Do you need the opportunity to learn and grow?
- Do you need advice and the voice of experience?
- Do you need trust?

These are very different types of support and they require different actions and behaviors from your boss. Before you ask, know what you're asking for.

Then, speak up. Don't wait around passively, hoping things will get better on their own. You need to let your boss know how you feel and the type of support you need.

- Be specific. Write it down, including all the details.
- Make a case for why it matters, not just to you, but to your boss and the organization.
- Emphasize how getting this support will help you do a better job and, in turn, make them look better to their boss.
- Don't hesitate to beat your own drum. Remind your boss of the good work you do. Let them know your importance to the team and how it achieves its goals.

Most, if not all, managers know that their success is dependent upon the people who report to them. If you can't do your job properly, neither can they.

Whether your boss becomes responsive or not, you should build your own support network. There's only so much you can do to get any single person to support you. Seek out allies wherever you can find them.

Finally, don't make it directly about you. Focus on how the lack of support impacts the team and the company. If a lack of resources is going to keep you and your team from successfully meeting goals and deadlines that impact the company or if you're being denied the skills and training to do your job properly, your boss's peers and supervisors ought to know these things.

Don't be vindictive. Don't point fingers.

Simply explain the situation and its potential negative outcomes. Then you've done what you can and it's out of your hands.

# Navigating a Boss Who Is Jealous of Your Success

*"The jealous are troublesome to others,
but a torment to themselves."*
*William Penn*

Maybe lately you've noticed some changes in your manager's behavior toward you. He always finds something to criticize about your work, even when others praise it. The other day your boss belittled your accomplishments in front of the team. Two weeks ago, you got assigned a project that no one else wanted. You're concerned that your recent string of successes may be to blame. You worry that your boss sees you as a threat and resents you.

In the workplace, comparisons are frequent. There are times when we feel envious of a coworker's impressive achievements or we are resentful because someone else was chosen for a high-visibility assignment. We also experience others' jealousy directed toward our own achievements.

But what if the feelings of jealousy or bitterness come from your supervisor?

Your boss, like everyone else, is human and shares the same desire for recognition and esteem in the workplace. Witnessing you surpass them can evoke a sense of vulnerability, particularly if they believe their own standing and reputation are being eroded, leading to feelings of jealousy, envy or irritation.

## Why Does It Matter?

When your boss is jealous of your success, it can cause a host of problems. Jealousy creates tension and strain in a relationship. A jealous boss may consciously or unconsciously withhold opportunities for your professional development and career advancement. A boss's jealousy may also lead to increased scrutiny, criticism or unrealistic expectations, which can adversely affect your work performance and morale. Your boss may treat you unfairly or unfavorably compared to your peers. Constantly dealing with a jealous boss can affect your motivation and overall happiness at work.

## Action Steps

Know that your boss's jealousy is not your fault, but you do need to address the situation. Here are a few things to consider.

- **Don't brag.** Be mindful of how you present your achievements. Focus on being humble and expressing genuine gratitude for the opportunities and support you receive at work.
- **Show appreciation and share credit.** Reflect on how often you express gratitude or give credit to your manager for their contributions to your success. When was the last time you acknowledged your manager not only in private conversations but also in public settings?
- **Share your influence with your supervisor.** Include them in important events and meetings. Whenever possible, elevate your manager's standing while you have the limelight. Embodying this collaborative spirit is the essence of being a team player.
- **Support your boss's team.** When receiving praise, emphasize that the success was a team effort and mention key team members who played crucial roles in the project. This reinforces the idea that you're working *together* toward a common goal. Your manager will likely view these actions favorably, perceiving you as a valuable team member rather than a potential rival.
- **Stay professional in your interactions with your boss.** Focus on your job responsibilities and deliver quality work.

If these strategies don't improve the situation and if your boss's jealousy becomes toxic or unmanageable, consider discussing the issue with a mentor, a higher-level manager or HR. They can help you explore your options.

Working under a boss who is jealous of your accomplishments can be difficult, but by adopting a mature and conciliatory attitude, you can handle this demanding situation. And remember to never let anyone's envy—even your boss's—detract from your sense of pride in your accomplishments.

## Section 6

# Advocating for Yourself at Work

This section delves into the crucial practice of advocating for yourself at work. Having a more centered association with your boss gives you the confidence to stick up for yourself. Central to this advocacy is the principle of authenticity. More than a buzzword, being your authentic self at work is akin to laying down a strong foundation on which your professional house stands. This authenticity lets you wear your identity with pride, enabling you to communicate and assert your unique voice and vision with unshakeable confidence. This isn't merely a step in the process; it's the cornerstone to earning genuine respect.

When you're rooted in authenticity and you command the respect you deserve, the landscape of opportunities expands before you. This isn't a passive stage. With this newfound clarity, you're better positioned to actively seek out avenues for professional growth, not just in terms of position, but in skills, network and influence. Feedback becomes your compass. But I'm not talking about mere words of affirmation or critique here; I mean rich and constructive feedback that provides clear direction, offering actionable insights that refine your path and purpose.

When contributions aren't heeded or heard, not only is individual morale affected, but teams also risk overlooking vital insights that can drive success. Highlighting your achievements isn't about singing your own praises to an echoing void. It's about strategically showcasing your value, ensuring your contributions don't become background noise. This strategic visibility acts as a propulsion system, giving you the drive and momentum to edge ahead in the race, whether it's for a coveted promotion or getting that well-deserved raise.

Of course, the path of self-advocacy isn't devoid of hurdles. There will be challenges from missed promotions and unattributed credit to the occasional shadows of baseless blame. These aren't mere setbacks; some challenges will test your professional resilience and commitment to growth. They push you to question, to adapt and most importantly, to grow.

By truly understanding the power of self-advocacy, you set yourself apart. Your voice, contributions and worth are your legacy. Every challenge faced, every piece of feedback acted upon and every achievement highlighted serves as a testament to your journey's unique significance. Remember that in the grand narrative of your career, you are not just a minor character; you're the author. It's imperative to ensure your story is celebrated.

Let the party begin.

# How To Be Your Authentic Self at Work

> "Authenticity is the daily practice of letting go of who we think we're supposed to be and embracing who we are."
> *Brené Brown*

If you see yourself as a kind and intelligent person who is unfairly judged for your identity, tattoos, piercings or hair choices, then consider this: Are you actively showing the world the person you believe yourself to be? It's one thing to say, *I'm being my authentic self,* and it's another to be seen by others as someone who is authentic.

Being authentic requires more than just showing up at work with your Pride shirt, your purple hair or your full-sleeve tattoos. It involves doing some deep introspection to develop the story of who you are and then sharing it with others.

## Why Does It Matter?

Being real at work isn't just about being different; it's about letting your true colors shine in everything you do. When you're true to who you are, your choices match up with what you really believe in. This not only makes things clearer but also gives you a big boost in self-esteem and confidence.

And when you're feeling confident, you'll do your best work. You'll also see the workplace in a brighter light. This upbeat vibe isn't just something you feel inside; it spreads around, making work more fun and collaborative for everyone. Being genuine doesn't just benefit you, it benefits those around you too.

## Action Steps

If you are seeking a path toward becoming more authentic at work, these six steps will help you on your journey.

1. **Examine your fears.** You may be well practiced in masking your personal life because you fear what may happen if people knew the real you. But in your quest to be authentic, it's time to see your fears as barriers you're imposing on yourself. While admittedly you might not be universally accepted by your colleagues, it's unlikely you'll be fired because you're perceived as different.
2. **Consider the gap between you being your real self and the self you currently show at work.** There probably aren't a lot of differences, so maybe there are ways you can inject a little more of your real self while still staying within whatever boundaries your workplace imposes. Show your sense of humor. Wear big jewelry or bright socks. You might be surprised and find your colleagues like the more authentic you than the one you've been pretending to be. (Keep in mind, though, that you should always make sure you follow your organization's dress code guidelines.)
3. **Consider the benefits of being yourself.** If you're still having a little trouble pushing your fears to the side, then flip the script and look at the benefits you get by being yourself. Being authentic means you're automatically taking a stand for integrity. If you're brave enough to be your honest self, then you're showing people that you're not afraid of doing the right thing.
4. **Believe that you belong.** If you're going to show others who you are, begin by believing that you have a place in the room, in the organization, in society. But also consider what sets you apart.
5. **Let others see your humanity.** Nobody's perfect and the journey toward authenticity means allowing people to see your imperfections which they may not see as imperfections at all. It's okay to be vulnerable because it gives people a

glimpse of your humanity, and it allows them to feel safe in being vulnerable themselves.
6. **Keep some boundaries.** While sharing stories and insights into who you are as a person can help build connections with others, it's healthy to have boundaries. Dumping the drama of your life history into the lap of someone who isn't ready to hear it isn't any more authentic than keeping it all hidden. Instead, be thoughtful about the type of relationship you have with someone before choosing to share personal details.

While becoming your authentic self is a personal journey, remember to listen to what other people share, and be the friend who acknowledges their story and truth. When someone shares their authentic story with you, emulate the type of attentive listening you seek from others.

There is no finite end to the journey of authenticity. Keep working on the story of you and see how being authentic will enrich your work life.

# How To Assert Yourself in the Workplace

> "It's not harsh to be assertive,
> it's harsher when people take advantage of you."
> *Janna Cachola*

Assertive people are direct and honest with others. If something is bothering them, they speak up; if they want or need something, they ask.

Assertiveness is about taking ownership over your thoughts, feelings and actions without blaming others or apologizing. Assertive people are forthcoming, clear, secure, responsive, positive and approachable.

## Why Does It Matter?

Being assertive helps you express yourself effectively and stand up for your point of view. It can help you do this while respecting the rights and beliefs of others. An assertive communication style keeps people from taking advantage of you, while also preventing you from acting like a bully toward others.

If you communicate in a way that's either too passive or too aggressive, your message may get lost because people are busy reacting to your delivery. Being overly passive or overly aggressive can get in the way of being assertive.

When you're too passive, you allow others to ignore your wants and needs. In contrast, if your communication style is aggressive, you may come across as a bully who ignores the needs, perspectives and opinions of others. Using an aggressive style weakens trust and mutual respect, and people may avoid, oppose or even resent you.

## Action Steps

I've found ten effective strategies to help you become more assertive without being too aggressive in your approach.

1. **Assess your current personal style**. Do you voice your opinions or remain silent? Do you say yes to additional work even when your schedule is full? Are you quick to judge or blame? Understand your current style before you make changes to your approach.
2. **Use "I" statements**. Using "I" statements lets others know what you're thinking or feeling without sounding accusatory. Keep your requests simple, specific and clear.
3. **Practice saying no**. If you have a hard time turning down requests, try saying, *No, I can't do that right now.* At first you might feel uncomfortable saying no if you are accustomed to always saying yes—but the goal is to build up your tolerance for that discomfort.
4. **Prepare and practice what you want to say**. Write out what you want to say during general work situations and then say it out loud. Practicing will help you organize your thoughts, be less anxious leading up to the conversation and be more confident during the actual conversation.
5. **Start small and low risk**. Practice being more assertive in situations that are low risk before tackling more difficult situations. Evaluate yourself and adjust your approach as needed. Over time you will build up the confidence to tackle more challenging situations.
6. **Use body language**. Communication isn't just verbal. Keep an upright posture and make regular eye contact. Practice assertive body language in front of a mirror or with a colleague.

7. **Keep emotions in check**. Conflict is hard for most people. If you get angry or frustrated and feel too emotional going into a situation, wait it out if possible. Then try to remain calm.
8. **Don't apologize for expressing a need, a want or a right**. Politely state what you need or want and wait to see how the other person responds. Don't apologize simply because you are uncomfortable with the fact that *someone else* might be uncomfortable.
9. **Take initiative**. Being assertive means taking initiative. Assertive people show a willingness to confront and resolve. They take ownership of their behavior and point of view.
10. **Pick your battles**. Assertiveness is situational and contextual. Know that there may be cases when being assertive won't get you anywhere and taking a more aggressive or passive stance is actually the better option.

Being assertive shows that you respect yourself because you're willing to stand up for your interests, opinions and perspectives. It also demonstrates that you're aware of others' rights and are willing to work on resolving conflicts. Becoming more assertive takes time and practice, but with persistence, your efforts will pay off.

# How To Garner Respect at Work

*"When you are content to be simply yourself and
don't compare or compete, everybody will respect you."*
*Lao Tzu*

If you're looking for ways to get more respect at work, you might feel like Rodney Dangerfield in one of his famous stand-up routines constantly complaining about how he doesn't get any respect.

Jokes can be made in any situation—and it's always good to be able to laugh at yourself—but feeling a lack of respect at work really isn't funny.

Perhaps your ideas are ignored or maybe stolen and attributed to others. Maybe you feel invisible or discounted. Maybe your efforts are taken for granted or you sense a patronizing attitude toward you. In all cases, a lack of respect is frustrating and can be hurtful.

## Why Does It Matter?

Let's be real; respect at work isn't a bonus, it's a must-have. Everyone, and I mean everyone, deserves it and that goes for *you* too.

No one wants to feel like they are just a small, insignificant part of a larger machine or a mere statistic on a financial report. The amount of money the company pays you and the level of value you are expected to produce in return should not be the only measures of your worth. Even if you work diligently and perform your job exceptionally well, feeling unappreciated, undervalued or disrespected can be really disheartening.

That's because feeling valued at work matters. When people feel respected, they're more motivated, collaborative and innovative. But when that respect is missing, it can tank morale and hinder creativity and productivity. So, fighting for the respect you deserve isn't just about personal pride—it's crucial for you to bring your best self to the table.

## Action Steps

If you feel that respect's in short supply, it might be tempting to lash out, but blowing up isn't the answer. Here are some steps you can take.

*Make sure people know your worth.*
Chronicle your performance. *Seriously.* Take notes. Others may choose to ignore your accomplishments, but you shouldn't. A common employee failing is that we often only show off our successes when we're asking for a raise. And while getting a raise is great, it's not the only way to feel valued. Let your boss and others know you're proud of your work so they can be proud of it, too.

Think of letting others know what you can do as a form of networking. Recognize that your boss and immediate team members are not the only individuals with influence within the company. It's perfectly fine to let others know you're good at what you do. Maybe some other boss will value you more than yours does. These are the things career advancement is made of.

Women are often conditioned to be modest. Openly expressing your accomplishments can sometimes feel like you are being overly boastful or trying to assert dominance. But it's perfectly okay to be proud of your work. Share your victories far and wide. *If you done it, it ain't bragging.*

*Stand up for yourself, but do it respectfully.*
Know your own worth. You have a job because you fulfill an important role in your company. If your company didn't need you, it wouldn't employ you. Don't allow yourself to be treated like a doormat. If every time you attempt to share your perspective, a colleague interrupts or speaks over you, making you feel unheard and undervalued, address

the situation in a respectful manner. After the meeting, approach your colleague privately and calmly say, "I noticed during our discussion earlier that I was often interrupted when I tried to share my thoughts. I value our collaboration, and I believe it's important for each of us to have an opportunity to speak and be heard. Can we work on ensuring everyone's perspective is considered?" By directly yet respectfully addressing the issue, you advocate for your right to be heard.

If you disagree with someone, do it judiciously and be able to back up why. If a colleague proposes a strategy that you believe won't work, instead of outright dismissing it, you might say, "I understand where you're coming from, but based on my experience, I've found that using an indirect selling approach might be more effective. Here's why . . ."

### Show respect to others. Be a role model.

Jim in Purchasing has an eccentric way of expressing himself . . . who cares? He deserves to be treated with respect. Alisha doesn't get other people's jokes. What difference does it make? Treat her with respect for who she is. Leon is socially awkward and avoids eye contact. Consider being sympathetic instead of annoyed.

It's not hard for you to model respect. If it doesn't come naturally, then practice. Demonstrate trust with your boss and coworkers, even those who don't reciprocate. Praise people's good work. Celebrate their successes and show empathy and compassion when they fail. The golden rule really is golden: treat others the way *you* would like to be treated.

### Seek out respectful relationships.

Grow yourself a support group. Whether the lack of respect you experience is from your boss, some of your coworkers or part of your company's culture, there are other people who appreciate who you are and what you do. Find them. Introduce yourself. It's unlikely that you're the only person at work who doesn't feel respected.

Ask others how you can help them. Everyone has strengths and weaknesses. Offer your skills to those who struggle in your areas of strength. With a little time and patience, supporting others can create a circle of trust and mutual respect.

*Invest in yourself.*
Research suggests that people who experience a lack of respect at work, but who actively engage in non-work activities, report better mental and physical health.

Work is a major part of our lives, but it isn't, and shouldn't be, the *only* part. Don't waste your energy trying to win over people who don't want to be won over. Go home and fix a tasty dinner. Take a class in something you're interested in. Go to the movies with a friend. Form a band and jam in the basement. Write your novel. Take the dog to the park. Think about what makes you happy and invest your time and energy there.

You can't demand people's respect. There is a saying that respect must be earned and that's true. But no matter what you do, some people are simply unwilling to show respect to others for who and what they are. You may never win over those people. But you *can* control how *you* react to them. Always take the high road.

# How To Take Initiative in the Performance Appraisal Process

> "When performance is measured, it improves.
> When performance is measured and reported, it improves faster."
> *Thomas S. Monson*

Not every organization has a formal performance appraisal process. If yours lacks a formal appraisal process, you should request a performance review from your boss. Without some form of appraisal, you can start to feel adrift, unsure of your standing or how you can improve. You deserve clarity on where you stand and a structured opportunity for dialogue about your future goals and areas of development.

## Why Does It Matter?

In-person meetings with supervisors allow for thoughtful review, feedback and personalized advice on how you can continue to improve and grow. Your commitment to improve and grow professionally may also put you on your boss's radar for possible promotions.

Your willingness to take the initiative in the performance appraisal process will be interpreted by your boss and others as a sign of your dedication and commitment toward professional growth. No one is going to care as much about your professional growth as you do, so take the initiative and own the process.

## Action Steps

There are seven important points for you to consider as you prepare for a performance appraisal.

*Critical job elements*

During the meeting with your boss, agree upon and document elements that your supervisor considers critical for your success in your job. Write down your understanding of those elements and confirm that understanding with your boss. Be prepared to discuss your recent performance on those elements at the appraisal meeting.

*Negative feedback*

If your performance review does not start off on a positive note, accept all constructive criticism. Do not become defensive and avoid making excuses. Remember that constructive feedback is essential for growth. Listen carefully to any suggestions your boss has for how you might improve on the core elements of your job. Commit to take action in response to the feedback.

*Career aspirations*

Clarify with your supervisor how your current assignments fit in with your medium and longer-term career goals. You may have greater access to opportunities within the firm by expressing your career aspirations during performance appraisal meetings. This is a case where the squeaky wheel is more likely to get oiled.

*Necessary experience for career growth*

Once you have expressed your desire to grow, ask for a more specific description of the types of tasks, assignments, projects and performance metrics that will allow you to develop the capabilities and experience you need to move ahead.

*Additional training and development*

Ask your boss what kind of opportunities are available through the organization and express your interest in obtaining additional training and development. Attending courses and workshops or earning a certificate or a degree may be helpful.

*New professional goals*

Setting new objectives should be a two-way street, with input from both you and your manager. Make sure that any new goals you and your boss establish for your performance are SMART goals that are Specific, Measurable, Agreed upon, Realistic and Timely.

*Follow-up and feedback*

A formal performance review may happen only once or twice a year. Find ways to meet and communicate more often with your boss about your performance. Use interim performance check-in meetings to discuss your progress on specific goals, any obstacles you currently face and successes you've achieved since your last meeting.

# How To Ask for Feedback From Your Boss

> "I have discovered in life that there are ways of getting almost anywhere you want to go, if you really want to go."
> *Langston Hughes*

We grow the most when we have the opportunity to learn from feedback, both positive and negative. Feedback meetings with your manager are valuable opportunities for you to learn, grow and advance your career. You must make sure that you're getting the feedback from your boss that you need in order to continue to improve and grow in your role.

## Why Does It Matter?

To improve and develop, you need to receive **detailed and actionable** feedback from your manager. If you already have regular meetings, you have the opportunity to easily introduce feedback into your conversations. If you aren't meeting with your manager on a regular basis, consider asking if they might have a few minutes to meet with you. You <u>deserve</u> to receive feedback so don't be shy about asking for it.

## Action Steps

Let your boss know that you are eager to know how you are doing and if there are ways you can improve your work performance. Keep three things in mind as you ask your manager for feedback.

*Prepare in advance for the feedback meeting.*
Come prepared to answer a few key questions that your boss might ask you, such as:

- How are things going?
- How is your work progressing?
- What challenges are you facing?
- Where could you most use my help?
- What professional opportunities would you like to pursue?
- Where do you see yourself in the long term?

Think through answers to those questions before the meeting.

*During the meeting keep the discussion focused on feedback.*
Some managers treat a feedback meeting as a progress-update meeting. Make sure the meeting stays focused on providing *you* with feedback. Emphasize how much you appreciate your manager's input and value their opinions. Frame the discussion in terms of your desire to improve your performance and grow in your role. For example, say, *"I would love to learn anything I can about how to improve my work and position myself to take on additional responsibilities."* If your manager needs some additional prompting, you might ask a few simple questions such as:

- What should I start doing? Stop doing? Do more of?
- Am I on track with meeting your goals for the project I've been assigned?
- Am I on track to receive additional responsibilities or to get promoted?

Feedback is most valuable when it is specific and actionable. If you aren't learning enough from what your manager is saying, try pushing gently with some follow-up questions such as:

- Could you give me more specifics?
- What specifically would you suggest I do differently?
- What specifically should I improve on?

*Send the right signals during the meeting.*

Demonstrate that you are taking in all the feedback by nodding and taking notes during the meeting. If you unexpectedly hear negative feedback or are surprised by certain comments, avoid showing signs of anger or frustration. Don't disagree with your manager, but do ask for further clarification. At the end of the meeting, repeat back what you heard and clarify next steps. Let your manager know you want to engage in more frequent feedback discussions and even ask him if he'd be open to setting a recurring calendar invite.

# How To Get More Constructive Feedback

*"Feedback in the breakfast of champions."*
*Ken Blanchard*

Did you know that 75 percent of employees believe that feedback is valuable and 92 percent of people believe that constructive criticism is effective at improving their performance? Despite those stats, people often don't proactively seek out feedback. I'm always surprised when people don't because constructive feedback is a gift that keeps on giving.

## Why Does It Matter?

Getting specific and constructive feedback is vital to your professional growth. Although everyone likes positive feedback, we tend to grow the most from constructive feedback. This type of feedback pinpoints areas of improvement, allowing us to recognize and address our blind spots. When delivered with care and genuine intent, constructive criticism is a powerful tool which paves the way for continuous learning and improvement.

## Action Steps

By following these five steps, you can learn how to get the kind of feedback that will help you grow.

1. **Ask for feedback in real time**. It's best to ask for feedback often and as close to completion of a task as possible. Don't be afraid to approach your manager, colleagues or mentors and ask for their honest feedback on your performance.
2. **Pose specific questions**. Instead of asking, *Do you have any feedback for me?* ask, *What is one thing I could improve upon?*

Using open-ended questions is the best way to secure actionable advice.
3. **Press for actionable examples.** Feedback such as, *I just think you need to be more assertive* or *You should be more of a team player,* are too ambiguous. Pose follow-up questions such as, *Can you explain exactly what you mean by that?* or *Could you give me an example of how I could be more assertive on the project?* or *What specific actions should I take to become more assertive?*
4. **Turn to colleagues.** There are a lot of people qualified to give you feedback, not just your boss. You want to receive feedback from anyone who has valuable insight on how you can improve. When seeking input, look not only upward but also to the left, right and occasionally downward on the organizational chart. Make it clear to those around you that you value their feedback and are willing to listen to it.
5. **Be proactive in virtual settings.** Because physical distance frequently prevents informal exchanges, feedback gets lost in the shuffle and it can be particularly challenging for members of a virtual team to receive regular feedback. If you work virtually, make an extra effort to request more feedback from those you interact with on a regular basis.

# How To Play Up Your Achievements at Work

*"It's not bragging if you can back it up."*
*Muhammad Ali*

We all possess unique talents and capabilities that make up our personal brand. For some people, touting their accomplishments comes naturally. Maybe a little too naturally, like for Ron Burgundy in the movie *Anchorman*. Ron is a shameless self-promoter. For most of us, we feel at least some level of discomfort when it comes to self-promotion or boasting about our accomplishments.

Wherever you fall on the spectrum of self-promotion, knowing how and when to promote your achievements is important to marketing your brand and advancing your career.

## Why Does It Matter?

You need to be able to demonstrate your value and contributions to the organization. And you deserve the recognition and advancement opportunities that come in the wake of success.

It's important to get recognized for your capabilities and accomplishments—but you don't want others to see you as a chronic show-off or braggart. People who brag too much are often perceived as egocentric, insecure and insensitive.

By showcasing your achievements and marketing your brand effectively, you have the power to leave a lasting impression on those around you and the organization you work for. Just as a company must carefully cultivate its image to succeed, *you* must work to present yourself in the best possible light to thrive in your career.

## Action Steps

So how can you promote yourself in a way that won't end up backfiring? Here are five strategies to keep in mind.

1. **Share your achievements when directly asked.** When you talk about an accomplishment in response to a direct question, people won't perceive it as bragging. In fact, the opposite is true. If you avoid answering the question, people might perceive you as uncollaborative, closed and untrustworthy. So, next time you have the chance to talk about your successes in response to direct questions, view it as a gift and make the most of the opportunity. Work to remain humble, though. Avoid using superlatives or exaggerating your success. Instead, be factual in describing your accomplishments and let the results speak for themselves.
2. **Share your achievements when others share theirs.** If your team is debriefing a successful project in front of senior leadership and others are talking about their specific contributions to the success, you can and should chime in with yours. When doing so, talk about the steps you took to achieve your success, rather than just talking about the outcome. This shows that you're willing to share knowledge and help others succeed as well.
3. **Find someone to promote you.** If you find it challenging to promote your own achievements, even when directly asked about them or when others are sharing theirs, you can ask others to promote them for you. Peers, bosses, sponsors and mentors can all advocate for you and your successes. If someone gives an unsolicited compliment or unexpectedly praises you, smile graciously and say *thank you*. You don't need to back up the compliment with even more evidence of your superpowers. But you also don't want to shrug it off or downplay it.

4. **Walk the middle ground.** While the majority of what you say can be positive and self-promoting, you should also acknowledge difficulties, mistakes and blunders. It makes you less likely to come across as arrogant and boastful. No one believes you are perfect, so it is better to acknowledge both your strengths and weaknesses along with successes and failures while discussing an overall positive outcome.
5. **Focus on the team and share credit with others.** Most successes are a team effort. Make sure to acknowledge the contributions of others who helped you achieve your success. Highlight how your success, in turn, helped the team or organization achieve a goal, rather than just talking about your own accomplishments. And allow others to share their successes and celebrate their accomplishments with them. This creates a positive and supportive team environment.

# How To Ask for a Promotion at Work

> "Know your worth. Don't ask for it.
> State it once and never accept anything less."
> *Unknown*

Did you know that 82 percent of employees want to discuss moving up in their careers, but 40 percent do not follow through? Don't be in the 40 percent.

## Why Does It Matter?

Taking the initiative toward career progression sends a positive signal because employees who are confident enough to ask for a promotion are more likely to stay with the company. It is also important to understand the ecosystem of the position and with whom you may want to forge alliances or create a stronger relationship.

Knowing the right way to ask for a promotion demonstrates your goals, skills and confidence. It helps you avoid saying things such as, *I deserve to get promoted because I'm a top performer, just like Tom who got promoted this year.*

## Action Steps

Take the initiative and follow six pieces of advice that can put you on the right track to getting the promotion that you're after.

1. **Thoughtfully research the position you want.** For the position you're interested in, you need to know exactly what is expected in terms of skills and competencies. Analyze where the company is focusing its efforts and allocating its resources. Growth areas of the business are where future promotional opportunities will be.

2. **Put your interest out there**. Plant the seed in your manager's mind that you may be interested in a new opportunity. When your boss knows your specific career goals and interests, they can spell out what you need to do to be successful. When an opportunity arises, your boss will be more likely to consider you for the opportunity if you've made your aspirations clear. You might say something such as, *I feel I've been meeting all the expectations in my current role. I'm proud of the impact I've had, but I would welcome your advice on how I can assume more responsibility and progress to the next level in my career.*
3. **Track your achievements**. Present logical reasons why you are a good fit for the position you covet. Focus on areas where you have made meaningful change or progress. To make your arguments stronger, use metrics such as revenue gained, savings achieved or new customers acquired to demonstrate the scope of your accomplishments. Make sure you don't overlook accomplishments that at the time might seem trivial to you. When the time comes to make your case for a promotion you want all the ammunition you can accumulate.
4. **Make sure your accomplishments are known to others in your organization**. Write progress reports for your boss that can be circulated to others, share your work by participating in knowledge-sharing events, informally let those around you know more about the projects you've been working on. Also, while you don't want to sign up for "can't win" assignments, you do want to raise your hand for high-profile tasks that increase your visibility beyond your immediate team.
5. **Create persuasive arguments**. Identify and advocate for improvements you can make. Focus on what you uniquely bring to the position. Frame your argument around taking on more responsibility. Make it clear how the promotion is a win-win for both you and your company.

6. **Create a plan for the future**. If your manager says no or not yet, ask for the specific reasons why your promotion was postponed or denied. Then, ask if you can meet again to create a development plan that outlines the steps you need to take to get the promotion in the future.

There's a final point I want to make here. Don't necessarily reject lateral promotions. Horizontal moves can help you gain valuable additional experience. The more skills you can develop in as many areas as possible, the greater your value is to your organization.

# How To Ask Your Boss for a Raise

> If you want to fly, you have to give up
> the things that weigh you down.
> *Toni Morrison*

Companies give employees raises when they create value, demonstrate hard work and exhibit potential for future success within their roles. While asking your manager for a raise may be uncomfortable and stressful, the investment you make in preparing for the conversation will pay dividends.

## Why Does It Matter?

You might know the quote *Shoot for the moon. Even if you miss, you'll land among the stars.* Securing a pay increase isn't just about padding your wallet; it's a testament to the value you bring to the table. By advocating for a raise, you're not only recognizing your own growth and contributions but nudging your boss to do the same. Asking for a raise is a proactive step toward aligning your compensation with industry standards and ensuring you're not undervalued. After all, your paycheck should reflect both your current efforts and your future potential.

## Action Steps

I'm the first one to acknowledge that asking for a raise isn't easy, but there are six simple steps that will help you.

1. **Reflect honestly on your work contributions**. Before you request a raise, make sure you can explain *why* you deserve a raise *at this time*. If you don't have enough good reasons, you may want to wait until you have adequate data to back up

your request. On the flip side, it is important not to be too humble. Be proud of your success and accomplishments!

2. **Gather all the evidence to make a strong case.** Provide specific numbers or statistics on your performance. For example, you could say, *In the past year, I generated 1,000 leads for the company, which is an increase of 12 percent from the previous year. This resulted in $64,000 in additional revenue.* If you keep track of your accomplishments throughout the year, it is easier to summarize the evidence you need when it comes time to ask for a raise, so keep weekly or bimonthly logs of your contributions.

3. **Find out what people in your role are paid across the industry.** Conversations with coworkers and peers can help you gain a better idea of what appropriate compensation is for your role. Glassdoor.com reports pay ranges for companies based on role and location. LinkedIn also shows salary ranges for job listings. If you work in a state such as New York that has already adopted pay transparency laws, you can see the salary that your company is advertising to new talent. Having data from reliable sources to show that you are currently underpaid for your contributions can provide powerful support when it comes time to have the conversation with your boss.

4. **Choose the right timeframe to make your request.** Most companies have timelines for hiring, performance reviews and salary increases. It is best to put in your request for a raise *before* annual budgets are set so that management can factor the raise into the new budget. After budgets are set, there is usually little wiggle room for additional expenses. Asking for a raise is also best timed directly following a positive performance review and after receiving good feedback or recognition from management. Other good times to bring up

conversations are around your work anniversary with your company and during periods when the company is experiencing financial success.
5. **Outline the conversation and schedule the meeting.** Establish the order of the points you want to make and consider any objections that your boss may have. Make sure to prepare responses to any objections. When you are ready, schedule a discussion with your supervisor. Choose a convenient time and ask to discuss your compensation. Give your boss a heads up on the topic.
6. **Have the actual discussion with your boss.** Start the conversation on a positive note by expressing appreciation for your manager, your job and the company. Then clearly and concisely make the case for why you deserve a raise, using the data you've gathered.

Here are a few other suggestions. When discussing a raise, it is best for *you* to anchor the conversation and have as much leverage as possible. Research shows that you should try to be the one to go first and propose the raise amount. It is also better to give a solid number, either a percent increase or dollar value, as opposed to a range. If you give a range, most managers will focus on the lower end of the range.

Asking for a raise that exceeds what you expect to get can help you land more money. For example, if you are seeking a 5 percent raise and you ask your manager for 5 percent, he may try to negotiate a lower number. However, if you go into the meeting asking for 7 percent, your manager may end up settling closer to 5 percent. Plus, there is always the possibility that he may be impressed with your work and rationale and agree to the 7 percent anyway!

Finally, if the answer to your salary increase request is not immediate, inquire about the timeline for a decision, and respectfully follow up at the agreed-upon time. Also, be open to alternative solutions if the company is not able to grant a raise. If you're working for a start-up, you may be able to negotiate some equity which could be worth a lot in the future depending on the company's growth trajectory. Perks and benefits are another great element to negotiate. More PTO, flexible hours, the possibility of doing your work remotely and reimbursement for additional training and education are all great ways that companies can reward employees for excellent work.

# How To Handle Not Getting the Promotion

*"For every minute you are angry,
you lose sixty seconds of happiness."*
*Ralph Waldo Emerson*

It's disheartening and humiliating to learn that you were passed over for a promotion. It's natural to feel disappointed, frustrated, sad and angry. Experience your emotions and then move forward.

## Why Does It Matter?

Things like this will happen in your career. You won't always be picked first. Sometimes, you may even be the last choice. Learning how to cope with loss and activating your internal drive to do better next time are two essential skills in growing as a professional.

Remember there may be other opportunities for advancement in the future; even around the corner.

## Action Steps

There are six things to keep in mind when you don't get a promotion.

1. **Talk to your boss about it**. Once you have processed your immediate emotions, it can be helpful to talk to your manager to get more insight into why you were not selected for the promotion. You want to gain clarity into areas where you can improve to increase your chances of getting promoted in the future.
2. **Remain professional and show grace**. Criticism can be hard to take. Remember that not getting promoted is *not* a reflection of your worth. Resist the urge to compare yourself to the person who got the promotion. It won't change the outcome

and you may come across as petty. Remain calm and focus on listening and learning from the conversation.
3. **Establish goals to address feedback.** Set specific goals for yourself based on the feedback you receive. Track your progress toward achieving those goals. This can help you demonstrate the progress you are making and show your boss that you are taking his feedback seriously.
4. **Stay positive.** After receiving disappointing news, it's easy to get down on yourself. Take your manager's feedback and use it as motivation. Reframe negative thoughts in a more positive light. This will increase your chances of getting promoted in the future.
5. **Put it behind you.** Don't dwell on the news that you didn't get a promotion. Focus on the present and the future. Looking in the rearview mirror is a waste of your precious time.
6. **Check back in to show how you are progressing**. Share your progress with your boss regularly. Provide updates on your progress toward achieving your goals, share examples of how you have applied the feedback and ask for additional support or guidance if needed. Doing this shows your boss you are committed to do whatever you can to be considered for promotion in the future.

# How To Deal With Unfair Treatment at Work

*"A person's a person, no matter how small."*
*Dr. Seuss*

Unfortunately, the workplace can sometimes feel like a dark and twisted dinner menu where unfairness is the main course. Everything on the unfairness menu is unappetizing, from nepotism and favoritism, to being passed over for promotions and interesting assignments, to performance evaluations based on personalities to being denied opportunities for training. The specials can be particularly unpalatable and vile—lies and rumors being spread about you and racist or ethnic jokes and offensive comments. Unfortunately, any of these and more can be on the unfairness menu at work.

## Why Does It Matter?

Don't be afraid to stand up for yourself. We all deserve fair and just treatment at work. It can be intimidating to challenge unfair treatment, especially when it's coming from those in positions of authority. However, standing up for yourself ensures that you receive the respect and recognition you deserve. Remember that you have rights as an employee, and it's up to you to advocate for yourself when those rights are being violated.

## Action Steps

Your first step is to do your best to stay calm and evaluate your situation. Does the treatment rise to the level of harassment or discrimination? Is it worth fighting? Will you feel better by taking the high road?

How you answer these questions may determine what you do next. But no matter the level of severity you're facing, there are some follow-up actions to take.

Document the situation. Write it down in as much detail as possible. Be a journalist and note the who, what, when, where and how. Record everything and be specific. This includes the names of people who might have witnessed it or be experiencing it also. Stay away from posting about the unfairness on social media, though. This isn't the kind of documenting that you should engage in. A rant can ultimately put you in a disadvantageous position. Don't provide ammunition to the opposition.

Even if it's less of a potential legal issue and more of a serious conversation with your boss, you need to have detailed information to reference. Joe's sexist jokes may not constitute harassment, but they're still demeaning and propagate unfair attitudes and treatment. The CFO's niece may be a delightful person, but that doesn't mean she should automatically get the promotion when you are more qualified and have more experience.

Once you've gathered your documentation, talk to your boss. Some bosses are not very good at handling sensitive issues related to unfairness. If you feel that you aren't getting anywhere with your boss you can try to talk with other managers at work or to HR. This is especially true in cases where illegal harassment or discrimination may be present.

To be clear, there is a difference between being treated unfairly and being harassed or discriminated against. Unfair treatment of any kind is no joke, but harassment and discrimination are both unethical and illegal. HR representatives are trained to handle these types of situations in a confidential and sensitive manner. Your HR department will likely take your situation very seriously. Help them do that. Insist that they do that. This may involve disciplinary action against the offender or changes to company policies and procedures. By insisting that HR take your situation seriously, you're not only advocating for yourself but also for the well-being of your colleagues. Harassment and discrimination of any kind shouldn't be tolerated.

# What To Do When Someone Takes Credit for Your Work

*"Soldiers generally win battles; generals get credit for them."*
*Napoleon Bonaparte*

We've all had this happen at one point or another: you share an idea with a colleague only to hear him repeat it in a meeting or you take the lead on a project and bring it to completion and then overhear your boss telling higher-ups it was her doing. It can be infuriating when someone takes credit for your work.

## Why Does It Matter?

It matters who gets credit for a job well done, especially when raises, promotions and bonuses are at stake. You deserve to get credit for work you complete, the projects you contribute to and ideas you come up with. How should you handle situations when someone else takes credit for your contributions?

## Action Steps

You can't just assume that people will notice the time and effort you put in, but handling the situation poorly can lead to conflict or damaged relationships with colleagues, team leaders and managers. Here are four tips that can help.

**Take time to calm down and properly assess the situation.** Before responding when you feel someone has unfairly taken credit for your work, you need to be in the right frame of mind. You might be tempted to call the person out right away, but this can be a mistake. Don't automatically presume that the person who took credit had malicious intentions. Credit stealing is often unintentional. You also need to take the time to ask yourself how much the credit-stealing act really matters. Not every piece of work you do has to have your name written all over it. If after reflecting you feel you need to set the record straight, take constructive action without making accusations. Ask questions to figure out why it happened and then jointly figure out how to make things right. Maybe your colleague can message the team thanking you for your contributions or you can both meet with your manager to clarify who did what.

**Practice "assertive modesty"**. There's a difference between bragging and keeping others informed of your contributions. People are often too passive and reluctant when it comes to sharing their contributions and accomplishments. Use every opportunity to demonstrate your involvement with the project and be clear about your contributions. If you have trouble speaking up about your contributions, consider approaching a colleague for help. Your colleague can ask you questions about your work in a meeting which can provide public proof of your contributions. Your confident knowledge-sharing will solidify in everybody's mind who was actually responsible. Ask colleagues to mention your name when the idea or project comes up in conversation. Take credit for your work but also give credit to others. The key is to learn to walk the tightrope between taking credit for your own performance and sharing credit with others who helped make your performance possible.

**Don't feel like you need to get credit for *everything* you do.** You need to be aware that others, especially your boss, may also have strong reasons for claiming at least a share of the credit for the work you do. Try to remember the saying, *credit shared is credit multiplied*. While your effort, creativity, insights and decisions may have brought the project to a successful conclusion, you are seldom a total solo act in the workplace. In most organizations you play a role as part of a broader team effort. Even though you believe that you performed the majority of the work that resulted in a successful outcome, others have probably contributed in important ways as well.

**Keep detailed records of your successes and accomplishments.** You'll want to be able to review your accomplishments with your boss at meetings and performance reviews. Having detailed data to reference during performance and promotion discussions is invaluable. Also, send periodic updates about your work to your boss even before a project is completed. That way even if someone tries to take credit for your work, your boss will know the reality.

We all deserve to get credit for the contributions we make in the workplace. It can be discouraging and frustrating when we feel others are trying to take the credit for our contributions, but by following these tips you can help preempt these incidents and deal better with them when they occur.

# How To Shoulder and Prevent Unfair Blame at Work

*"All blame is a waste of time."*
*Casey Stengel*

Did you know that we are all naturally wired to blame other people or circumstances when things go wrong, that people often blame others to try to increase their own self-esteem, and that research shows that people in the workplace tend to copy blaming as a behavior? This research suggests that we have to fight against natural tendencies and make the conscious choice *not* to blame others.

When you find yourself in a situation where your manager or a coworker unfairly blames you for something, you need to know how to respond. You also should adopt preemptive strategies to reduce the number of times that this happens.

## Why Does It Matter?

No one likes to be blamed for mistakes at work, so it's important to know how to respond effectively when this happens. There are three rules to follow when you are unfairly blamed for a mistake.

- Listen attentively and avoid becoming defensive or emotional. Remain calm, polite and collected. Take notes so you can respond thoughtfully when you are ready.
- Don't get defensive and take the time you need to gather your thoughts and information before responding. Make sure you follow up on the opportunity to state your case.
- If you didn't do what you are being accused of, you should calmly—but directly—say so. Provide evidence in the form of emails or other documentation, but don't come across as defen-

sive or accuse or assign blame to others. Focus on the fact that shedding more light on the situation creates the opportunity for everyone to learn. Make it clear that while you were not responsible for the mistake, you would be happy to help resolve it.

While it's important to know how to respond in the event that you are unfairly blamed for something, the best course of action is to preempt unfair blame from happening in the first place.

## Action Steps

There are four things that you can do to reduce the likelihood that you will be unfairly blamed for things that happen in the workplace.

*Maintain a reputation for doing quality work.*
If you are well-known for the quality of your work, others will be less likely to believe those who try to shift blame on you. Also, if you are known for doing quality work, your manager will be less inclined to select you as the target of blame. Consistently doing great work allows you to weather false accusations.

*Keep a record and organized files of what you do.*
Documentation is your best defense. Keep written records of your work in easily accessible digital files. Also, check in with your network contacts frequently, especially with those inclined to believe in you and publicly support you.

*Be someone who owns up to your mistakes.*
Don't engage in lengthy apologies or excuses. Succinctly admit your mistake and state, *"I will do my best to ensure this doesn't happen again."* People who deny responsibility chip away at trust. Owning up to your mistakes insulates you from unfair accusations.

*Accept that catching some amount of blame is part of life in the workplace.*
While being blamed for something when you didn't do it is frustrating, recognize that a certain amount of blame, even if it's unfair, happens in the workplace. While it's best if you take preemptive steps to minimize that you will be on the receiving end of unfair blame, you can't dodge being blamed for things 100 percent of the time.

## Section 7

# Making Strides in Your Career

In this section, I dive deeper into the playbook of progressing professionally—on the nuances that can set you apart in the workplace. That's an almost impossible task if you don't have the confidence to advocate for yourself.

You need to understand your company's inner workings—the unsaid dynamics, the hidden hierarchies and the cultural undertones. It's akin to a seasoned sailor reading the wind and the waves. It's not just about playing by the rules; it's about understanding the game, its players and the subtleties that can mean the difference between winning and losing.

However, awareness is just the beginning. The professional landscape is ever-evolving, and to remain competitive, you need to continuously hone and update your skills. What's deemed innovative today might be elementary tomorrow. By staying updated, you don't just ensure relevance; you position yourself as a proactive player, always leading in the game.

As you enhance your skills and knowledge, you also need to focus on cultivating your personal power in the workplace. Beyond the confines of a job description, it's the respect and influence you command, stemming from consistent delivery, unwavering reliability and the expertise you bring to the table. This influence becomes your currency to increase your visibility and effectively pitch your groundbreaking ideas. When you're seen and heard, your work gets the acknowledgement it deserves. This leads to recognition by senior executives—game-changers who can propel your trajectory, be it through mentorship or sponsorship.

Navigating the intricate maze of professional advancement requires more than just hard work. It's a calculated dance of self-improvement, organizational understanding and strategic visibility. By mastering this dance, you set the stage for your success.

Ready. Set. Let's tango.

# How To Activate Your Company Intelligence Radar

*"I would encourage you: be informed—knowledge is power."*
*Matt Bevin*

Your organization is where you spend most of your waking hours. Depending on your role, you may only have access to the people and information in your office, your specific department or your functional area. Perhaps you hear information about other departments, other divisions or different functions, but you don't have any first-hand experience with people in them.

How do you gain the intelligence you need to stay on top of what is happening more broadly at your organization?

## Why Does It Matter?

It's important to be attuned to possible changes in leadership, upcoming challenges, shifts in policy or external pressures on your company which may impact your livelihood and professional future.

After tapping into any information that your company provides directly to you on its intranet, in emails or through other forms of communication, there are four sources of information you should check out to activate your company intelligence radar.

## Action Steps

Start with publicly available reliable sources. Access your company's website. Learn what customers have said or posted on social media sites. Read the positive and the negative comments which you may not hear about at work. Trade magazines and journals provide valuable data about your company, its suppliers and its competitors. If your company is publicly held, you could buy as little as one share of stock in your name and get the annual report and attend shareholders meetings.

Next, your company's public relations office probably provides regular updates and information about the company to business journalists. Read any recent press releases. You may find out more information about the company's achievements or setbacks. Read what the press says about your company and its leaders. Google your company's executives and board members to find out more about their previous employment histories and what they have said publicly about the company.

If you work in a federal or state agency, you can access the annual budget. If you work for a publicly traded company, you can find extensive financial information in SEC filings which are available on line. You may wish to compare your company's data against its competitors. You can also obtain information on changes in the number of employees and other metrics.

Finally, every organization has a rumor mill. Hopefully, you will be able to discern mere gossip from facts about events which may impact your professional future. If you have a circle of reliable colleagues, tap into what they say during coffee breaks or at lunch. Actively listen for any information that could affect your future. Not everything you hear will be reliable, but you may be able to put important pieces together.

Knowledge about your organization is power. Make a habit of gathering and analyzing any and all reliable information and intelligence.

# How To Identify the Hidden Keys to Success at Work

*"The ladder of success is best climbed
by stepping on the rungs of opportunity."*
*Ayn Rand*

Almost every organization has hidden keys to getting ahead. Everyone is promoted for a reason, whether it's their competence, people interaction skills, relationships they form or specific work accomplishments.

## Why Does It Matter?

Beyond the explicit rules and standard operating procedures, every organization has its unique, often unspoken, dynamics and cultural nuances that drive decision-making and influence outcomes. These covert elements can range from the relationships and networks that facilitate information flow, to the unwritten codes of conduct that determine who rises and who doesn't. Think of your organization like a big game. Sure, there are clear-cut rules, but there's also a ton of behind-the-scenes stuff that can really change how the game's played. It's like knowing the secret shortcuts in a video game. By figuring out these hidden success hacks in your company, you're getting the inside scoop to getting ahead.

## Action Steps

There are a few steps you can take to identify and unlock the hidden keys to success.

- **Take initiative whenever you can**. Many organizations promote individuals who regularly show initiative. When a job needs doing, step in and do it. Taking initiative means going above and beyond your current job description, offering to take on new responsibilities without first being asked and showing ownership over the success of the business. Someone may be watching to see who decides to take initiative and who doesn't.

- **Look carefully at the backgrounds, experience and styles of individuals who have succeeded in moving up the ladder in your organization**. Reasons that people are promoted are often good indicators of hidden keys to success. Try to discern common patterns. Asking questions to discern patterns helps, too. Did the people who got promoted in front of you all gain some experience in a specific functional area such as operations or marketing earlier in their careers? Did they begin their careers in a specific division at the company? Do they share common interests or have similar capabilities? Are there personality characteristics that they share? Have they all forged close relationships with certain senior people? Is there a common pattern in tenure, credentials or specific training?
- **Get a mentor**. Mentors can help you identify the right kinds of opportunities to go after within your organization. For many reasons, it's very important to your success to find a mentor who can guide you in your career. One of the most valuable services a mentor can provide is tipping you off to the hidden keys to success in your organization. Ask probing questions to better understand organizational dynamics and promotion criteria. In addition, people with good networks and strong mentor relationships gain knowledge faster about how to get ahead because any number of people within their network can take them aside and explain the inner workings of the organization.
- **Build your internal network**. The more people you know at your organization the more insight and information you can gain.

# How To Keep Your Skills Current in Today's Changing Workplace

*"The more that you read, the more things you will know. The more that you learn, the more places you'll go."*
*Dr. Seuss*

Rapid innovation and automation mean that the half-life of existing skills is shrinking. Skills that were once in high demand can become outdated quickly, so it is increasingly important for individuals to continuously learn and adapt to stay competitive in the job market.

For example: in the tech sector, there is an increasing demand for roles and skills related to artificial intelligence. AI developers design and build systems that can analyze vast amounts of data and make predictions. These roles require skills in working with large data sets and writing algorithms. On the other hand, network engineers are becoming less in-demand as more companies move to cloud-based services.

All of us need to keep our skill sets diversified and up to date.

## Why Does It Matter?

Keeping yourself and your skills relevant to the industry is one of the most important factors of workplace success. It means not only are your skills still relevant—*you're* still relevant. And don't only focus on the technical skills of a job. In a recent study, research found that 85 percent of job success is attributed to soft skills, or what some might call social skills, while only 15 percent of job success is rooted in technical expertise.

## Action Steps

There are four steps you can take to keep your skill set current and of value in the workplace.

1. **Inventory your skills.** Take ten minutes to write a list of the skills you bring to the table and add an example of how you add value through each skill. For example, a person who is skilled in data analysis might be able to analyze sales data to identify trends and patterns that could help a company improve its marketing strategies or better target its products to specific customer segments.
2. **Ask for feedback from your manager.** See if the skills your manager identifies align to your self-assessment. Then ask your manager what skills you do not have that would be helpful for you to develop. You may find you would benefit from developing project management skills because you need to become more competent at planning, organizing and managing projects. That, in turn, enables your ability to better manage time, resources and stakeholders.
3. **Identify the skills that matter in your current field or industry of interest.** Look at which roles in your industry have increased in hiring and which have decreased. This will show momentum on which roles and associated skills are potentially no longer valued—or which are being automated and which are in demand.
    - Do some research on skill predictions and current trends.
    - Do not discount soft skills.
4. **Find resources for skill development and use them.** The key is to identify training materials and then hold yourself accountable for completing the training. There are many resources for skill development including attending conferences and workshops, working with an experienced professional

who can provide guidance and feedback, tapping into webinars and live online training tutorials, reading books, viewing videos and attending in-person classroom-based training sessions.
- Take advantage of any on-the-job training opportunities your company provides, such as job rotations, cross-training and mentoring programs to gain new skills.
- Join professional organizations and attend their events.
- Stay abreast of the latest technologies and tools used in your industry and learn how to use them by accessing vendor training content.

# How To Sell Your Ideas at Work

*"A little progress every day adds up to big results."*
*Satya Nani*

When you join a new organization or start in a new role, you may feel pressure to impress your boss. Or if you've been in your role for a while, you may have ideas on changes to improve operational efficiency or effectiveness.

Despite how good you think your ideas are, it may be hard to sell them to others. They may be interpreted as critical of the status quo, too costly or too difficult to implement. Your boss may feel that the ideas cannot currently be executed. Your boss may believe you don't understand the issue well enough to provide recommendations. They may even feel threatened by your idea or believe that you are making old problems look easy to solve.

## Why Does It Matter?
When you propose a new idea, you don't want to make a CLM—a Career Limiting Move.

So, what do you need to consider when you have a good idea you want to sell to others? An idea is only as valid as it is viable and likely to be implemented.

## Action Steps
Address these questions before proposing your idea to your boss and others.

1. Do I fully understand the situation?
2. Who is going to feel threatened?

3. How much credibility and support do I have?
4. How many ideas should I tackle?

Before proposing the idea, gather insight on how likely it is to be accepted. There may be blocking factors related to timing, budget or legal constraints. To get a full picture, pay attention to the decisions senior leaders make and the reasoning behind them. Talk to members of senior management and ask about their goals, priorities and challenges. Seek out mentors or trusted colleagues who can provide insight and advice on the inner workings at your organization. Stay up to date on the latest news and developments within the organization, as this can provide valuable context and clues.

Next, remember that everyone has different motivations and your analysis needs to take potential objections or concerns into account. Observe how decisions are made and who is involved in the decision-making process. You want to consider your idea from the perspective of important decision-makers and influencers to be ready for objections and know what you might be walking into.

Finally, it's essential to prioritize your ideas to maximize your chance of success. You can build a track record of achievement by successfully proposing and implementing smaller and less polarizing ideas. With time you will build the confidence and the credibility to tackle bigger problems.

As you establish a stronger reputation within the organization, you'll naturally earn increased respect, trust, and support. You'll also gain greater confidence in freely sharing your ideas for collaborative exploration with others and even for others to explore independently.

# How To Capture the Attention of Senior Executives

*"There is no better way to establish a reputation for excellence than by delivering excellent results."*
*Brian Tracy*

Are you captivated by the idea of climbing the corporate ladder and making your way into a more senior position? The process of getting promoted can be complex, with many factors influencing the outcome, including responsibilities, requirements and expectations. It's also necessary to get on the radar of senior executives.

So go ahead and pursue your goals with gusto, determination and resilience, and one day, those senior executives will take notice of your hard work and achievements.

## Why Does It Matter?

Senior executives play a key role in deciding who gets promoted, who will be given new responsibilities, and who will be offered opportunities for growth within the company. Being recognized by senior executives can raise your profile and visibility, which opens the door to new opportunities. Senior executives also have access to resources and information that can help you achieve your goals and advance your career.

Successful people aren't afraid to go after what they want. They understand that recognition and success come to those who are willing to put in the effort and take calculated risks.

## Action Steps

From what I've seen in the workplace, several crucial steps can help you capture the attention of senior executives.

1. **Demonstrate your commitment to the company.** How would your work change if you performed as if you owned the company? To show commitment, you must understand the bigger picture, the purpose of the organization and its overall goals. Once you internalize organizational goals and organizational purpose, you'll increase your contribution and show that you are committed to making a positive impact.
    o Show that you are eager to contribute every way you can to the success of the company.
    o Add value at every turn by contributing ideas and participating in initiatives.
    o Go above and beyond your manager's expectations.
    o Make sure that the way in which you add value aligns with the company's goals and priorities.
2. **Focus on learning from your network rather than simply completing tasks.** At the end of the day, simply churning out work is not enough to gain management's attention. Instead, ingrain yourself in the fabric of what your company is. By talking to your network, you will gain important insights into how they were able to get ahead—and which speed bumps to avoid on your journey toward success.
    o Proactively network with coworkers, higher-ups and people more experienced than you.
    o Learn about others' experiences in the industry and at the organization.
    o Inquire about higher-ups' successes and failures.
    o Attend company events and engage in conversations with senior executives whenever possible.
3. **Challenge existing norms and find new solutions.** Many companies struggle to implement change and don't challenge the status quo as often as they should. Don't blindly accept

the status quo as unchangeable. Look for inefficiencies and areas of improvement along the way.
    - Can a task you do be performed faster or more efficiently?
    - Can you automate a process?
    - Can you improve quality or reduce cost by performing a task differently?
    - Can you eliminate a task?
4. **Ask questions**. Asking questions demonstrates your interest and engagement in the company and shows that you are taking initiative to learn and grow. The answers to the questions you ask help you gain critical insights and information which help you contribute more effectively to the company's success.
5. **See how you can take on more responsibilities**. The only way for others to trust that you can take on more responsibility is to prove yourself in the workplace. Once senior executives see that you have leadership potential and can successfully complete complex tasks, they'll be inclined to give you even more responsibility.
    - Focus on delivering outstanding results in your role, taking ownership and exceeding expectations.
    - Look for opportunities to assume new responsibilities, lead projects and demonstrate leadership potential.
    - Frame your request to take on more responsibility as a route to lighten your boss's workload.

# How To Find a Great Mentor

> "A mentor is someone who sees more talent and ability in you than you see yourself, and helps bring it out of you."
> *Bob Proctor*

A good mentor can make a huge impact on your career. If you ask most successful people how they got to where they are, they can point to mentors who they credit, at least in part, for their success. Mark Zuckerberg was mentored by Steve Jobs; Bill Gates was mentored by Warren Buffett and Oprah Winfrey was Maya Angelou's mentee. Most people, including me, will tell you that their mentor(s) made all the difference in their career success. So, if no one has ever told you this, let me be the first: mentors are very important to your professional success.

## Why Does It Matter?

A great mentor can help you take charge of your career path, boost your confidence to try new things, clue you in on untapped opportunities and show you the ropes when things get tricky. Their advice can be a game-changer, helping you see more and do more than you possibly could have without their advice.

Don't deny yourself the important career boost that a mentor can provide.

## Action Steps

Here are a few tips on how you can find mentors and maintain and nurture those relationships.

**Find and select the right mentor.**
Identifying an appropriate mentor is the first step in the process. Before you identify a mentor, think carefully about the specific kinds

of skills or experiences you are looking for in a mentor. Ideally, your mentor should be a role model and someone who has been in your situation or a similar situation, a number of years before you.

Large corporations often have formal mentoring programs. If your workplace doesn't, consider the informal networks or groups where more experienced colleagues are willing to offer guidance. Attend internal workshops and conferences. These are prime opportunities not only for learning but for mingling with potential mentors.

Websites such as LinkedIn can be ripe hunting grounds for identifying a mentor. Engaging with professionals whose careers or posts you admire can be the starting point. Your alma mater also likely wants to see its graduates succeed and might have structures in place, like mentorship programs or networking events, to facilitate this.

Once you've identified a potential mentor, you're ready to set the ball into motion.

**Ask for that first meeting.**
According to numerous studies, 76 percent of people agree that mentors are important, but only 37 percent have one. Why the disparity? Most people are afraid to ask for that initial meeting with a possible mentor. The fear of rejection is real, but you shouldn't let it get in your way.

Approaching someone you look up to, especially when you're not very familiar with him or he's in a higher position than you, can be daunting. However, you can ease your nerves by remembering that most successful people had mentors. They've benefited from this guidance and usually are eager to pay it back by offering assistance to others. Why not you? If you're keen to build a connection, initiate with a modest request: a short fifteen-to-thirty minute chat, either in-person or online.

A concise email is often the most effective approach. Highlight a couple aspects of their work that impress you, provide a brief introduction about yourself and clearly state your purpose for reaching out. Share what you hope to gain from their insights and conclude with a direct request: "Could we possibly schedule a short conversation over coffee in the upcoming weeks?"

A casual coffee catch-up or a brief video chat requires minimal commitment from your prospective mentor and allows you to get to know them better, assess your rapport and determine if their experience and knowledge align well with your needs.

**Make the most of the initial meeting.**
Consider your initial coffee meetup or online chat as a chance for relaxed dialogue. Keep in mind that you're both in the process of getting to know each other, so the conversation shouldn't solely revolve around work. Delve into their personal interests, such as their weekend activities, pastimes or where they spent their childhood. Everyone appreciates the occasional diversion from routine work topics. This also helps you identify shared interests or experiences.

Midway through your conversation, transition to career-focused questions and discuss your aspirations. At the end of the conversation, reflect back on the insights they shared, indicating your appreciation for their advice. For example, you could say, "From our chat, I gather that networking with peers played a pivotal role in your career. I'll explore some online gatherings to connect with peers in my domain. I'm grateful for that tip."

**Show appreciation and follow up.**
After your discussion, send a thank-you email within the week. Highlight a few pivotal insights you gained from the chat and express your intent to touch base again in several weeks.

Around a month after expressing your thanks, update your potential mentor on the steps you've undertaken, rooted in your initial conversation's insights. Use the intervals between these interactions to actively work toward the objectives you co-established with your mentor. Periodically share with them (through a brief text or email) the impact of their counsel on both your professional and personal growth. However, ensure you're not overwhelming them with too many updates. A monthly check-in is ideal in the beginning, but once a stronger mentorship bond is formed, reaching out quarterly is adequate. The primary aim is maintaining communication and updating them on your career trajectory.

**Offer to help**.
As with any relationship, mentoring relationships are a two-way street. What you're giving back to your mentor is really your progress, but there's also no harm in checking in with your mentor during your meetings to see if you can help them in any way. Maybe they're working on a presentation and could use an outside perspective, or perhaps you know someone they were looking to connect with.

**Have realistic expectations**.
Mentors typically have a job, a family, hobbies and multiple mentees. In other words, they're not there just for you and to meet your needs. Be mindful of the competing demands on your mentor's time. You should seek their guidance and advice as a process toward your own personal and professional growth. Your mentor is not there to do your job.

**Engage multiple mentors**.
While appreciating your mentor's role, keep in mind that there are other important sources of teaching, advising and support. Other contacts, both in the organization, such as leaders, peers, subordinates or customers, as well as outside the organization, can play a role in your professional development.

Multiple mentors, in different fields and at different stages of your career, enhance your chances of success.

The right kind of mentorship can be life-changing. Staying in the driver's seat and being proactive will make your relationship with your mentor a successful one.

# How To Become More Visible at Work

> "If you build the guts to do something, anything,
> then you better save enough to face the consequences."
> *Criss Jami,* Killosophy

There are many reasons why you may want to become more visible in the company you work for. If you are seeking to advance in your career, increasing your visibility can make you more visible to decision-makers who may be considering promotions or new opportunities.

## Why Does It Matter?

By increasing your visibility, you can also learn from more experienced colleagues and develop new skills that can help you grow in your career.

Increasing your visibility can also help you build relationships and connections within your organization, which can be valuable for finding new opportunities and getting support for your work.

Increased visibility can lead to recognition for your contributions and achievements, which can be personally rewarding and help boost your confidence as you can also become more influential within your organization.

## Action Steps

There are three things to focus on to increase your visibility in your company.

*If you work remotely, be seen and heard.*
- Develop a strong relationship with at least one person who works on-site. Doing so allows you to have greater awareness of what's going on and this person can act as an advocate for you when you aren't physically present.

- Use video chats instead of phone calls whenever possible so that people associate you with more than just your voice.
- Be more active and responsive over instant messenger and in meetings and offer status updates more regularly than you would if you were working in person.
- Select a few important meetings where you commit to attending in person.
- When you are physically present, be extra visible by greeting as many people as you can and sitting next to people you want to get to know better.

*Volunteer for projects that allow you to work with different people.*
- Sign up for projects involving people you haven't met yet or would like to get to know better. Large, cross-team projects and initiatives can be efficient ways to expand your network.
- Volunteer for low-commitment activities that give you a way to interact with people you wouldn't meet otherwise. Before volunteering, though, make sure that you can handle the additional work in light of your existing workload.
- When in doubt about whether to volunteer for something, ask a seasoned coworker you trust about the task. There may be a reason no one is signing up for something or it might be a hidden opportunity that others don't recognize or need.

*If your coworkers organize social events, join early on.*
Workplace social events can sometimes help you meet future mentors and influential individuals who can consider you for interesting assignments.
- Try to show up, at least for part of it, especially when you are new to the team or the organization.

- If you establish a pattern of absence at these events, your coworkers may assume that you are not interested, and you may not be invited in the future.
- If you choose to attend, remember that you are still "at work" during these events, so act professionally.

# How To Build Personal Power at Work

> "The most common way people give up their power
> is by thinking they don't have any."
> *Alice Walker*

Personal power is the ability to be winsome and influence the outcome of events. Rather than relying on formal authority, personal power comes from solid interpersonal skills, self-esteem and confidence.

## Why Does It Matter?

Owning your power gives you the credibility to be successful. Owning your power also gives confidence and an understanding of how you can help others make decisions and achieve their objectives. It allows you to create and maintain strong relationships both in and out of the workplace. Most importantly, it enables you to stand up for yourself.

## Action Steps

There are seven steps to building your personal power.

- **Take initiative to build a track record**. Look for opportunities to improve processes, solve problems or take on additional responsibilities. Once you have identified an area where you can take initiative, come up with a plan for how you will tackle the challenge. Let your boss know what you are planning to do and why you think it is important. It is not just what you have done that matters, but also how you have done it.
- **Develop relevant skills and competencies**. Those who have expertise have more power. The more unique your expertise,

the more important it will be as a source of power. Technical expertise is important but so is expertise in soft skill areas such as managing interpersonal relationships and conceptual ability.

- **Engage in positive self-talk.** Negative self-talk paralyzes you from taking action, holds you back from sharing your thoughts and ideas and prevents you from taking risks and exploring new opportunities. Don't let limiting beliefs inhibit your success. Focus on your strengths and accomplishments, and remind yourself of all the things you are capable of.
- **Be likable.** Research suggests that people who are liked have greater personal power. "Likability" is associated with behaviors found in friendships. People are drawn to others who are positive and upbeat. By looking on the bright side, you can make yourself more likable.
- **Acknowledge your fears.** Your fears, as with your negative thoughts, sabotage your success and rob you of your power. We all have fears, but we lose our power when we let our fears overwhelm and paralyze us from taking action. Acknowledge your fears and then face them head on. Each new risk you take brings you closer to owning your power.
- **Maintain a growth mindset.** Knowledge is power and those with a growth mindset are open to learning. Be curious, keep an open mind and listen and learn from others. Every day provides a new opportunity for personal growth. You can't be an expert in everything, but when you have a growth mindset your willingness to learn leads to personal power.
- **Practice self-care.** Effort is important and you need energy to fuel effort. But you can lose steam if you don't take the time to refuel and re-energize. To take care of your physical health, get enough sleep, eat a healthy diet and exercise regularly. To take care of your mental health, set aside time to

relax and unwind, practice mindfulness and seek support. To take care of your emotional well-being, identify and express your emotions in a healthy way, practice self-compassion and set healthy boundaries with others.

Remember that building personal power is a process that takes time and effort. Be patient, persistent and consistent in your efforts, and you will eventually see results.

# How To Challenge the Status Quo in Your Workplace

*"Here's to the crazy ones, the misfits, the rebels, the troublemakers, the round pegs in the square holes . . . "*
*Steve Jobs*

The world of work is ever-changing. If a company fails to adapt to the waves of change, it will be swallowed up by them. However, research suggests that 72 percent of leaders say they never, or rarely, challenge the status quo in their organizations. Less than 10 percent of employees affirm that they work in companies that encourage non-conformity.

Conformity is prevalent in the workplace. We model others' behaviors and agree with managers' opinions to survive. Let's face it: the status quo is comfortable. Nobody wants to make the extra effort to change if things are going smoothly, even though the status quo may be planting the seeds of problems for the future. Finally, conformity occurs thanks to our personal tendencies to dismiss information that contradicts our own views in favor of information that reinforces them.

## Why Does It Matter?

Challenging the status quo can be a difficult and risky endeavor, but it can also be rewarding and necessary for progress. By challenging the status quo, you can bring about positive change and lead your team or organization to innovation.

## Action Steps

There are seven steps you can take to challenge the status quo in your organization:

1. **Recognize the presence of status quo bias**. Intellectually test your decisions to see if you have a rational reason behind them—or if you just don't feel comfortable breaking the mold. If there are no solid reasons to maintain the initial decision, try switching things up.
2. **Identify the problem and the opportunity for improvement**. Take some time to understand the current state of affairs and the reasons why things are the way they are. Although a company may have numerous opportunities for change, start by concentrating on one particular opportunity. Choosing exactly what you want to alter is key to challenging the status quo.
3. **Gather evidence and conduct research**. You need to clearly identify what the problem is and its negative consequences. Look for data, research and other evidence that supports your belief that the status quo is not working and that change is needed.
4. **Seek the opinions of others**. Get feedback on your idea from others who can bring fresh perspectives or highlight concerns. This helps you identify and address any flaws in your idea.
5. **Create a plan**. Write a detailed plan on how to implement the strategy to show that you put considerable effort into the process and are genuine and serious about making a positive change. It also helps you stay focused and organized.
6. **Present your plan to leadership**. Present your proposal for a change and your implementation plan with confidence and respect. To improve your chances of success, be ready to respond to any questions that the management may have regarding your proposal. Leave more time for questions than for the actual delivery of your presentation.

7. **Stick with it.** Changing the status quo can be difficult and may require persistence and determination. Keep pushing for change, even when you encounter obstacles or resistance. Don't give up because you're frustrated that things aren't happening exactly the way you want them to or as quickly as you would like.

# How To Become an Intrapreneur at Work

"A ship in the harbor is safe, but that's not what ships are built for."
*John Shedd*

Did you know nearly 50 percent greater productivity is achieved in businesses created by serial entrepreneurs? Entrepreneurs have many great qualities. They are willing to go through the process and take on the risk of developing, organizing and running a new business.

What names come to mind when you think about successful entrepreneurs? Steve Jobs? Bill Gates? Jeff Bezos? Henry Ford? Elon Musk? Oprah Winfrey?

Entrepreneurs are dreamers who turn their vision into reality. They are not afraid to take risks, to fail and to start again. They inspire us to think differently; to never settle and to always strive for more. They remind us that anything is possible, if you have the courage and determination to make it happen.

## Why Does It Matter?

You can apply an entrepreneurial spirit to how you operate within your company in the form of intrapreneurship.

Intrapreneurship is about discovering new ways of doing things at your job and then doing them. You can bring the "start-up" vibe to your office. You may not be the CEO of your own company yet, but that shouldn't stop you from thinking and acting like an entrepreneur. By constantly pushing boundaries and by adopting the mindset and practices of an entrepreneur, you can not only make a difference in your current workplace—you pave the way for your own successful venture in the future.

Soon, you'll add your name to the list of people who reach for their goals, hold fast to determination and push the limits of what's possible.

## Action Steps

Here are three steps you can take to become an intrapreneur in your everyday work.

*Develop an entrepreneurial mindset.*
Always be on the lookout for growth opportunities. An entrepreneurial opportunity might come in the form of an unsolved problem or an unmet customer need, or it may just be a new and innovative solution to an old problem. Entrepreneurs are defined by their ability to identify new opportunities. They are always on the alert, looking for the chance to capitalize on change and disruption in the way business is done. Don't be afraid to challenge the status quo. Entrepreneurs constantly ask questions such as, *What if? Why?* or *Why not?* See addressing customer needs as an evolving process and a moving target which continuously requires innovative solutions. View setbacks and failures as learning experiences. Entrepreneurs are not deterred by the risk of failure. They see setbacks as bumps on the road to success. They focus on what they can learn from every single mistake, setback or failure. Maintain a learning attitude, regardless of outcome.

*Ask probing questions and be curious.*
Ask yourself questions every day about how you might better meet your customers' needs. Ask your colleagues questions about their ideas and their struggles. Ask your customers what would make their experience better or what aspects of your product or service might be improved. Ask them what additional problems your product or service could solve.

Practice your abilities to sense opportunities, to exploit existing assets and to develop ideas to meet emerging needs or trends. Surround yourself with supportive people who encourage your curiosity. Maintain an inventory of unexploited opportunities and regularly revisit your inventory.

*Approach new ideas you want to pursue with discipline.*
People with an entrepreneurial mindset execute—they get on with it instead of analyzing new ideas to death. They are also adaptive—able to change directions as the real opportunity evolves. When they face setbacks, they bounce back and continue moving forward.

    The most successful entrepreneurs are also disciplined about limiting the number of projects they take on so they can execute well on those they pursue. They are disciplined about putting in long hours and hard work that it takes to make their idea a reality. They involve many people, both inside and outside the organization, in pursuit of an opportunity. They create and sustain networks of relationships rather than going it alone, making the most of the resources other people have to offer. And they inspire and motivate others to want to work toward achieving their goals.

# How To Grow in a Dead-End Job

"There is no such thing as a dead-end job. It is just a job that you haven't found a way to make more interesting yet."
*Tim Fargo*

At some point in your career, you may find yourself in a situation where there is little or no hope for professional advancement. You may experience feelings of frustration and discouragement and you may even believe that you will need to give up your dreams of progressing professionally.

## Why Does It Matter?

In a dead-end job, you can still take control of your career and work to improve your skills and prospects. It may not be easy, but with dedication and hard work, you can work toward a better future. Working to find purpose, meaning or even a different, more engaging task helps you cultivate the soft skills of dedication, perseverance and positivity.

## Action Steps

Despite your feelings about the situation, you do have options to grow your skills and develop even while remaining in a dead-end job. Here are a few suggestions for how to handle the situation.

*Seek out new responsibilities and challenges within your current job.*
Talk to your manager about ways you can expand your responsibilities within your current role. Is there a task or project that would allow you to learn something new or develop a new skill? Can you become an internal coordinator or external representative for your area or department? Can you offer to train or mentor new hires? Is there any opportunity to become involved in activities that are central

to your organization's top priorities? Is there a task force you can lead? By expanding the scope of your job, you create a more rewarding role for yourself.

*Make sure you are recognized for all the work you do.*
Maybe you're completing others' work and your boss doesn't see everything you do. Share updates on your projects and accomplishments through regular meetings, email updates or presentations. Get recognized for every responsibility you take on.

*Take on the tough tasks.*
Some tasks no one wants to take on, so you might gain extra visibility from taking them on. At a minimum, your boss will be grateful. At a maximum, it will expand your network and maybe teach you new skills. This strategy can prepare you for openings in another division within your organization.

*Participate in training and professional development opportunities.*
Many companies offer in-house training or allow employees to attend conferences or workshops. These can be a great way to learn new skills and stay up-to-date with developments in your field.

*Network with others in your industry.*
Building connections with people in your field can help you stay informed about job openings and career opportunities. It can also help you learn from others who have more experience and can offer guidance and mentorship.

*Consider taking on freelance or part-time work in your field.*
If you are unable to change jobs right now, consider gaining additional experience and build your resume through freelance or part-time work. This is especially important if you're looking to switch industries

and need to start building a track record. Commit time outside of work to grow your skills, resume and portfolio so that when you *can* leave your job, you're more than prepared.

# Section 8

# Upping Your Productivity Game

To master task management, it's crucial to get the 411 on what's expected of you. Understanding your role isn't just about knowing your job description. It's about achieving clarity on the nuances of your position, which sometimes means proactively seeking that clarity from your boss. You're not alone if you've ever felt a twinge of hesitation before knocking on your boss's door with a slew of questions. Yet, the best professionals know the value of clarity and they prioritize it.

Once you've got the lowdown on expectations, it's time to bring the hustle and truly excel in that role. This journey often starts with a solid foundation of time management, discipline and focus. We all have days when procrastination whispers in our ears or when an impromptu office chat eats into our productivity. But with a roadmap of goals and priorities, navigating the waters becomes less daunting. It's not about always working harder, but working smarter.

Of course, work life can be unpredictable. Maybe a coworker departs unexpectedly, leaving you with their workload, or perhaps you've found yourself staring blankly at your screen, unsure how to reignite passion for the repetitive tasks you do every day. And let's not forget the challenge of adapting to remote work—ensuring your home environment is just as productive as the office, if not more so. The beauty is that each challenge, whether it's seeking clarity or maximizing output, is a piece of the puzzle that adds up to a fulfilling, dynamic professional journey. And the more adept we become at fitting these pieces together, the more seamless and rewarding our work life becomes.

Dive into section eight, and you'll snag the inside scoop on supercharging your productivity. I've got your back. Every hack is curated to amp up your efficiency game and push the limits of your performance.

You in?

# Asking Your Boss for Clarity in Your Role

"Seeking clarity today paves the path for success tomorrow."

How much of what you do every day is what you originally thought your job would be? If you're like most people, the position you were hired to fill has evolved into an amalgam of the roles that two or three other former colleagues used to do.

It may make economic sense for an organization to be choosy about whether they replace someone who's left the company, but if there was a staff reduction due to layoffs, it's unlikely those jobs will be filled. What's been piled on your plate is now yours to manage, at least in the short term.

## Why Does It Matter?
Where does that sort of role-smushing leave you?

Probably confused, maybe disorganized and possibly thinking about when the situation will change. None of that is good for your employer—and feeling confused and uncertain isn't good for you. When you lose sight of how you fit into the big picture, you can lose sight of your purpose and your motivation.

Gaining clarity from your boss about what your role really is now enables you to get your work done faster, more efficiently and with fewer headaches along the way.

## Action Steps
You might feel as if it will be a difficult conversation, but there are specific questions you can ask your boss to help you gain clarity and try to create some order out of the chaos. These questions aren't confrontational; instead, they seek to come to a shared understanding.

*"How is my work important to the business?"*
This is especially good to ask if you've amassed additional tasks that weren't part of your original job. Answering this question might also be the first time your boss really thinks about what you're doing and whether it makes sense to have you doing the tasks you've been assigned. As you discuss your priorities and how those tasks relate to your role, you can take the opportunity to negotiate with your boss about reallocating tasks that don't fit into your purpose.

*"What am I responsible and accountable for?"*
If your role has grown and you've taken on more tasks, it helps to go through each task and talk about exactly what you're responsible for and define the specific goals or targets you need to meet. Engage in a constructive dialogue with your manager to establish a set of goals that is both challenging and attainable, reflecting a mutually agreed-upon, manageable number of goals. Focusing on too many goals dilutes your focus and effort which can make it challenging to achieve any of them. Also, if you share responsibility with others on your team, ask for specifics about who is ultimately responsible and accountable among the group members.

*"How are you measuring my performance?"*
If you don't already have goals set for you, ask your boss to provide you with specific goals and the way they'll be measured. You should also ask your boss how they personally measure performance.

Are they more concerned with timeliness or quality? What is your boss's view of hard work versus your understanding of it? What does it take to be seen as a high-performer?

As you get answers, you can put together your own report card and measure yourself against it on a regular basis.

*"How well am I performing now?"*
This is your opportunity to learn what your manager thinks versus what *you* think about your performance. It's not about trying to persuade your boss that you're performing better than they think; instead, you should see this as an opportunity to learn where the bar is for your performance and how you can refocus toward that measurement.

*"How do I need to improve?"*
This question should delight your boss because it demonstrates that you genuinely want to excel in your job. This is a good conversation for each of you to summarize what you see as your individual action items and agree on a timeline for revisiting your progress.

Now that you've opened this dialogue, it's in your best interest to keep it going on a regular basis. And congratulate yourself for being brave enough to take on a tough conversation. Here's hoping that your newly acquired clarity will be rewarding in more ways than one.

# Clarifying Expectations at Work

> "It's a lack of clarity that creates chaos and frustration. Those emotions are poison...."
> *Steve Maraboli*

"*What do they want from me?*"

It's a good question. The expectations for some jobs seem pretty straightforward. Take, for example, the delivery of a package to a customer. The customer needs a package delivered. You deliver the package. Everyone's happy. But even then, other things are still expected of you. Proper scanning and processing of the package, adhering to the rest of the delivery schedule, regular reporting on delivery progress and swiftly addressing any issues that may arise such as delivery to the wrong address or missing packages.

But what if your job entails working with two or eight or ten others, in two or three different departments to carry out a project the CFO just handed down? In that kind of situation it might be a lot harder for you to understand what is expected of you.

## Why Does It Matter?

Situations and conditions change. Projects, stakeholders, teammates and even bosses come and go. Expectations will change with them. If your company's or the boss's priorities shift then so will yours. You need to know when this happens. If you get a new boss or a new project, you'll probably need to start all over again. But that's okay.

Learning how to clarify exactly what's expected of you lets you be efficient, effective and productive. Otherwise, it's just chaos.

## Action Steps

**First, find out who your stakeholders are.** This is anyone who has skin in the game. Your boss and maybe their boss, too. Maybe it's other departments in the company, internal and external customers and/or investors. This is a *finding* out process, not a *figuring* out process. Instead of guessing, engage with your boss. They are your first line of clarity.

**Second, work together to form a common understanding of what's expected of you.** Give an example of something you're unsure about. Getting one concrete instance cleared up can be a springboard to greater, more open and transparent communication.

**Ask for details.** Not just what and when, but how the work is expected to be done and who needs to be involved in doing it. Ask about milestones and benchmarks you need to meet. Negotiate for resources. Get answers to what happens if the situation changes. Will there be reasonable adjustments in the expectations?

**Write things down.** Document what's expected of you in case it becomes an issue later on.

**Ask for your priorities when multiple bosses are involved.** Trying to serve many masters is a losing game. If there are multiple expectations, find out which of them is the highest priority. Ideally, your direct supervisor will be able to sort this out, but it may take somebody high up in the company hierarchy to make the final call.

**Finally, revisit and re-clarify expectations.** Regularly touch base to ensure you remain aligned with your boss's and team's expectations and are still on the right trajectory.

Nailing down expectations at work is like tuning an instrument; it sets the stage for harmony and peak performance. When everyone's on the same page, productivity soars, and misunderstandings take a back seat.

# Asking for Help at Work

*"None of us is as smart as all of us."*
*Ken Blanchard*

Asking for help ought to be the most natural thing in the world, but many of us resist the very thought of it. In the U.S., there tends to be a cultural stigma around needing help. Self-reliance and the myth of the lone-good-guy-facing-the-hostile world still have a powerful hold on the national psyche.

Self-reliance is fine, but its utility is severely limited in the real world. If you need help at work, and who doesn't sometimes, ignore the three myths that hold all of us back from advocating for what we need.

- *"It will make me look bad or stupid or weak or lazy."* Research suggests that asking for help can actually make you look like a more trusted and trustworthy colleague. We all struggle once in a while. When you acknowledge it, so can those around you.
- *"He'll just say no."* With so many of us already stretched like rubber bands, most people are willing to help a coworker out if they can. Again, we're all in the same boat.
- *"She might say yes, but she'll be upset about it."* We don't want add to somebody's workload, so we project that on to her. However, most people like to help others. It creates a sense of kinship and camaraderie.

If you do get a *no,* which isn't outside of the realm of possibility, it's more likely that the person you asked simply *can't* help rather than that they *won't* help.

## Why Does It Matter?

We all need help now and again. When it's you, have the confidence to ask for it. You might be surprised at how much easier and more enjoyable your work can be when you open yourself up to the support and guidance of those around you.

## Action Steps

Define what you need and when you need it. *"I'm drowning here,"* is not going to get you the help you need, so be specific.

- If you need someone to help complete your quarterly report by the end of the day, they need to know where the report stands now, what specifically is missing and what needs to be done.
- Don't automatically assume that Jake in Operations doesn't know anything about a fulfillment problem and can't help. Carol in Marketing may be a spreadsheet genius. Sometimes one person you know will know ten other people who can help.
- Be willing to help in return. It's much easier to reconcile asking for help when you've been helpful in the past. The surest way not to get the help you need is to acquire a reputation for always taking, but never giving.

A workplace is like a village. It takes everybody pitching in to function properly. When somebody's house catches fire, everybody grabs a bucket and hose. When a ship is caught in a storm, every sailor mans a post. Asking for help is not a sign of weakness but rather an acknowledgment that collective effort often leads to the best outcomes.

# Avoiding Procrastination on the Job

*"The future depends on what you do today."*
*Gandhi*

The key to getting things done is to avoid procrastinating. This can be hard to do if you find a task boring, challenging, ambiguous or unstructured. However, the most critical thing to avoid procrastination is to simply begin the work.

As the saying goes, *"A job begun is a job half done."* Do something—anything—to just get started.

## Why Does It Matter?

We all procrastinate but when you use techniques to help you overcome your tendency to procrastinate you simply get more done, and over time you gain the confidence to tackle your work without delay.

It's easier to keep going with a task after you've overcome the initial hump of starting it. That's because the tasks that induce procrastination are rarely as bad as we think.

## Action Steps

How do you begin?

- **Look at the full scope of what needs to be done by a specific date.** Many people procrastinate because they look at the scope of work, panic, and then put it aside. That's why *divid*ing the task is so critical. Divide the scope of work into doable chunks and establish interim deadlines.
- **Limit yourself to short work periods.** Sometimes we think marathon work sessions are the only way to get something done but that's not necessarily the case. Try instead to work

on doable chunks for thirty minutes today and pick up the work again tomorrow. Doing a little today will get you over the emotional hump of starting. Then try a strategy such as adding an extra ten minutes each workday to the time you spend on the task until you get to three hours total.
- **Disable digital distractions ahead of time** so you have no choice but to work on what's really important. Silence your phone and don't check email for a stretch of time that you block off on your calendar.
- **Find a location where you can be productive**. Sometimes just changing your physical work location can help push you to start a task, whether it's a conference room, a coffee shop or your home office with the door shut.
- **Avoid prioritizing your small tasks**. Many of us fall into the trap of first tackling things we can readily tick off our to-do list, such as answering emails, while leaving the big, complex stuff untouched for another day. Force yourself to think about the downside of putting off the big tasks.
- **Pre-commit publicly to others**. By daring to say *"I'll send you the report by the end of the day,"* we add social benefits to following through on our promises which can successfully nudge us to get going.
- **Don't let expecting perfection get in your way**. A task might seem unachievable if you imagine having to get it done perfectly the first time. Any task will seem easier if you accept that missteps and imperfections will occur.
- **Acknowledge and address your emotions**. You might be anxious or fearful about the task you need to tackle. Admit to yourself that those emotions may be getting in your way and then tell yourself that just getting started will help you overcome those feelings.

- **Don't forget to reward yourself after you complete work.** Let yourself take a break or engage in an activity you enjoy for a few minutes after completing an assignment.

Procrastination is productivity's silent saboteur! Let your achievements speak louder than your to-do list.

# Staying Focused on the Job

> "Don't judge each day by the harvest you reap
> but by the seeds that you plant."
> *Robert Louis Stevenson*

Being easily distracted is often played for laughs in movies such as *Up*, where Dug the dog gets distracted when he senses a squirrel or in *Elf* where Buddy the elf gets easily distracted by the sights and sounds of New York City.

Distraction is a familiar problem for all of us; we react instantly to the sound of a ping or familiar ringtone, even if it's not actually from our own phone. The temptation to look at your phone to read the notification or see who's calling can be nearly impossible to resist.

Minor distractions don't create as much disruption. For instance, you may be distracted by an itch on your arm, but once you scratch it, you can go right back to what you were doing. However, if you're working and suddenly receive a message from a coworker, the time it takes you to read and respond has created a full interruption.

## Why Does It Matter?

Research states it takes about twenty-three minutes to regain your focus when you resume working after a full interruption. Three interruptions in an hour means you've lost the entire hour of productivity!

That's distressing because you need to fully concentrate on your tasks to perform quality work. In addition, staying focused lets you work efficiently and boosts your motivation to move onto additional tasks. As you continue to make progress, your stress level is reduced because deadlines become achievable.

You'll never eliminate interruptions or distractions at work, but you can make some changes in *how* you work.

## Action Steps

It will take some effort to train yourself out of work habits that are deeply ingrained, but adopting a new and better set of habits will more than pay off in terms of improved job performance.

- **Modify your habits within your work environment.** If you work in an open office, let your colleagues know you wear headphones when you're focusing on work. You'll reduce the chances that someone will interrupt you. If the headphones aren't enough, you can also put up a sign that says something such as, *"Focusing, please do not disturb."* Or, if possible, reserve a small meeting room or private collaboration area to minimize distractions.
- **Turn off notifications in your email, cellphone and chat applications.** You may only need to do this on a short-term basis if you're trying to break an established habit, but if making it a regular practice helps you stay on track, then you're better off keeping it that way so that you don't get tempted.
- **Organize your calendar into blocks of work time and break time.** Take a look at the tasks you need to focus on each day, and estimate the amount of time you think each one will take. Using the Pomodoro Technique*, schedule a block that's around twenty-five minutes, and then schedule a five-minute break. Once you've completed four cycles or two hours, give yourself a longer break of fifteen to thirty minutes. Don't skip break times; they are necessary recovery periods for you to reset yourself.
- **Don't let meetings overload your calendar.** Choose whether you want to accept a meeting invitation if it coincides with a focused work block. Your primary job is to do the work that helps you meet your team and corporate goals, not to attend a bunch of meetings that only require you to passively register

what's being said. Virtual meetings can always be recorded with a transcription, and for in-person meetings, someone can take notes for those who can't attend.
- **Respond to email, texts or phone calls <u>once or twice a day only</u>**. Let your colleagues know that your response time will fall within a specific window. You can use an away message in chat applications and add your response time to your email signature so that everyone is aware that your response may be delayed.

Technology will continue to evolve and create more enticing ways to distract us. Take control of your mental focus so you can be successful in your job and preserve your well-being.

*For further detail regarding the Pomodoro Technique refer to page 324.

# Upping Your Task Completion Game

> *"Eat a live frog first thing in the morning and nothing worse will happen to you the rest of the day."*
> *Mark Twain*

Scientists have studied the body's natural cycles for decades. During the course of a workday, we all experience peaks and valleys in our productivity which run in ninety-to-120-minute cycles. The ups and downs of these cycles explain why you can start a task feeling excited and alert and then two hours later, you find yourself checking Instagram or hunting around for a snack.

## Why Does It Matter?

These energy peaks and valleys are normal and unavoidable, and it's important to map your own rhythms and work with them so that you don't find yourself working against them. Some experts call your most effective time your "prime time".

To up your task completion game, you need to identify your prime time and then use a structured process to document, prioritize and plan your tasks.

## Action Steps

The best way to identify your own rhythms and pinpoint your prime time is to rate your energy, focus and motivation at the end of every hour, using a scale from one to ten, over the course of a work week. Once you map out your energy, you'll quickly see patterns in your natural cycles, which will help you identify your prime time. Tackling your most important, difficult and strategic tasks during your prime time will enable you to be more productive.

Once you've identified your prime time, you can prioritize and plan your tasks by following these five steps:

*Get in the mood.*
Before setting priorities, put yourself in the right frame of mind. Breathe in, breathe out and tell yourself that the next few minutes are some of the most important minutes of the day. Tell your brain it needs to filter out distractions and stay focused.

*Document your tasks.*
Don't worry about writing the most important task first. The goal is to get everything out of your head and into the real world on paper or in an electronic document.

*Prioritize your tasks.*
Order your priorities according to importance. Use the Eisenhower Matrix to group your tasks into four categories:

- **Category 1**: Urgent and important tasks to do it as soon as possible, preferably during your prime time.
- **Category 2**: Important, but not urgent, tasks which you should try to tackle during your prime time.
- **Category 3**: Urgent tasks which are less important that you should do as soon as possible outside of your prime time.
- **Category 4:** Less important tasks which are also not urgent. Complete these tasks outside of your prime time or delegate them to someone else if you can.

*Plan your tasks.*
At a high level, think through how you will approach each task and estimate how much time you will need for completion. Then block

off time slots on your planner for each task with a few breaks built-in in-between tasks.

*Complete your tasks.*
The final step is to work through the tasks you've planned and to execute them to the best of your ability.

Congrats! You did it.

# Meeting Deadlines and Completing Tasks on Time

> "In every job that must be done, there is an element of fun.
> You find the fun and–SNAP–the job's a game!"
> *Mary Poppins*

Another day, another deadline. And another day. And another deadline. And yet . . . you're struggling with them. You've been late one or ten times too often, and it's becoming a problem.

Maybe your time management is . . . poor. Maybe there's always too much on your plate. Maybe you can't say no. Maybe your boss doesn't give you much choice in the matter. Maybe you feel so overwhelmed that you sit and stare at the work while your mind burrows deep into a void.

## Why Does It Matter?

There are always going to be reasons for missing deadlines. Somebody gets sick. Somebody forgot to add their PTO to the schedule. Massive storms hold up shipments. Systems go down.

But the reason shouldn't be your performance. It shouldn't be because you forgot something or assumed you'd be able to spend the afternoon with League of Legends and figured you'd just catch up later. You probably won't. But it won't be an issue if you don't have to in the first place.

Whatever the reasons, if you're missing deadlines and it's becoming a problem, you need to deal with it. And you can.

## Action Steps

You first need to answer a question: Why are you missing deadlines? How you handle meeting deadlines and finishing tasks on time will depend largely on the answer to that central question. Is it . . .

- Procrastination?
- Distractions?
- Too much due at the same time?
- Do you lack necessary skills?
- The goalposts keep moving?

You can't solve a problem until you get to the root of it. If you're wasting time, take steps to stop it. It's easier said than done, but you know what you're doing instead of working.

Otherwise, consider using this handy checklist to help you build self-awareness and meet deadlines.

- Make sure you know *exactly* what's expected of you and by when.
- Think about that and identify potential problems ahead of time—and tell your boss.
- Be realistic and don't agree to something you know you can't accomplish.
- Work with your boss to see if there's a way to either give you more time or lighten your expected load.
- Ensure everyone's on the same page and understands how their part affects and interacts with the other parts.
- Ask team members for realistic estimates and expectations.
- Take the project or task, break it down into smaller parts and make a timeline.
- Block off time for your tasks at hand.
- Monotask and focus on one piece at a time.
- Build in buffers where you can.
- Communicate any issues as soon as possible.
- Start right now. You have two weeks to finish? Great, start today anyway. Your schedule buffers are for when you *need* them, not when you'd rather be doing something else.

Action leads to more action. Momentum is powerful. Once set in motion, it's easier to maintain the pace. Be proactive. Whenever possible, get a jump start on tasks. Ask yourself, would you rather have your report ready a day early and wait or scramble to complete it by the next morning's deadline?

You shouldn't really have to think about it.

# Accomplishing More at Work

*"We have a strategic plan. It's called doing things."*
*Herb Kelleher*

Successful people are usually identified as the ones who can either produce a higher quantity of work, work of a higher quality or both. Productive people have the drive, the motivation and the ambition to distinguish themselves and they believe in improving their own luck. They agree with Thomas Jefferson's quote: *"The harder I work, the luckier I get."*

## Why Does It Matter?

It may go without saying, but indulge me. The more you can accomplish, the better your resume looks and the more favorable your boss and coworkers will view you. Over time, you will also discover that you can increase your productivity while simultaneously improving the quality of your work.

With greater work productivity and quality comes success

## Action Steps

If you want to be more successful and productive at work there are three actions you should take:

### Dedicate more time

If you want to achieve more at work you may simply have to devote more hours to your work. This doesn't mean logging excessively long hours. But it might mean figuring out if you can start your day earlier or work a bit later to extend the time you have available.

Maybe you can spend less time in meetings or engaging in other activities where you are not actively working on assigned tasks. However, make sure that you're not working *too* much or without breaks, as this can lead to burnout and have other negative effects.

*Use available time to the maximum benefit*
If you can't increase your hours, you can try to work more efficiently during your available work time.

To gain time, eliminate distractions such as repeatedly checking email or social media. Create a comfortable and organized workspace. Delegate as much as possible to others and don't be afraid to ask for help when you need it. Also become comfortable with saying no to tasks that are not a priority. And ruthlessly eliminate any tasks that don't move the needle against your goals.

Try using time-management techniques, such as the Pomodoro Technique. The goal is to break your work down into smaller, focused blocks of time to help you stay motivated and focused. Here's how it works:

1. Choose a task that you want to work on.
2. Set a timer for twenty-five minutes (that is the "pomodoro") and work on the task until the timer goes off.
3. Take a short break (usually five minutes) to stretch, grab a snack or do something else to recharge.
4. After four pomodoros take a longer break (usually fifteen to thirty minutes when possible) to rest and recharge.
5. Repeat the process until you have completed your work.

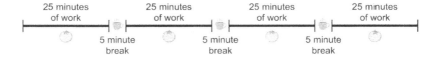

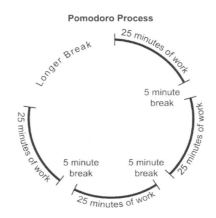

*Increase your productivity by upskilling*

Knowing how to use technology effectively can help you work more efficiently and get more done. Identify the routine aspects of your work that could be automated or streamlined by using productivity and collaboration technologies. Once you understand what can be automated or streamlined, figure out the most appropriate tool to use and then train yourself in how to use it. Microsoft Office, Google Workspace, Slack or new and emerging technologies that can automate aspects of your work are all great pieces of technology that can help you accomplish more.

In general, the best way to learn how to use a software tool is to just start using it and to be willing to experiment and try new things. The more you use the tool, the more comfortable and proficient you will become.

When you unlock smarter working methods, you multiply your milestones.

# Maximizing Productivity When Working Remotely

*"Productivity is never an accident. It is always the result of a commitment to excellence, intelligent planning, and focused effort."*
*Paul J. Meyer*

According to a McKinsey survey from June of 2022, 35 percent of all job holders can work from home full-time and 23 percent can do so part-time. Furthermore, 87 percent of workers offered remote work accept the opportunity and spend an average of three days a week at home.

And these numbers are growing steadily.

Long before the COVID pandemic forced many of us to work from home, remote work was already becoming ingrained in the business world. Some jobs will never be able to be done remotely, of course, but many businesses and workers have discovered that what seemed like a temporary inconvenience is actually a practical, beneficial and permanent change in how and where people work.

## Why Does It Matter?

Along with benefits come challenges. Some companies worry that people working at home will be less productive. And some individuals who are already working remotely or considering it, worry about that, too.

Remote work isn't going away. It's now an established reality, and there are ways you can make sure you're maximizing your productivity while working remotely.

## Action Steps

**Establish your workday and stick to it**. Remote work generally allows for some flexibility, which is one of its most appealing aspects. However, it also offers the potential for blurring the lines between work time and home time.

In a world where work-life balance is always an issue, failing to establish or not following a set workday can be problematic. Keeping regular hours devoted solely to work will help keep you focused on what you should be doing and when you should be doing it.

**Establish a regular workspace.** Being able to work at the coffee shop is wonderful now and then, but research and anecdotal evidence both indicate that it's a poor day-to-day strategy. You need to have a set, predetermined space to work in that you can set up to reflect and promote how you work best.

Limit or avoid multitasking. What often feels like handling multiple things at once is actually just switching back and forth between doing two things without giving either thing the proper attention. Studies show that multitasking decreases productivity. Close the open tabs on your browser. Turn off your phone, or at least set it more than arm's length away. Empty the dishwasher later. Focus on doing one thing at a time and doing that one thing well.

**Schedule your day.** Plan out what you need to get done and when to do it. Whenever that prime time is for you, use it for your most challenging tasks; the ones that require your greatest focus and most intense concentration. Some of the benefits of remote work are a reduction in commuting time and longer periods of uninterrupted work time. Capitalize on those benefits.

As part of your schedule, take breaks when you need them. Know when it's the best time to go get that coffee. Maybe you have to fight against dozing off in the middle of the afternoon. Go check the mailbox. Take a few minutes to mentally and physically step away, stretch your limbs and clear your head.

**Know when it's the end of the work day.** Working from home will always pose a challenge to conscientious employees. You want to be productive. You want to do a good job. You want to look good to your boss. But part of being productive over the long run is to avoid burnout in the short term.

Our jobs will always encourage us to do that one more thing, answer that additional email or look over the report that just came in. Acknowledge when it's time to go home. Shut off the laptop, turn your phone on, get up and walk away for the night. To be productive for years means taking care of yourself daily.

# Getting Through a Busy Time at Work

"Beware the barrenness of a busy life."
*Socrates*

Getting thrust into a busy time at work is not fun. You might be working later into the night, your inbox is overflowing and any hope of eating regular meals is gone. But it won't last forever and finding a coping method to get you through is the most painless way to complete your work well without losing a piece of your soul.

## Why Does It Matter?

Every industry and function has busy periods. Accountants, school teachers, marketers, lawyers—pick a job and you can find some seasonality and cyclicality to the busyness.

When faced with a busy time in your job, it's vital to understand how to get through with minimum exhaustion. Days or weeks of busyness without a good coping mechanism can lead to sloppy work, built-up resentment and burnout.

## Action Steps

Yes, there will be busy times at work, but by taking some steps to control the impending hurricane, you can navigate your way through it.

*Prepare yourself.*
You're about to head into the storm, so get ready for it.

- Prepare yourself with a ready supply of easy-to-prepare food and frozen meals, or ask your partner or roommate if they could take over the cooking responsibilities for the time being.

- Look at your personal and work calendar for the next few weeks and identify your "can't miss" events.
- Reschedule less-important personal events, and see if a colleague could take on some of your work assignments or cover a few meetings for you.
- Give your friends and colleagues a heads up that you're heading into a busy time, and apologize in advance if you're less engaged with them.

*Set your boundaries and ground rules.*
The first person who has to respect your boundaries is you. Decide the time you're going to end your day and stick to it.

- Communicate the limits on your time for others in your life.
- Explain there are certain times you'll do things with your family or friends or certain times when you'll only respond to important texts or emails.
- Confirm that everyone knows when it's okay to interrupt you, and commit to honoring your agreed time to stop working.

*Find your work groove.*
Your wiring might make you a morning person who likes to run headlong into the day or a creature of the night whose energy boost comes in the evening. When you're in a busy period, lean into your biological rhythms and your prime time.

- Follow a workflow built on science. Research shows that most adults perform at their best during the late morning. Your body temperature starts to rise just before you wake up and increases into midday. During that time, your mental alertness and concentration improve too.

- A short nap can do wonders to refresh and reset your rhythm. Conversely, it's been shown that fatigue may boost creativity, so if you've grappling with a problem that requires creative thinking, maybe you want to save that for the evening when you're getting tired.

*Manage your stress.*
When you're tense about work, sometimes you can lash out at things that wouldn't normally be a big deal. Unwitting friends, partners or children will not understand why you have flown into a rage about a minor incident.

- Be mindful of how you're channeling your stress.
- Stop and ask yourself if something is really worth being upset about.
- Take time in your day to shake off stress, even if only for a few minutes.
- Consciously unclench your jaw and drop your shoulders and stretch a bit.
- Take a few minutes to do something pleasurable such as taking a walk outside or grabbing an indulgent snack.

*Don't forget your personal life.*
Yes, your career brings a certain amount of meaning and purpose to your life, but your personal relationships are what sustain you emotionally. You may make choices to decrease your social life over this busy period, but don't sacrifice your personal relationships and lose the restorative powers they have on your mental health.

*Mark the end of your day and unwind.*
When you reach the end of day, develop a ritual that allows you to move from the focus of work to the calmness of home. Let your

loved ones know that you need this time to help you find yourself again.

- Choose an activity that will allow you to fully set aside thoughts of work.
- Spend ten minutes focusing on your breathing, and as work thoughts creep into your head, acknowledge them and let them leave.
- Pick up the book you've been reading and get lost in a chapter or two.
- Seek out the warmth and love of your partner, friends, your pets; whoever fills that space in your life.
- Focus on them and forget about this busy period for a while.

If you're navigating a work rush, these strategies can be your lifeline to smoother sailing, so use them.

# Handling More Work When a Coworker Quits

*"The strength of the team is each individual member. The strength of each member is the team."*
*Phil Jackson*

Quitting a job is sometimes depicted in the movies or on TV to give a long-suffering character a chance to finally stand up to the boss and make a dramatic exit.

While it may be satisfying to watch these kinds of scenes on TV, in real life when a colleague quits, the work they perform doesn't walk out the door with them. Their workload and responsibilities still must be handled by someone.

### Why Does it Matter?
When your boss informs you that you're going to need to take on additional work, you will probably feel some combination of anger and panic. You might even silently curse your quitter colleague for dumping their job on you. And while all those feelings are natural, what you should do is pause and take a deep breath. If this is happening then you need to know how to handle it properly right from the start.

At best, you've picked up new skills and your responsibilities have expanded. You've proven that you're willing to take on a big challenge and thrive. These are all great things you can add to your resume. With your new responsibilities you might even be better aligned for that promotion you've been eyeing. At worst, you can decide the position doesn't really fit you anymore. More on that in a minute . . .

### Action Steps
If you find yourself juggling new responsibilities thanks to a newly quit coworker, there's a six-step plan you can follow.

1. **Acknowledge the situation**. When you accept the situation as a challenge you need to meet, then you can think more clearly about what's being asked of you versus what you can reasonably do.
2. **Work out a plan with your boss**. Meet with your boss and be prepared with questions to help you gather information.
    - **Is this change in your responsibilities permanent or temporary?** If it's temporary, then you can be a good employee and pitch in. But if it's your permanent workload, you have to look at your current workload and figure out how much you can realistically take on and how much you will politely request to be delegated to others.
    - **If the company is hiring a replacement, what's the timeline?**
    - **Who's your key contact if you have questions?**
    - **Who can train you?** Are there documents, spreadsheets or other materials that you'll need access to?
3. **Prioritize urgencies**. Even if you get some help ramping up, it's still going to take time to feel comfortable. Your new tasks will be unfamiliar and you may have difficulty figuring out your priorities. Keep a conversation open with your manager, and ask for guidance on which of your tasks now take precedence.
4. **Set limits on extra hours**. Once you have the chance to settle in, be careful not to end up sacrificing your personal life just to keep up with your increased workload. Don't neglect going to the gym after work if that was always your routine or meeting friends for lunch or for drinks after work. Ignoring the social aspects of your life may cause you to resent your job, decrease your motivation and increase your stress.
5. **Don't burn yourself out**. And, yes, use all the paid time off provided by your company. Taking time off not only allows

you to recharge, relax and take care of yourself, but it also enhances your productivity as you regain the energy required to tackle your responsibilities.

6. **Take the long view**. Finally, once you're well established in your expanded role and time has passed, take a hard look at what your job has turned into and decide if it's the job you really want. After all, you were given someone else's role. While it might be something you can do, is this the direction you want your career to go in? It's okay to move on to something else—either in your company or somewhere else. The choice is yours. Just make sure you don't make a rash decision.

# Combatting Job-Related Boredom

*"Is life not a thousand times too short for us to bore ourselves?"*
*Friedrich Nietzsche*

Picture this scene: you glance over at the clock and see that it's only 9 a.m., and you still have seven long hours to get through before you can go home. The thought of spending another hour, much less another day, staring at the same computer screen and slogging through your never-ending to-do list is soul-crushing. You take a deep breath and remind yourself to focus on the tasks at hand, but the slow tick of the clock seems to taunt you with each passing second.

Sound familiar?

We've all experienced boredom at some point in our work lives, thanks to a slow day or repetitive tasks. Handling boredom starts with figuring out why you're bored. Is it procrastination? Do you not have enough work to do? Are you bored by your job duties? Do you think you're in a mid-career malaise?

Being bored at work is frustrating, but boredom doesn't have to be chronic or terminal. It can be a great catalyst for reexamining your job and making positive changes.

## Why Does It Matter?

Avoiding boredom at work is essential, not only for your job performance but also for your overall well-being. When you're engaged in tasks you view as meaningful you're more likely to produce high-quality work, exhibit greater problem-solving abilities and contribute positively to the work environment. Consider this: stocking shelves at a grocery store may feel tedious and mind-numbing when viewed simply as a task. However, when you step back, you realize that your work simplifies and enriches the lives of potentially hundreds or even thousands of customers. Your effort ensures that shoppers can find exactly what they need to nourish themselves and their families. This principle applies across the board, whether you're repairing carburetors, sorting sales data, mopping floors in a hospital or managing a telemarketing team.

Your work has a ripple effect, extending far beyond just you and your immediate supervisor. It contributes to the ease and quality of other people's lives, making what you do meaningful and impactful. Combating boredom isn't just about making it through the workday; it's about understanding and valuing the greater purpose your work serves in the grand scheme of things, laying the foundation for a fulfilling and successful career.

## Action Steps

First, identify the root of your boredom. If it's clearly temporary, consider making little changes in your routine.

- Rearrange your schedule. Move your morning tasks to the afternoon and vice-versa.
- Finish the Wednesday report you hate on Monday instead and push your Monday tasks back.
- Choose a different time, place or group of people with which to eat lunch.

If your boredom is more entrenched or complex, you may need to take bigger steps to address it.

- Ask your boss for new projects that will let you stretch yourself and learn new skills and processes.
- Help the new hire or a struggling coworker.
- Look for ways to make the work you do more efficient.
- Take advantage of any training your company offers.

Of course, you might need to consider a new job. This doesn't necessarily mean quitting your current one—maybe you can request a transfer or go after a promotion. If dissatisfaction with your role is at the root of your boredom, consider sharing how you're feeling with your boss. Get his advice on how to remain an asset to the company while identifying new opportunities where you can be fully engaged and grow as a professional.

There's a chance that your boredom isn't from your job at all, but rather your life. Take a good, hard look at your life outside of work. It's possible that the root of your boredom lies there and addressing your leisure and extracurricular activities could be the key to rejuvenating your sense of engagement and fulfillment. So, learn something just for you. Use your down time, breaks and lunch to engage your spirit in something that brings you joy.

Maybe you've always wanted to play the saxophone or do card tricks. Maybe creative writing is your thing. You can use downtime productively to make your life more fun and interesting.

Finally, look for meaning in what you do every day. Every job provides something positive for someone else. All you have to do is identify the meaning and remember to tap into it the next time you get into a rut.

# Succeeding Without Working Long Hours

*"The key is in not spending time, but in investing it."*
*Stephen R. Covey*

At some point in your career, you may find yourself spending more time at work without feeling more productive or more recognized for it. There may be different causes contributing to that issue including:

- Your boss stays at work late and you feel compelled to stay, to follow-the-leader. The boss's day may start later than yours, but you can't change that.
- Your colleagues may stay late just to impress the boss, without actually getting much work done. You feel pressured to stay with them to fit in and not be viewed as an outlier.
- You may be getting paid overtime for staying late. That was attractive to you in the past, but no longer is now. Now you would prefer a more manageable schedule.

## Why Does It Matter?

Extended hours at work can encroach upon your personal time, sometimes to the extent that it affects your mental and physical well-being. A healthy balance between work and personal life ensures rejuvenation, allowing you to return to work with a fresh perspective.

Consistently long hours can also lead to burnout putting you in a state of chronic physical and emotional exhaustion.

The quality of your work doesn't necessarily correlate with the number of hours you put in. In many cases, working smarter, not longer, will yield better results.

## Action Steps

Here are four suggestions for how to perform your job as well or even better than your peers, without having to stay later than you want or need to. Use each mini-checklist as a guide to help you navigate your job by building efficient, productive work habits.

*Control interruptions and set boundaries*

Your colleagues may stop by to chat about non-work-related issues. Others may just want to take a break and socialize with you. Some may come to you for help with their own assignments. People taking up your time may be less productive and trying to stretch out their day so they can stay late and impress the boss.

- Count how many times during the workday your work is interrupted and for how long.
- Practice being firm and polite in limiting the number and duration of these kinds of casual interactions.
- Tactfully discourage and stop rewarding others' interruptions.
- Set and politely communicate your specific work hours to colleagues to ensure respect for personal boundaries.
- Stop others from passing the buck.

People pass the buck for any number of reasons. Coworkers may realize that they cannot do their assignments well on their own. They may not have any ambition to advance in their roles and are just trying to get by. They may be slackers who may flatter you with compliments to redirect their duties to you.

- Say no to colleagues who are simply passing the buck.
- Consult your boss directly.
- Verify requests and be recognized for your extra work.

*Prioritize high-impact tasks*

You may feel that everything you do needs to be done *now*. It doesn't. Some things can wait. Remember the Eisenhower Matrix we referenced a few chapters ago. Get your daily duties done on time by analyzing your major tasks and ranking them in order of importance and urgency.

- Focus on the most impactful work.
- Avoid wasting time on low-priority tasks.
- Talk to your boss about reassigning certain tasks to others when appropriate.

*Focus on efficiency*

You can save time by focusing on optimizing your efficiency.

- Reduce the number and duration of phone calls.
- Use efficient, effective technology to replace manual tasks.
- Organize your files, desk and working tools.
- Protect your most productive time for creative, hard tasks.
- Set aside specific blocks of time for focused work.
- Attend meetings on an as-needed basis only.
- Delegate tasks whenever feasible.

*Gain your boss's support*

At the end of the day, a good boss should not waste your time micromanaging your schedule.

- Persuade your boss to allow you to have a more predictable schedule (which *you* control).
- Prove to your boss that your work ethic and efficiency allow you to perform your tasks at a high level of quality and productivity without staying late at the office.

You don't have to burn the midnight oil to achieve big success at work. By following these strategies, you can succeed without logging excessive hours.

**Section 9**

# Nailing Your New Role: Taking Charge of the Next Chapter

This section addresses how you can set yourself up for success when you take on a new role. It includes tips from making sure you ask the right questions in the interviewing process to ensure "fit" to outlining what you need to do in your first ninety days on the job. The focus is not on tactical concerns such as updating your resume or writing a cover letter, but rather on important strategic considerations.

Embarking on a new role can be like setting out on a new expedition. Every phase requires careful planning, keen observation and smart execution. It all starts with making a pivotal decision—choosing the right quest or, in this case, the right next position. Just as an explorer wouldn't dive headfirst into unknown terrain without a map, you shouldn't accept a position without first ensuring it's a great match. One surefire way to do that is to pose pertinent questions during the interviewing process.

But what's a grand adventure without its treasures? Once you're convinced about the journey, your next crucial step is negotiating the treasures you deserve, meaning your compensation and benefits. Remember, this isn't about greed; it's about ensuring you're valued fairly for the expertise and passion you bring to the job.

So, let's say you've got the map (the right job) and the treasure (the right compensation package). Now comes the actual quest—your first week at the new job. It's the foundation of the grand structure you're going to build. A few well-planned actions in the first week can set the tone for your entire journey. Dive into your role with the enthusiasm of an adventurer uncovering hidden secrets. That's where tackling the new role with confidence comes into play. And don't forget that every adventurer needs allies. And in the workplace, your allies are your team members. Integrating smoothly into a new team can make all the difference.

Like every memorable adventure, setting yourself up for success in a new role requires strategy, courage and the heart of a true explorer.

You'll notice that this section's format is a little different from the previous chapters. It doesn't have the signature "Why Does It Matter" and "Action Steps" paragraphs. Instead, these chapters are full of wholly-actionable advice.

So, gear up, adventurer, for your professional journey.

# How To Make the Decision To Take a New Position

In the past companies provided neatly staged career trajectories for their employees. Upon graduating, you'd enter the corporate world and, if you did reasonably well, you'd progress upwards over the decades, benefiting from promotions and pay raises along the way. This consistent, predictable journey is now nearly extinct in the modern workplace. In today's context, you need to own your journey.

Deciding to take a new position is not easy. Why? Because it can impact your career trajectory, your personal life, your finances and your overall well-being. You need a structured approach to help you make an informed choice.

You need to reflect on a few things before you decide that a job change is in order.

**Reflect on your attitude**: Before blaming your job, reflect on your mindset. Ask yourself honestly if you are predisposed to dissatisfaction. Ask yourself if it's genuinely the job or just your nature to feel discontented. Make sure it really is the job. Are there simple ways you can feel better about the job without making a change?

**Tweak your role**: If you're struggling to change your outlook on your current role, try reshaping your job responsibilities. Talk with your boss about redesigning your current role so that it better aligns with your passions and strengths. Maybe you can take on an exciting new project or change the clients you engage with.

**Change up your interactions**: If colleague interactions are draining, change that dynamic. Simply changing who you interact with more on an everyday basis can improve your job satisfaction. Prioritize relationships that empower you. Of course, if your relationship with your boss or your coworkers is especially difficult, you may not be able to work around them.

There are, however, situations that you should pay attention to that indicate it might be time to make a change. Here are some examples.

1. **You are not being recognized for your work**. You feel ready for a promotion and you know you deserve one. But there are several, more qualified candidates ahead of you. The situation is not likely to change for quite some time.
2. **Your salary does not compensate for your dissatisfaction**. Maybe you took a new job and it turned out to be completely different from what you expected, even though you gave yourself ample time to adapt. Perhaps you have been in a job for a while, but you find yourself so bored that you cannot imagine doing the same tasks over-and-over again for years to come. Or maybe the workload and stress in your current job make you feel seriously overworked and underpaid.
3. **There are no growth opportunities or upward mobility in your company**. Maybe your entire department was just relegated to a lower status within the organization. You see and hear that the opportunity for funding, investment and growth has shifted to other parts of the organization. You explore your options to move to an area poised for greater growth in the company but your inquiries are not met with a level of interest matching yours.
4. **You cannot work for your boss**. You and your boss may have been peers in the past and you were the one who was not promoted, your personalities may clash or there may be other, hard to define, incompatibilities between you. If the relationship has no hope for improvement and if your boss is not expected to go elsewhere anytime soon, you may

have to seriously consider looking for another employment opportunity.

If any of these apply to you, you may need to consider a job change.

If you've decided that it is time to make a change, reflecting on the following five things can help you to make the best decision for your next step.

*Understand exactly what is not working.*
Ask yourself some pointed questions about what isn't working in the job you have now. What is the driving force behind your dissatisfaction? Does it stem from the work the company does? Or is it more closely related to the company's culture, your coworkers or bosses?

Find the general source of dissatisfaction and then dive deeper to find specific aspects of your job that are not working well. Depending on the source, you may decide the only way to address the issue is to make a change.

*Understand exactly what is working.*
Then ask yourself some pointed questions about what is working in your current role. What motivates you? Which aspects of your work have been positive contributors to your productivity, fulfillment and enjoyment in your workplace? What skills does your job allow you to employ and how has your job allowed you to develop new skills?

Identifying these things will help give you direction in finding a new role that is compatible with the positive aspects of your current job.

*Identify your strengths and skill gaps.*
What areas of your job and academic experiences have you found particularly engaging and been able to grasp well? How can you use those skills and experiences to pivot into something new and what is needed to supplement your existing knowledge? It may not be

practical to make a dramatic change right away. Options such as graduate school or other programs are a great way to fill in skill gaps and direct your learning with a detailed focus. Someone interested in gaining computer science skills, for example, can participate in a coding bootcamp, take online courses, enroll in an undergraduate program or pursue a master's degree. The idea is to gain the credentials and close any skill gaps so that you can take on a new position that interests you.

*Decide if you want to switch companies or just switch roles.*
Taking a new position doesn't necessarily mean wandering far from home. Look for positions you want within your current company that will set you up for future success and complement your skill set.

*Identify your values and clarify your priorities.*
Figure out your core values, priorities and the factors that make up your ideal working environment. Then, examine how a new position complements them (or doesn't) and enables you to grow professionally (or doesn't). What do you value most in any job? Is it salary, job responsibilities, company culture, opportunities for growth, work-life balance or something else? What are your short-term and long-term career goals?

Once you've reflected on the above and you are considering a new role, here are some important dos and don'ts to consider.

## Dos and don'ts to keep in mind

- **Don't ignore cultural fit.** Learn as much as you can about the company, its culture and its reputation in the industry. Use platforms such as Glassdoor or LinkedIn to see reviews and get a sense of employee sentiment. Make observations during the recruiting process to assess fit. Sometimes gut instincts can be powerful indicators. How do you feel when you think about working at this new place? Excited, anxious, indifferent? Ask direct questions throughout the interviewing process. Is the work environment collaborative, competitive, relaxed, structured, innovative? What is the company's approach to work-life balance, flexibility, diversity and inclusion?

- **Do your research**. In my experience people often neglect to do thorough enough research when considering a new role. This can lead to unrealistic expectations. They overlook the financial health and market standing of a potential employer, assuming that the job offer comes from a stable company. However, some companies recruit for roles even when facing economic uncertainties. Understand the company's financial health and growth potential.
- **Do make sure the job title reflects the actual role**. Is there clarity about the role or does it seem ambiguous? Candidates for new roles often wrongly believe that job titles and descriptions capture the full essence of the role. In some firms, roles can be vague or mislabeled. It's crucial to clarify exact responsibilities and performance metrics before making a move.
- **Don't let money be the only factor**. If compensation is the only issue and you leave to do the same job elsewhere for a small bump in pay, you might regret leaving behind a boss you admire and coworkers you adore. If money is the only factor in your decision, you might want to think twice about making the move and make sure you've exhausted your compensation options in your current role.
- **Don't flee from a situation; run toward a new one head-on**. My dad used to say, "Don't run away from something. Run toward something." There's a lot of wisdom in that advice. I've observed so many people who were frustrated in

their current roles and chose to impulsively jump ship without a clear plan. Blinded by the allure of a fresh start, they hastily chased a new opportunity without thoroughly vetting it. Don't make that mistake. Make sure you're running toward something.
- **Do take time to reflect.** Sometimes, stepping back for a day or two provides clarity. It's essential to ensure that the decision to take a new position aligns with both your professional goals and personal circumstances. Will you be taking on responsibilities that you enjoy and that align with your career goals? Consider the potential for growth and advancement in the new position. Discuss the opportunity with trusted friends, family, mentors or colleagues. They might offer a different perspective or point out pros and cons you haven't considered.

Moving on from your current job may end up being a very good decision for your personal and professional future. Be aware, though, that a rapid succession of short-term employments can be a red flag for future employers. Prospective employers will usually ask you why you left your last job and will seek references from previous jobs.

Also, if and when you decide to move on, make sure you maintain your professionalism and follow the appropriate steps to achieve a smooth transition and start any new job on the right foot.

Lastly, remember that no job is perfect. Every position will have its challenges and rewards. The key is to find a role where the benefits outweigh the drawbacks and where you can see yourself growing and being content.

# How To Ask the Right Questions To Ensure a Job Match

As with people on dating apps, employers are going to paint the best picture they can of the position they're looking to fill. And just like dating, once you meet and start asking questions, you find out how much of the position profile or job description is rooted in reality—and whether or not it's a good fit.

There are twelve key questions to ask to help you figure out if an open position is the right one for you. I've given this list of questions to friends who have interviewed for jobs and every single one has been happy with the decision to accept the role. I'm hoping my track record of success with this list continues with you!

## Questions to ask

1. **Is this a new position or an existing one?** For a new position, ask why there's now a need for this role. A new role might mean team expansion due to growth or it might mean a gap or problem that they're trying to solve. If it's an existing position, ask what happened to the person you'd be replacing. If they moved up in the company, that bodes well for career advancement. If they've left the company, then see if you can find out if others have come and gone in the same role. High turnover might indicate trouble.
2. **What are the expectations for this role?** Dig into both the job responsibilities and expectations to get insight into whether the job aligns to your interests, skills and goals, as well as the hiring manager's expectations. You may find out if extra hours or weekend work is expected or if there are a lot of deadlines and demands in the role that might create a work-life balance concern.

3. **What's a typical workday like for this role?** This will help you understand what you can reasonably expect day to day. You should get a sense of how structured the job is, whether it's fast-paced or laid back, what the meeting schedule is like and how collaborative the team is.
4. **What are the biggest challenges for this role?** If the job has a lot of challenges and you don't like high-pressure situations, then it's probably not the right role for you—even if everything else about the company sounds great. But if you enjoy being challenged, then this is your opportunity to explain how your skills and temperament make you ideally suited to the role.
5. **How is training provided and how long is the ramp-up period?** If you're told there is no formal training needed for the role, then it's probably expected for you to get up to speed quickly. If you feel you need training, then find out whether it's available during the onboarding period. Training and career development tells you a lot about whether a company invests in its employees and wants to retain them over the long term.
6. **What are the goals to accomplish within the first ninety days?** Getting an understanding of what you'll be responsible for accomplishing in those first ninety days will let you prepare for expectations if you're offered the job. It will also let you gauge whether those expectations are realistic.
7. **What can you tell me about the team associated with this role?** You can learn not only about who they are, but also their work ethic, how well they work together and what the team culture is like. As you listen, consider whether you're hearing things that make you feel like you'd fit in well.
8. **Are there other skills you're looking for to help round out the team?** Perhaps the team has been handed a new project that requires skills they don't possess. Or maybe you realize

you have a skill that sounds like it would be highly useful on the team. Either way, the responses you get to this question help you evaluate not only how you'll fit into the role, but also into the team.

9. **What are the company's goals, and how does this role and the team contribute to those goals?** The company goals provide insight into the long-term plans and direction for the business. Consider whether their approach to business aligns with your own values and goals.
10. **How is job performance evaluated and measured?** It's critical that you understand the measurements by which you'll be assessed. It's not enough to ensure you get the job; you must understand what's expected so you can keep the job.
11. **What is the career path for advancement beyond this role?** At a larger organization, you should be working toward a change in title and responsibilities about every three years. For smaller companies, your title and role may change more often. Inquire about how often promotions occur and whether there are other positions you could advance to in the company.
12. **What's the one thing you think I should know about this role or this company?** This might catch your interviewer off guard and end up providing you with a bit of unexpected insight. If they speak candidly and honestly, you may learn something that will either swing you toward or away from the company.

Whether it's your dream partner or your dream position, it takes diligence to find the right match. Give yourself the best chance of success by asking these twelve questions, listening carefully to the answers and reflecting on whether the dream can turn into a happy longer-term reality for you.

# How To Negotiate Compensation for a New Position

When you start a new job, you have a unique opportunity to position yourself as a valuable asset and to set your level of compensation accordingly.

While not everyone is motivated by money, studies suggest that job satisfaction and overall happiness in the workplace are linked to financial compensation. Avoid selling yourself short because it's likely that your compensation upon hiring won't change significantly for a little while.

To make sure you receive the best compensation possible for a new role, there are certain steps you should take prior to a negotiation, as well as some dos and don'ts to remember during the actual negotiation process.

## Steps to take

Every compensation negotiation is different, and every employer has a different set of thresholds. Understanding the context in which your negotiation is going to take place and being sensitive to the culture of the organization are essential.

- **Don't immediately engage in a negotiation over compensation.** If you receive a job offer over phone call or via video conference, *do not negotiate the offer right away*, even if the offer is unreasonably low. And regardless of how you feel about the offer in the moment, thank the person making the offer.
- **Have an accurate estimate of your value to a company.** Advocate in a convincing way for the package you want. You have to provide evidence that you're worth the price you're asking for and can back up your assertions with facts.

You risk putting off a prospective employer by pitching yourself too high, so you need to get your level right. If you position yourself appropriately, the prospective employer will not want to risk losing you.
- **Consider several factors when evaluating compensation for a job**. Your experience, the job location, the level of the job and general macroeconomic trends all contribute to fair compensation. There are plenty of online resources to help you gain an understanding of what you should expect to make. You can also ask for advice from people in your professional and personal networks. Check multiple sources to make sure the information is not biased.
- **Decide your salary or wage "bottom line" and "optimal outcome"**. The bottom line is defined by the absolute lowest salary or hourly wage you will accept. Any offer below that number you should walk away from. The optimal outcome is defined by your desired salary or wage. This number should be in the upper range of what you can expect to make. The employer will likely negotiate down from this number. Research suggests that providing a specific number such as $64,750 is more effective than a general number such as $65,000. This will show your employer that you have done your research and that you know *exactly* what you are worth.

Of course, salary is not the only aspect of a job offer that you need to consider. You want to consider the entire compensation package, including bonuses, benefits, job location and other factors. All the variables in the total compensation package can be used as negotiating leverage or concessions.

Know what you are worth. Know exactly what you will ask for. Know what you will not accept.

## Dos and don'ts to keep in mind

- **Do be likable and self-confident.** It is easier to negotiate an offer if the other party truly likes you and wants you to take the job. This is already likely, since you received an offer, but it is nevertheless important to remember during the negotiation process itself.
- **Do be prepared for any questions or pushback from the employer.** The employer might ask if you have other offers or even propose ultimatums.
- **Do rehearse what you are going to say and how you plan to say it.** Ask for feedback from trusted friends, family or advisors. You need to supply ample reasons to support your demand and practice articulating your reasons in advance to a friendly audience.
- **<u>Do not</u> negotiate serially.** If you successfully negotiate a higher salary, do not try to negotiate a higher bonus or more vacation time without mentioning those requests beforehand. At the start of the meeting, lay out all your requests and their relative importance to you.
- **<u>Do not</u> negotiate everything.** Employers know that you want a fair package, but you need to be balanced. You likely won't get *everything* you want. Remember to view the outcome holistically—and to show a genuine desire for the job.

At its core, good negotiation is about getting the best deal you can while at the same time keeping the goodwill of the other side.

# How To Succeed in the First Week at a New Job

Maybe you're only a couple of days into your new role, but you already feel like you've been thrown into the deep end of the pool and you don't know how to swim.

The ramp-up period in a new job is not always structured and leisurely, it can be unstructured, frenzied and hectic. Instead of feeling overwhelmed, you can make a splash in your new role by following some straightforward advice.

## Steps to take

1. **Clarify expectations for your new role**. Ask your manager to clarify any responsibilities that are not 100 percent clear so you can do the job just as well—or even better—than your predecessor. Discuss the following four areas with your manager:
   - High priority tasks and deliverables.
   - Expectations regarding accomplishments for your first ninety days in the role.
   - The definition of success for someone in your role. For instance, are there specific success metrics against which your performance will be evaluated?
   - The key people you should meet during your first two weeks.
2. **Define a regular interaction schedule with your manager**. Recurring check-ins ensure that you are on track to meet your goals and that any issues you face are addressed in a timely manner. If your manager hesitates to establish regular check-ins, find ways to informally interact after meetings, over lunch or casually during the course of the workday.

3. **Introduce yourself to coworkers**. Walk around the office and introduce yourself to coworkers. Learn about their roles and responsibilities. If you work remotely, send your teammates a short email or instant message introducing yourself. You can also ask your manager to introduce you in a team meeting.
4. **Understand your coworkers' priorities**. The better you understand what everyone is working on—and what they consider to be their top priorities—the better you can align your own work to the broader goals of the team and department.
5. **Establish your day-to-day work schedule**. Ask your coworkers when employees typically arrive at and leave the office. Observe patterns in work practices such as when people typically take breaks, go to lunch and acceptable hours for sending work emails. Get a sense for routine business hours and cultural practices so that you can establish your own schedule and habits accordingly.
6. **Set up your workspace and access to hardware and software**. Install any required software like email, instant messaging, video conferencing, file sharing applications. If you work remotely, establish a dedicated workspace where you can minimize distractions and ensure your backdrop for video calls is professional.
7. **Gain access to any necessary files and calendar invites**. Make certain that you have any folders of old work that are available for review. If your team uses a shared drive, ask coworkers to grant you access. Ask your coworkers if there are any upcoming meetings that you should attend and request to be included on the calendar invites.
8. **Familiarize yourself with your physical work environment**. Make a note of managers' offices, coworkers' workstations, meeting rooms, bathrooms, break rooms, stairwells,

emergency exit, and any elevators. This will help you avoid getting lost on your way to meetings and help you identify locations where people informally gather to engage in casual discussion and information sharing.

9. **Establish a daily routine.** Take care of arrangements in advance so that you can be focused and productive at work. For example, arrange for transportation to and from work and for childcare if you have children. Ensure you have planned for a routine regarding when you will take breaks and how you will structure your workday.

By following this template during your first week on the job, you'll ensure that you get off to a great start every single time you take on a new role.

# How To Tackle a New Role With Confidence

You've been pulled from your familiar surroundings, yanked from your very reality, torn from the arms of all you know and hold dear. And thrust mercilessly into the existential dread and cosmic horror of . . . a new job.

Taking on a new job or a new role *shouldn't* be terrifying. You've done it before, and you'll almost certainly do it again. But at the same time, it *can* be unnerving. It can feel like you're starting over, from scratch, at level one. You may not know your new colleagues; they may not know you.

However, you can take a few simple actions on your first day to tackle your new role with confidence.

## Steps to take

- **Keep your lunch and after-work plans open for a few weeks**. If you get asked to lunch, go. If the group invites you out after work on Friday, accept. It's in everyone's best interest for you to become part of the team as seamlessly as possible. For extroverts, don't force yourself or your conversation on others. For introverts, go forth and do your best. It will be good enough.
- **Ask a lot, listen more and watch most of all**. Whether you're brand new to the company or your new role is with your old company, you have a lot to learn about how things work. What's the *official* structure and how do things *really* get done? What are the team dynamics? Who has influence with the boss and who doesn't?
- **Don't worry about asking a lot of questions**. Everyone expects the new person to be full of questions, and almost

everyone likes to show off their experience and insider knowledge. Ask people what they do and what's involved, then listen closely to what they say and what they may not say. You'll get a good idea pretty quickly of what people think of the company, the department, the boss and each other.

- **Start building relationships immediately**. If you want to build solid working and networking relationships, it's likely you'll need to be the one to reach out. The relationships with your boss, coworkers and direct reports are paramount, but you can also work on forming and strengthening relationships with people from all over the company. This will help you learn as much as you can about the company, its culture and its processes.
- **Relax and remember why you're there**. You already got the job. You earned a promotion. You transferred to a department that will give you new challenges. You started with a new company. Think about how much you've already accomplished—now's your chance to accomplish more. Be patient with yourself. Don't expect to master everything right away but do believe in yourself and your ability to succeed in the new role. You got this.

# How To Set Yourself Up for Success in a New Role

When starting a new role, you may feel like a contestant on the TV reality series *Survivor*. You're navigating a new environment, establishing relationships with colleagues and trying to avoid being "voted off" the team.

Whether you're a *Survivor* contestant or starting in a new role, you'll need to build alliances, master new skills, adapt to new challenges, align to group norms and demonstrate resilience.

## Steps to take
Here are six actions to take when you are in a new role.

1. **Form alliances**. Building relationships with key players involves understanding the political landscape of the organization and identifying the individuals who hold the most power and influence. To identify the movers and shakers, observe how decisions are made, who is involved in important meetings and projects and who has a record of success. Once you have identified the individuals with whom you want to form an alliance, focus on building relationships with them by finding ways to help and support them achieve their goals. You want to demonstrate your value to them and establish yourself as a reliable and essential member of the team. Building alliances can also help you gain access to resources and opportunities for growth and development. By building relationships with key players, you may learn from their experience, tap into their networks and gain exposure to new and exciting projects or initiatives.
2. **Shortlist a few quick wins**. Make a positive impact as quickly as possible in your new role. Some examples of quick wins

include: streamlining a repetitive process to save time and increase productivity, creating a dashboard of key performance data, suggesting and implementing a cost-saving measure or using technology to solve a nagging customer problem. Whatever quick wins you identify, systematically make tangible improvements and build momentum.

3. **Identify the skills you need to develop.** You will likely need to master both technical skills as well as soft skills to thrive in your new job. By understanding the specific skills and competencies required for success in your new role, you can create a plan for developing these skills and enhancing your performance. This may involve seeking training or professional development opportunities, working with mentors or coaches or seeking feedback from colleagues or supervisors.

4. **Align to cultural expectations.** A new person who violates the team's behavioral standards risks being viewed as an outsider. Observe and learn the unwritten rules of engagement, including the team's culture and behavioral norms. If the norm is to communicate important information to the entire team through a specific messaging platform, adhere to that protocol. Or if everyone wears business formal attire when customers are present in the office then you should also. Keep in mind that critical norms may vary throughout the organization and depend on the level of responsibility you have.

5. **Stay adaptable and open-minded.** You need to be willing to learn and adapt to new situations, challenges and opportunities as they arise in your role. Stay open-minded to new perspectives and ideas that can enhance your performance and contribute to the organization's success. Stay curious about the work you do and its impact on the organization. Ask questions, seek out feedback and be willing to challenge

the status quo to drive innovation and progress. Be willing to adapt to new responsibilities as your role evolves.
6. **Know all your stakeholders.** You need to know who the stakeholders are, what they expect you to achieve and in what timeframe. Priorities may have shifted since you accepted the role and they may change again as you gain experience. You will likely have various stakeholders to please, not just your boss. These stakeholders may have differing opinions about what constitutes success in the role, so gather your information and reconcile it into a plan that satisfies the most important priorities.

As you start a new role, it's important to keep these six factors in mind and regularly assess your progress in each area. Set aside fifteen minutes each week to reflect on whether you're still on track or if adjustments are necessary. By doing so, you can ensure that you stay on the right path throughout your transition and beyond and achieve your goals in your new role.

# How To Integrate Seamlessly Into a New Team

It can be tough being the new kid in town. Unfortunately, it doesn't get easier when you're a full grown adult taking on a new role. In fact, it can be harder.

You won't have recess or hallway passing periods to get to know your new teammates informally. If you're remote, you won't get invited to lunch, chat in the breakroom or share a joke in the elevator.

What if everybody loved the person you're replacing? You might feel as if you can never live up to Hassan. He was a superstar. Nothing is going to make the first few weeks of being the new kid on the team a party. But there are some ways you can make it smoother and easier to find your voice and your place.

**Steps to take**

To start, it helps to smile. Be open and approachable. Project a positive attitude and show genuine interest in getting to know your team members. Then follow this advice:

- Ask your team leader if he'll prep you ahead of time on how the team typically operates, who your teammates are, what roles they play and any team norms.
- Spend the first few days and weeks listening more than talking. This will help you understand team dynamics, ongoing projects and current challenges. Listening actively shows respect for your colleagues' knowledge and experience. Every team has its own culture, norms and unwritten rules. Pay attention to how meetings are conducted, how decisions are made and how team members communicate.

- Ask questions to display your eagerness to learn and integrate into the team effectively. It's okay not to know everything right away.
- Avoid gossip. Stay out of others' conflicts. These are things that can undercut you and instantly destroy your ability to build trust with your teammates.
- Be yourself, a little at a time. Let your new teammates get to know you a little at a time. Be friendly and show restraint. While you don't have to divulge personal details, sharing a bit about your background, experiences and interests can humanize you and help team members connect with you.
- Let your new colleagues know you'd like to get to know them better, but don't push. If you get an initial *no* or cold shoulder, relax, accept it and try someone else. If the team has social gatherings, lunches or outings, participate in them. It's an informal setting where you can get to know team members better.
- Be a willing collaborator. Technically, that's what you're here for. Listen to other people's ideas and work with them to achieve collective success. Offer help where you see opportunities, even if it's outside of your defined role. This can demonstrate your commitment and drive. However, avoid stepping on toes or making others feel like you're encroaching on their responsibilities. The best kind of teammate is a good teammate, the kind who helps, shares and collaborates.
- Teams often have established dynamics and relationships. Respect those while finding your unique space within the team.

People like to work with other people who do their job well and who are professional and reliable. You don't have to be each other's BFFs, but over time, you'll get to like many of your teammates and they'll like you. With a respectful nod to introverts, we're all essentially social animals. Most of us want to get along.

Integrating into a new team is a journey, not a destination. It takes time to fully understand the dynamics and build trust. As tough as it is to be the new kid, the good news is that eventually, you're not new anymore. Eventually, you're just part of the team.

## Section 10

# Staying Sane: Workplace Zen

Navigating the modern workplace can often feel like walking a tightrope, with pressures and challenges unbalancing you at every moment. To stay grounded and maintain your sanity, especially in a toxic work environment, you need to put into play strategies that prioritize your well-being. This section covers tips on how to stay sane at work—from addressing burnout to saying no when you can't take on more work.

Optimizing workplace well-being isn't just a catch phrase—it's the foundation for everything else. This means creating an environment, mentally and physically, where you can feel safe, valued and equipped to do your best. Part of this involves achieving a work-life balance, a delicate equilibrium where neither the demands of your job overshadow your personal life nor vice versa. This balance is a cornerstone that ensures you come to work recharged and ready, both of which are crucial to keeping yourself motivated and performing at your peak.

However, even in the most harmonious environments, there will be moments of intense pressure. Whether it's a project deadline or an unexpected surge in tasks, it's inevitable. It's in these moments that setting limits becomes vital. You need to recognize your boundaries and understand that you can't always do everything for everyone. Asserting yourself by pushing back on unreasonable expectations or saying no to additional work isn't about being difficult; it's about self-preservation. These proactive steps ensure you don't end up burned out and overwhelmed.

Now, let's add another layer of complexity: the digital age. With remote work becoming more common, managing burnout in a virtual environment presents its own challenges. The lines between work and personal time can blur, making strategies such as managing stress in the moment and handling anxiety crucial. Quick self-checks, deep breaths and brief moments of mindfulness are potent tools in your arsenal.

But what happens when the toxicity of the work environment seems all-encompassing? This is where getting more support at work becomes pivotal. We're not islands and even in the most challenging situations, there will always be allies—be they colleagues, supervisors or external networks. Leaning on them and seeking their advice can provide the fresh perspective and practical solutions you need to navigate the mire.

While every workplace has its challenges, a toxic environment can drain even the most resilient among us. By adopting a holistic approach, starting with individual well-being, setting boundaries, managing stress and seeking support, we can not only survive in such environments but carve out pockets of sanity and success.

Ready to weather the storm together? Here we go.

# Optimizing Your Workplace Well-Being

> "When I think of well-being, I don't mean a fleeting feeling of happiness. Rather, well-being is an individual's sense of satisfaction with their life as a whole, the feeling that "life is good." A person with high well-being has inner contentment, an enduring sense of fulfillment and a view that life is heading in a good direction."
>
> *Rob Cross*

Recent years have seen a significant decrease in workplace well-being. COVID, the so-called Great Resignation and other factors have contributed to a staggering rise in the number of people struggling with burnout, increased workloads, the lack of community and feeling that they have little control over their work and lives.

All of this makes workplace well-being a hot topic. Organizations large and small are making efforts to take better care of their employees, reduce their stress and support work-life balance. And that's a very good thing.

## Why Does It Matter?

Even with the best intentions, your company is still squarely focused on the bottom line. Work is always going to be stressful and your mental health is always going to require your attention.

Maybe you've heard this before, but it really is true: it's okay not to be okay. If you need help coping with the stresses of work and life, ask for it. Many employers offer access to mental health services. If your company doesn't or you don't feel comfortable reaching out at work, most communities offer free or low-cost counseling and other services. Use them. Your well-being matters.

## Action Steps

For your own well-being, ask not only what your company can do for you, but what you can do for you. Follow these steps to optimize your happiness.

*Develop and maintain a routine.*
This is especially important for those working remotely or in a hybrid workplace. Set a schedule for going to bed and getting up that you can maintain on a daily or at least work-daily basis. Eat lunch and dinner at about the same time every day.

To maintain your sanity, step away on a regular basis. Perhaps this means taking the dog for a walk or closing your laptop and practicing deep breathing or meditation. It might involve going out for a cup of tea or eating a slice of chocolate cake. Whatever form it takes, take a break.

*Insist on establishing and sticking to a work-life balance.*
Make going to work a discrete event and make going home a ritual. Even if both of them take place where you live.

When you log off at the end of the work day, tell yourself, *"I'm going home now."* Say it aloud twice if that helps. Remind yourself that you're entitled to a private life which does not include answering emails after midnight or taking work calls on a Sunday morning.

*Take care of your physical well-being.*
Our minds and bodies are intimately connected. Think about how you feel when you have the flu. You're weak, tired, achy and nauseous. Most of us also feel just as bad mentally when we are physically ill. Your physical well-being directly impacts your mental well-being.

Keep that in mind as you plan your daily and weekly schedules. Try to find time every day to at least walk around the block, climb stairs or engage in some sort of physical activity. Running marathons isn't required, but maybe you can arrange for a longer walk two or three times a week.

*Take a long, hard look at your finances.*
Financial pressures are one of the leading causes of stress in adults. Money worries affect us mentally, physically, emotionally and socially. To help ease financial stress, set and stick to a budget that you can afford. Consider financial planning even if you don't have a lot of money. Financial counseling can show you how to make money work for you, which really does reduce stress.

You can't predict when the car or the washing machine will break down and need repairs, but you can cut back on non-essential purchases. Look for areas where you can economize without making yourself feel deprived.

*Connect with people outside of work.*
Work friends provide support, encouragement and understanding. Cultivate these relationships and hold them dear.

Many of us focus so much on our work and families that we often allow other friendships to stagnate and fade away. This is especially problematic when we stop to consider that work and family are often the two greatest sources of stress in our lives. No matter how much we like our jobs and love our partners and kids, they can cause stress.

You need people with whom you have no financial or familial connection. You need people with whom you can share the fears, frustrations and joys of your families without risking hurt feelings and emotional damage. You need people whose relationships with you have no strings, with whom you can unwind without fear of repercussion. You, and all of us, need friends.

# Achieving Work-Life Balance

> "No one on his deathbed ever said:
> I wish I had spent more time at the office."
> *Paul Tsongas*

For most of us, work and life can be hard to separate. Technology makes us very accessible and friendships and personal connections are a part of our work. In fact, research shows that only about a third of people are able to draw a clear line between work and the rest of their lives. For two-thirds of the workforce, work is often looming in the background. People who fall into this group tend to agree with the statement: *"It is often difficult to tell where my work life ends and my non-work life begins."*

While the idea that there is a perfect work-life balance is a red herring, most of us want to achieve a reasonable level of work-life balance.

## Why Does It Matter?

It is harder than ever to accomplish that goal with today's "always on" workplace culture.

Some people feel pressure to work long hours or be constantly available in order to advance their careers or meet the expectations of their boss or company. In some workplaces, there is even a culture of overwork, where long hours and constant availability are expected and even celebrated.

Modern technology has added to the challenge of achieving work-life balance. The proliferation of smartphones and other devices allow people to stay connected to work at all times through email and instant messaging.

It's important to recognize that it's not healthy or sustainable to be "always on" at work. You need to find ways to set boundaries and prioritize work-life balance in order to maintain your well-being and productivity.

When you feel that you have achieved a good balance between your work and personal life, you are more satisfied with your job overall. This can lead to increased motivation and engagement in your work.

Achieving work-life balance can also contribute to overall personal happiness and well-being.

## Action Steps

Even in jobs in which work hours are relatively fixed and there is less of an "always on" culture, there may be life events that can make achieving work-life balance more difficult. Take a hard look at your work schedule and consider the following points to create a better work-life balance for yourself.

- **Assess your work situation.** What are your work requirements, both while at work and after returning home? How do they fit in with your career ambitions? Are you able to disconnect from work during personal time or are you constantly 'on-call'?
- **Assess your personal situation.** Who are the most important people in your life? Are there imminent family changes which may affect your balance? How is your physical and mental health? Do you have time for exercise, recreation and personal hobbies? How has your work influenced your relationships with family and friends?
- **Set boundaries.** Outline specific times when you will and will not check work emails or set limits on the amount of overtime you are willing to work.

- **Prioritize your time**. Make a list of your responsibilities and prioritize the tasks that are most important or urgent. This helps you focus on what really needs to get done and avoids feelings of being overwhelmed.
- **Use your time efficiently**. Look for ways to streamline your work processes and eliminate unnecessary tasks to free up more time for personal activities and responsibilities.
- **Reset expectations with your boss**. Have an honest conversation with your boss about the challenges you are facing. Make it clear that you recognize how important it is to support your team and be available for your colleagues, but that it shouldn't come at the cost of your mental, physical or emotional health.
- **Change your work arrangement**. Your boss might be able to reduce your workload or change the nature of your role. Research suggests that having more control over when work occurs and reducing variability can be key to increasing satisfaction, even more than the sheer number of hours worked.
  - Irregular hours cause stress because they affect the ability to plan—so you may want to talk to your boss about how to reduce variability in your work schedule.
  - Explore the option of flextime work, where you work the same total number of hours every week, but on a schedule that works better for you.
  - Ask to work remotely a few days a week to eliminate commuting time.
  - Consider enlisting the support of coworkers if you are struggling to manage all of your responsibilities.
  - Explore the option of sharing a full-time load with your coworkers in a job-share arrangement if they are experiencing similar challenges.

- **Find activities you enjoy**. Make time in your life for hobbies and activities that you enjoy and that help you relax and recharge your drained batteries.
- **Learn to say no**. It's okay to turn down requests or opportunities that would take up too much of your time or energy. You have a limited amount of time and energy, and it's important to prioritize your own well-being above everything else.

Striving for a balanced work-life rhythm is crucial. Remember that your career is a marathon, not a hundred-meter dash. Only with equilibrium can you expect to go the distance.

# Keeping Yourself Motivated at Work

"Ninety percent of adults spend half their waking lives doing things they would rather not be doing at places they would rather not be."
*Barry Schwartz,* Why We Work

A 2022 Bloomberg survey of college graduates reports that less than 50 percent are working in their field of study. Chances are you didn't grow up to be what you thought you'd be. And that's okay. It just means that you need to find ways to keep yourself motivated at work.

Some people are driven. They're filled with passion and desire. They know exactly what they want, where they want to be and happily go about doing whatever they need to do to get there. They wake up every morning determined to get one day closer to their goals.

These people have callings. Great for them.

The rest of us have jobs.

What we want is hard to define and harder to find. We're not always exactly sure what it looks like. And we're not always sure how we'll get there. In the meantime, we have to make a living.

## Why Does It Matter?

Every now and then motivation sags. We lose sight of why we're doing what we do. You're not the only one who goes through periods of low or non-existent motivation. Even the CEO has times when he'd rather be doing something else.

Unless you're independently wealthy, you need an income. Your job provides that. Maybe doing well in this job will help you get a better one in the future; one that pays more or that you'd rather be doing. You just need to find a way to activate your motivation to keep yourself engaged and doing good work in the meantime.

## Action Steps

So how can you revive or rekindle your motivation?

**On a purely practical level, start by planning your day and tracking your progress.** When your motivation lags, it's easy to feel overwhelmed when you look at the literal or figurative pile of work that lies in front of you. Where should you even begin?

- Make a list of what you absolutely must get done today. If you need to, begin small.
- Unless you have tasks that are urgent and should be addressed right away, look for tasks that you can quickly check off your list. It may seem childish, but there is pleasure to be had in seeing items crossed off your list.
- Build momentum that will help you make it through the longer and more challenging tasks.

**Next, reward yourself for getting things done.** Crossing things off your list may not be motivation enough. Research suggests setting up small rewards when working through long-term tasks is self-motivating. Give yourself a reward for getting to a preset milestone. Take a little walk. Grab a donut with that next cup of coffee. Why not make it a latte?

**Third, check in with your team or support system.** Camaraderie can be a great motivator. Most of us like our teammates, so take the time to connect with one or two. Or, check in with a friend or family member. Engaging in conversation can be a powerful tool in contextualizing and alleviating feelings of demotivation. While these discussions may not always yield concrete solutions, the act of vocalizing your struggles often brings relief and clarity. However, it's important to approach these talks with caution; remember, the goal is to rise above misery, not to wallow in it. By expressing and unburdening yourself of the emotions tied to demotivation, you pave the way to overcome them.

**Finally, look at the situation pragmatically and get back in touch with why you're working in the first place.** Remind yourself that you're working for reasons beyond the thrills and excitement of your job. Maybe you simply have bills to pay and people you're responsible for. Maybe you're building a career and your current position is one of the steps in getting to your ultimate goals. Remind yourself of the reasons you are working.

# Setting Limits When You Are Pushed Too Far

> "Caring for myself is not self-indulgence. It is self-preservation, and that is an act of political warfare."
> *Audre Lorde,* A Burst of Light

A crashing wave of resignation came after the COVID-19 pandemic. Service workers and professionals fled their jobs in droves.

The pandemic didn't so much cause underlying issues—such as punishing hours, mediocre pay, chronic labor shortages, toxic work environments—but brought them to a head. Employees weren't necessarily leaving for better jobs. They fled for their psychological and emotional well-being.

Some workplaces can be very stressful, especially those in professions such as healthcare, social work and education. The responsibility to go above and beyond in these professions can play on the emotions of those drawn to them. Sure, you're overworked, underpaid and unappreciated, but if you quit, what will happen to your patients and clients?

The service sector is also rife with stress. Workers often feel guilty or afraid of their jobs if they turn down a shift, call in sick or take their kids to the doctor. How can you leave your coworkers in the lurch when staffing levels are already too low? You care too much about your teammates to let them down.

## Why Does It Matter?

Whether it's your sense of following a calling, such as healthcare or education or your need to make a living and support your coworkers, you push yourself to and often past, your limits.

Coming to terms with these and similar work situations goes beyond popular catchphrases such as "wellness", "self-care" and "work-life balance." It enters the realm of self-preservation and survival.

Long-term stress, anxiety, burnout and depression all have serious consequences. They can lead to addiction, abuse and psychological or physical deterioration. Even if you manage to stay emotionally strong, think about the consequences of facing serious physical illness. Will it seem selfish if you need to spend time in the ICU or rehab?

Unfortunately, there isn't a tried-and-true method of escape from the pressure of a job. There are only some hard truths that you need to seriously consider if you want to keep your mind, body and soul intact.

## Action Steps

You may have heard these suggestions before, but they're important enough to reiterate. Pay special attention to how each may resonate with your attitude about work.

- Your work shouldn't be your life. It shouldn't cost your mental or physical health. It shouldn't mean sacrificing your family, friends, partner or your happiness. Write that down.
- Say *no* and mean it. Don't let anyone convince you that it isn't okay to say no when you need to.
- Everything has limits. But before you can set limits, you need to know what your boundaries are. Take some time to reflect on what is important to you and where boundary lines should be drawn.
- Use "I" statements to express how you feel and what you need, but avoid blaming or attacking others.
- You can't help others if you're not okay. You're not being selfish, you're potentially saving your life. You need to put on *your* oxygen mask first.

- If you want to get out of a toxic environment, run in the other direction. No one should force himself to stay in a toxic environment.

Overall, don't let *yourself* down. You need to take care of yourself when you've been pushed too far at work. This may involve taking a vacation, a leave of absence or seeking support from a therapist or trusted professional. Take a good, long look around. Then do what you have to do for *you*.

# Saying *No* to Additional Work

> "It's only in saying no that you can
> concentrate on what's really important."
> *Steve Jobs*

When you are a highly productive and effective member of your organization, you may find yourself at the receiving end of additional assignments. Your boss and others may try to flatter you with phrases such as, *"I know that if I ask you to do it, it will get done right!"* or *"Could you just take on one more thing?"* or *"Please handle this urgent project."*

## Why Does It Matter?

Being asked to take on additional tasks is often a sign that your boss trusts you and values your abilities. I acknowledge that that is a positive thing.

However, when you are already overloaded, you may start to see this pattern of constant additional requests as unfair, especially when others at your level receive the same compensation for doing a lot less work. And saying *yes* all the time can lead to increased stress and burnout and decreased work-life balance.

You can push back on additional work. By being judicious about when you push back and by being respectful in your request, you can define the parameters that allow you to maintain a workload that's manageable and achievable. Here's how.

## Action Steps

Follow these steps to handle the challenge of being asked to take on additional work.

*Temporize.*
Avoid a knee-jerk reaction of either saying *yes* or *no*. Take the time to think through the request.

While you must always acknowledge your boss's authority, you know better than anybody else, including your boss, what is currently on your plate. You have detailed information regarding your current assignments, the time it takes to complete them and the progress you've made on them.

*Gather the data.*
Be prepared to share the details of your workload. Your boss should generally know what you're working on, but that doesn't mean they understand the amount of time and effort it takes to do it. And if you take pride in making it look easy, then your boss has even less reason to think you can't take on additional tasks. To provide yourself with additional factual information, keep a list of all of the projects and tasks that you do in a given week, along with associated deadlines. When your boss comes to you with a new request, you can share your list and ask them how the new task fits in with your other priorities.

Having this information at the ready gives you a lot of room to negotiate and reprioritize your tasks. In addition, it allows you to honestly and directly explain that you're at capacity. And to clarify that for the sake of your work quality, you don't want to overpromise and not deliver what you're accountable for. You can set boundaries by agreeing that something can be added to your list if something else comes off, even if only until you complete the new task.

*Meet to discuss.*
Ask for a meeting with your boss to discuss the new assignment. You may feel pressured to say yes out of loyalty to your boss or your desire

to be a team player. However, you should make sure that you don't blindly give in to the pressure. Even if your boss tells you the new assignment is a top priority, you should be prepared to show the potential negative impact of the new project on your existing activities. A good boss should value your input and want to make sure that you are not overwhelmed by taking on a new assignment.

*Get all your questions answered.*
Ask pertinent questions about the new project and what the work entails so you know exactly what would be required if you commit to the new assignment. The worst thing you can do is say yes to something because you didn't take the time to fully understand the task.

Understand how you might benefit from saying yes to the new assignment. Ask specific questions about the project, such as its purpose in the bigger picture, the resources needed and the time table for completion.

Make sure you understand how your effort is going to be recognized, either financially or as a possible step toward promotion. Once you feel you have all the information you need, if you can, ask for a day or two to decide.

*Make a decision.*
Ultimately, you need to make a decision about the new assignment.

If after careful analysis you must say no, then provide a direct explanation for why you can't do what you've been asked to. And instead of simply stating *No, I can't,* or *No I won't,* consider one of the following.

- Not right now, but maybe in a month, after I finish this other task.
- Not with the current resources; I would need additional resources.
- Not if I will be blamed for neglecting other projects.

- Not without some appropriate recognition for taking on this extra work.

Provide your explanation in a way that leans on the details of the request and the factors that affect it. For instance, your boss comes to you on Wednesday afternoon with a request to complete a new task by Friday. You could say, "It would be really difficult for me to get that done by Friday because I know it will take me a couple of days just to gather the information." By framing your response that way, you deliver the message that the deadline is impossible for you, and you have a factual reason why it's not possible. By stating the facts, it doesn't sound like you're just trying to get out of it.

It is better to say *no* upfront to something you simply cannot take on than to drop the ball or underperform on an assignment later.

You may need to say yes to the assignment if your boss insists. As long as you have been clear in your communication with your boss by laying out the risks and consequences of taking on the new assignment, you have done what you can to address the request responsibly. And then remind yourself that taking on the project may bring unintended positive results. Albert Einstein once said, "*In every crisis, lies an opportunity,*" so try to find the silver lining.

# Pushing Back When Everything at Work Is "Urgent"

*"Action expresses priorities."*
*Mahatma Gandhi*

Many of us have encountered coworkers and supervisors who believe that every task is urgent and requires our immediate attention. *NEED ASAP!* is the subject line of every email you receive from them. They say the same phrase fifty times a day: *This is high priority* or *This is mission critical*.

These people have a sense of urgency that compels them to move quickly and demand prompt resolution to everything they encounter.

Having a boss or coworker who sees everything as urgent is like playing a never-ending game of whack-a-mole. The minute you address one task, a new one is thrown at you—which also requires your immediate attention. You find it difficult to keep up and resolve them all in a timely manner. It can feel demotivating, overwhelming and exhausting.

## Why Does It Matter?

Bosses and coworkers who view everything as a fire drill can be challenging and stressful to work for and with. They leave a trail of chaos in their wake. What exacerbates the situation is that these individuals are often highly productive and dedicated workers who may have received praise in the past for their responsive behavior.

Adopting a sense of urgency is sometimes necessary and important. However, if all or most tasks are treated as equally urgent, it can lead to negative consequences.

Voicing your concerns in this area can prevent burnout, reduce stress and ultimately improve your productivity and your job satisfaction.

## Action Steps
There are a few steps you can take to address this situation.

*Communicate your concerns about the constant urgency.*
Schedule a meeting with the party(ies) responsible for the constant urgency to calmly express your concerns about the high-pressure work environment. Let them know how it is affecting your productivity and well-being, as well as the quality of your work. Provide specific examples to support your case and, if they're willing and able, help them to change their ways.

*Help others see the full range of consequences.*
Discuss with those who frequently drive urgency the significant implications of their persistent demands.

- **Decreased quality of work**. When you rush to complete a task, you may overlook important details, make mistakes or fail to consider alternative solutions.
- **Burnout**. Working with a sense of urgency over a prolonged period can lead to burnout, decreased motivation and decreased job satisfaction.
- **Increased stress and anxiety**. Working under constant pressure and with an unending sense of urgency can lead to increased stress and anxiety.
- **A negative impact on relationships**. When you constantly rush through tasks, you may neglect communication and collaboration with colleagues. When you don't coordinate with others, relationships suffer.
- **Missed opportunities**: Acting with excessive urgency may lead you to overlook important opportunities or fail to consider longer-term planning and strategy.

*Offer solutions for better prioritization.*
If you can, propose solutions that may alleviate pressure your boss or coworker might feel. You can help him focus on the most critical tasks by sharing how to group tasks into one of four buckets.

- Urgent and important.
- Important but not urgent.
- Urgent but not important.
- Not urgent and not important.

Commit to do the urgent and important tasks as soon as possible. Establish a reasonable timeline to undertake tasks that are important but not urgent. If possible, delegate the urgent but unimportant tasks to others. Gain support to eliminate tasks which are not urgent or important by presenting a well-reasoned case highlighting how the tasks detract from productivity and divert resources away from more critical objectives.

*Set appropriate expectations.*
Clarify with your boss or coworker which tasks are genuinely urgent and which can wait. Then, set expectations for realistic timelines and workloads to help manage the pressure as you tackle the genuinely urgent tasks.

Be proactive in managing your workload. Maintain clear communication with your boss or coworker. Make a point of checking in regularly to ensure you are on the same page.

# Managing Stress in the Moment

> "The greatest weapon against stress is our ability
> to choose one thought over another."
> *William James*

Everyone who holds a job feels the pressure of occasional work-related stress. In fact, a quarter of all employees view their jobs as the number one stressor in their lives.

Even if you love what you do, your job probably has stressful moments. Any number of things can cause us to experience moments of acute stress.

- Maybe you're worried because you've been told that instead of having a week to complete the project you now have only two days.
- Maybe you're angry because in front of your peers your boss criticized the way you handled the meeting.
- Maybe you're frustrated because your budget has been cut by 20 percent.

There are times when worry, anger and frustration are justified. But it's difficult to respond effectively when you're in the grip of these emotions.

## Why Does It Matter?

A stress reaction can hijack rational thought. It cuts off communication with the prefrontal cortex, the area of the brain used to spot patterns, perceive nuance in a situation, remember past experiences and consider diverse options. When you've been *hijacked* by stress, you may say or do things you regret.

Left unchallenged, stress may prevent you from seeing the truth and contributes to an even higher level of stress. These thoughts can persist even after you practice relaxation techniques. Learning to release yourself from negative thought patterns like all-or-nothing thinking, overgeneralizing and personalizing will lower your stress.

## Action Steps

You must regain control of your prefrontal cortex by purposefully engaging the thinking part of your brain, so you can see things more clearly and take your next step thoughtfully. You can learn how by following these five steps.

*Hit the pause button.*
Before reacting to a stressful situation, take a moment to think things through.

If you're in the middle of a conversation say, "I'll *get back to you. I need a minute to consider that,*" or *"Could we revisit this topic? I need some time to think about it,"* to buy yourself the time you need to clear your head.

If you're unable to interrupt the conversation, simply remain silent and use body language to show you're taking a pause. Pausing for even a few seconds can prevent you from immediately acting in a way you might regret later. Similarly, don't respond immediately to your coworker's email or the instant message or the voicemail your boss just left. Take a step back and give yourself a moment.

*Calm your mind.*
Use a three-pronged calm down strategy to make the best decision.

**Pause and breathe**. You need to help your body relax and reduce the amount of cortisol running through your bloodstream. You can do this by taking a few deep breaths to initiate a relaxation response.

**Reflect and label.** Notice what you are feeling and then name it. *I'm feeling upset and fearful* or *I'm worried about how my boss will respond.*

**Analyze and decide.** After you calm down, it's time to think objectively about the situation and how to proceed. Ask yourself, *"Have I assessed the situation correctly?" "Are there any other possibilities that I need to consider?" "What are my options for moving forward?"*

*Release yourself from unproductive thinking patterns and mind traps.*
While deep breathing can alleviate the physical symptoms of stress, it may not address the root cause of anxiety-inducing thoughts. During periods of high stress, it's common to get stuck in a negative thought loop that doesn't reflect reality. You may start to feel more self-critical, anxious or irritable and struggle to maintain a positive outlook.

To avoid getting caught up in mind traps do three things.

1. **Examine the facts**: What does the evidence say?
2. **Identify alternative explanations**: Are there any other possibilities?
3. **Gain perspective**: What would a neutral observer say?

*Let go of what you can't control.*
A common source of workplace stress is feeling like a situation is out of your control. While you can influence many things, you can't influence or control *everything*.

The next time you feel overwhelmed, ask yourself what lies within your influence and what lies outside it. When something is outside your influence, you need to let it go. Accept the fact that there are simply some problems you can't solve. It's better to focus attention on areas where you can actually make an impact.

*Maintain perspective.*
Sometimes simply talking about a stressor can be a relief and sharing your experiences with others can help you gain perspective and find solutions. Find a colleague or mentor with whom you can talk about the situation. Keep a journal. Getting things out of your head and on paper can help you work through difficult feelings more objectively.

It's never fun to deal with episodes of acute stress when they happen at work, but it is important to learn how to effectively manage them.

# Handling Times When You're Anxious at Work

> "Anxiety's like a rocking chair. It gives you something to do, but it doesn't get you very far."
> *Jodi Picoult*

*Relax! Don't be so shy! There's nothing to worry about. What's the worst that could happen?*

We've probably all heard this countless times but somehow it just never seems to help.

Regardless of whether you have a diagnosed anxiety disorder or your anxious response is simply triggered by certain situations, how you feel and how you react in social or stressful situations isn't something to be dismissed lightly.

## Why Does It Matter?

Anxiety is a crippling, debilitating state of mind that can have profound emotional and physical effects. It can cloud your judgment, destroy your confidence and paralyze you. It's hardly fun to experience anxiety at parties, let alone work.

Anxiety manifests itself in many forms, from assuming the worst in everyone and every situation to self-sabotaging thoughts such as, *If I screw up, I'll get fired. They all think I'm an idiot anyway.*

The fact that you probably won't mess up and they certainly don't think you're an idiot may be of little help. Instead, finding logic- *and* feelings-based healthy coping mechanisms can lessen the pain of day-to-day workplace anxiety.

## Action Steps

At the outset, try to make friends with your anxiety.

Most of us tend to view the quirks and pitfalls of our mental health as the enemy. Try to quit framing your anxiety as a problem and view it simply as a part of who you are. Instead of constantly battling it, look for ways to work with or around it.

*Create an anxiety-response ritual.*
Think of it as dropping an anchor to keep your boat from floating into the shoals. The familiar helps to ground and comfort us. So, the next time a stressful situation triggers you, have a plan for how to react as best you can. Common rituals include:

- Getting a glass of water or cup of tea.
- Opening your journal or laptop to write a positive, calm message to yourself.
- Getting up and walking around your desk five times.
- Closing your eyes and taking ten deep breaths.

It doesn't matter what the ritual is. It only matters that you choose one that works for you and do it with consistency.

One of the most insidious parts of anxiety is that it feeds on itself. You become *more* anxious *because* you're anxious. Think about what you'd say to a friend or coworker who comes to you about their anxiety. You wouldn't blow them off or tell them to just suck it up, as you usually do to yourself. What would you say to them?

Now say that to yourself.

Finally, don't wait to be ready to take action. You may never be fully ready. Confidence isn't something that happens to you; it's something you build.

At the end of the day, your anxiety isn't something you cure—it's something you learn to live with by minimizing its effects on your behavior. When you make yourself move forward today, you make it a tiny bit easier to move forward tomorrow.

Please note, though, that if anxiety is a significant disruptive factor in your life, you should address it with a mental health professional. You deserve more relief than the simple steps I'm presenting here.

# Taking Steps To Reduce Your Burnout

*"Burnout is the result of feeling like you have nothing more to give."*
*Arianna Huffington*

If you feel burned out at work, you are not alone. According to a survey by Gallup, 23 percent of employees report feeling burned out at work very often or always, while an additional 44 percent report feeling burned out sometimes. That means most of us.

## Why Does It Matter?

Burnout can have a negative impact on both your physical and mental health. It leads to feelings of exhaustion, cynicism and a decreased sense of personal accomplishment.

Burnout can negatively affect your productivity, relationships and the quality of your life. Taking steps to prevent burnout can improve your well-being and your performance in your job and personal life.

## Action Steps

You don't need a new job or a month-long vacation if you're burnt out. Namely, because that isn't realistic for many (most) people. Instead, here are six steps to reduce burnout.

*Reduce your workload.*

- Find ways to delegate more and say no to new tasks by following the advice laid out in previous chapters.
- Take stock of how frequently you turn down additional assignments when you have the option. Make sure you're not just always blindly accepting every assignment.

- Consider evaluating the way you handle your tasks. Can you improve your organization and delegation? Are you efficiently prioritizing your responsibilities?

*Seize more control.*

- Recognize what aspects of your work environment are within your power to change and what will remain unchanged no matter what you do.
    - Are you frequently interrupted by your boss at all hours, making you feel you always have to be available?
    - Do priorities at work frequently change, making it hard to plan and stay on track?
    - Do you lack the necessary resources to effectively do your job?
- Reflect on what actions you can take to address these issues. Often times it will involve a conversation with your boss to obtain more resources or to stabilize your priorities. Gather the information you need to prove your point and then have the conversation.

*Seek greater reward for your effort.*

- Evaluate what you need to feel valued in your job.
    - Ask for a raise or promotion.
    - Seek more positive feedback and, if helpful, increased interaction with your supervisor.
- Determine which rewards would make your job more fulfilling for you—and if those rewards can be obtained in your current work environment.
    - Use the rewards you have already earned such as paid time off.

*Improve collective morale and group spirit.*

- Inquire about someone's day.
- Express gratitude for a peer's contributions.
- Communicate in a manner that is respectful and non-judgmental.

Burnout can be contagious, and by elevating your own engagement and morale, you can positively impact the group. However, if despite your best efforts the relationships and morale of the group cannot be improved, it may be worth considering a job change.

*Seek equitable treatment.*

- Advocate for fair treatment in the workplace by making sure your contributions are recognized, speaking up when you feel overlooked and asking for what you need.
  - Address bias by requesting acknowledgement, resources or extra time.
- Bring up unfair biases in a polite and professional way by asking for explanations and clarifications. For example, you can ask for an explanation as to why someone else was given extra time on a project, while you were not.

*Take breaks.*

- Take a vacation. Even a single day off from work can be beneficial.
- Step away from your work for a few minutes every hour or two to clear your head and refocus.
- Engage in physical activities such as taking a walk, stretching or socializing with coworkers.

- Walk away from your work and allow your mind to relax and wander.

Remember: You are the master of your own well-being, and you have the power to prevent burnout.

# Managing Burnout When You Work Remotely

> *"Learn to say no to demands, requests, invitations and activities that leave you with no time for yourself. Until I learned to say no and mean it, I was always overloaded by stress."*
> *Holly Mosier*

Remote workers often find they're more, not less, productive, than their co-located counterparts. This presents a challenge: too much work can lead to burnout and have dastardly consequences.

## Why Does It Matter?

When you work from home, you live in (or very near) your office. That brings the results of burnout (such as stress, lashing out at others and general misery) to your front door.

Learning how to handle work-from-home burnout ensures that you have an escape from your day-to-day life and can prioritize yourself and your family.

## Action Steps

I've found a few simple ways to reduce burnout when working remotely. Refer to the checklist below.

- **Set formal business hours**. When you work from home, you can easily find yourself working well into the night or early morning. You don't have to keep the same hours you would if you were in the office, but figure out what hours work best for your schedule and then keep to them.
- **Develop an after-work ritual**. When business hours end, do something akin to leaving the office. When you work from home, you benefit from having a similar "shut down" routine.

Perhaps you turn off the lights in your home office and lock the door or simply shut off your computer.
- **Change devices when you change modes from work to personal time.** If you can, have a computer designated for work and a tablet with social media and entertainment apps.
- **Get outside when you take breaks.** Step away from your computer and do something that helps you relax, such as going for a walk or stretching. However, if you always take breaks right next to where you work, it can feel as though you are never able to get away from your work. Research shows that breaks taken in nature are the most restorative. Even a short five-minute break walking outside and around trees or near a body of water can have a huge effect on your brain's ability to rest and recharge. So try to take your breaks outside if at all possible.
- **Stay connected.** Working remotely can be isolating, so stay connected with your colleagues and friends. Set up regular check-ins or virtual happy hours to maintain a sense of community. Virtual coffee or lunch dates with coworkers can help you build personal connections, too.
- **Seek support.** If you're feeling overwhelmed, don't be afraid to reach out to your manager. Set up a one-on-one meeting to discuss your feelings of burnout and provide specific examples of how burnout is negatively impacting your work.

# Getting More Support at Work

> "If you want to lift yourself up, lift up someone else."
> *Booker T. Washington*

If you have a job, you're going to need all kinds of support. It might be support you need to perform a task or support for growing your career and developing new skills. Maybe it's support for acquiring the resources you need to do your job well or getting supportive feedback.

If you're human, you also have emotional and social support needs. Work demands a lot from you—and it's okay to ask for support at work. *Everyone* needs help at times.

## Why Does It Matter?

It can be hard to ask for support. It can make you feel vulnerable or weak.

Unless you're John Wayne riding the range alone, you'll need help now and then. You need support to be happy and productive at work. To get it, you have to identify when you need it and how to ask for it.

## Action Steps

**First, figure out what kind of support you need.** This requires knowing what you really need. You may feel like you need a lighter workload when what you really need is more collaboration. What seems like a bad fit may be a lack of proper training.

Look closely at where you're having troubles. What will really help you solve the root of the problem instead of just treating the symptoms? When you put your finger on it, that's the support you need.

**Second, build a case for why you need support.** Don't focus on you; focus on us. For example, explaining how flexible hours or working remotely will help you get work done more efficiently will get you support because your boss will see that it benefits you and the company.

**Third, talk to your boss**. Frame it as looking for feedback to open the conversation. Explain the challenge you're facing that necessitates the support. Then ask your boss for *their* ideas.
They might even come to the same conclusions as you. If they have no ideas for adequately supporting you, the stage is set for you to present your case. Show them how supporting you is also good for them.

**Fourth, talk to your coworkers**. Chances are that others have gone through something similar compared to what you're going through. Most teammates know what it's like to need support in times of personal or professional challenges. Some things they can't help with, but your teammates can help cover if you need to go to a doctor's appointment or talk with your kid's teacher. They can also provide a great deal of moral and emotional support.

**Fifth, build peoples' trust in you**. If your teammates are supporting you, show them that they can count on your support when they need it. If your boss is giving you a flexible schedule, show them how it's enabling you to be more productive.

A happy, positive workplace is a place of mutual trust, respect and support. Ask for support when you need it, and offer it to others when you can.

# Staying Sane in a Toxic Work Environment

*"Remember, you were created to be a champion and ready for any battle."*
*Pernell Stoney*

Working in a toxic environment can feel like being trapped in a horror movie. To paraphrase writer Leo Tolstoy, all happy workplaces are alike, but every toxic workplace is toxic in its own way.

A company that wouldn't dream of tolerating sexual harassment may still have a culture of employee abuse and bullying. Or vice-versa.

Some companies tolerate a lot, but you shouldn't have to. You owe your job your best efforts. You don't owe it your sanity and dignity.

## Why Does It Matter?

Work shouldn't be an emotional battle zone, but sadly, sometimes it is. When it is, you have to do whatever is necessary to keep yourself sane.

Whether you're coping with a bully, an abuser, chronic gossip, malignant negativity, routine disrespect or some combination of these, a toxic workplace can make you question your capabilities, your competence, your motivation and even your self-worth. Living with toxic behaviors can even make you question your personal safety and sanity.

## Action Steps

To stay sane in a toxic environment, follow these steps:

1. Define the toxic behavior.
2. Document the behaviors.
3. Report, report, report.
4. Create an action plan.
5. Be kind to yourself.

*Define the toxic behavior.*
You can't just say *"This place is a horror show."* You have to be able to point to and articulate the specific reasons why it is so awful. Bad behavior encompasses a lot but consistent demeaning, sexist and inappropriate joking and comments is a specific behavior that can be addressed with specific actions.

This also helps you understand why you react the way you do and how you can further protect yourself. Directly identifying the problem is the first step to solving it.

*Document the behaviors.*
Write things down when they happen or as soon as possible afterward.

On February 13th at 2:45 p.m. in the warehouse, person X did Y and said Z. Make note of any witnesses who can help back up your story. This allows you to build a case for possible action. It demonstrates that a pattern of bad behavior exists and it wasn't a one-time misstep.

Many toxic people will try to gaslight you. They'll deny bad actions or claim you're imagining things. Documentation lets you point directly at their behaviors, if only to remind yourself that you're not crazy or imagining things.

*Report, report, report.*
Nothing changes until someone declares enough is enough. Take your documentation and show it to someone who can help.

- Start with your boss. Part of their job is being responsible to the people who report to them.
- If your boss is the problem or refuses to handle the issue, go over their head. They might get mad, but so what? You have yourself, your job and your well-being to think about. Remember, there are laws in place to protect you from retaliation.

- Talk to HR. For HR, it's a lot easier to address toxic situations in an office than it is to bring in lawyers and PR professionals. This works to your advantage.
- Report harassment or abuse to local or federal authorities. This also applies to cases of discrimination due to sexual orientation, gender identity, age, race or religion. Labor departments and agencies exist to help and protect you.

*Create an action plan.*
The best solutions are in-house. Maybe it can be handled by you or your boss having a serious talk with the bad actors. Maybe it needs more intervention than that.

Push for and cooperate with any company investigation. Your documentation and witnesses again come into play here.

Know your outs. Resolution may not be forthcoming, so you must figure out if you need to leave your job. Most of us can't easily just up and quit because we need to make a living. However, some working situations cannot be lived with. Only you can decide that for yourself.

*Be kind to yourself.*
If you need or want to stay in a toxic work environment, take steps for self-preservation. Use the checklist below to help.

- **Keep it at work and don't bring it home**. Being treated badly tends to make us behave badly. Don't let it happen, especially not at home.
- **Create a support system**. You're almost certainly not alone in suffering and are bound to have sympathetic coworkers. Be their friend and let them be yours.
- **Avoid ongoing drama**. Walk away, at the earliest opportunity.
- **Learn to say *no* in a respectful and assertive way**. Set limits on how much time and energy you're willing to give.

## Section 11

# Handling Special Situations in the Workplace

We're generally taught the core skills necessary for our roles—how to manage a project, negotiate with vendors and analyze the data in a spreadsheet. Yet it's the unpredictable and nuanced situations that can truly test our adaptability, emotional intelligence and resilience. The workplace isn't a sterile arena for task execution; it's a complex web of personalities, challenges and unique scenarios. You need an equally diverse set of coping strategies. This section delves deep into these less-discussed but equally crucial unicorn situations.

The modern workplace is a microcosm of society at large with similar politics, interpersonal dynamics and societal pressures. Knowing when to raise a concern or even merely recognizing when something is amiss are important skills. It's about distinguishing between what might just be an annoyance and what violates the very ethos of a healthy working environment.

This section explores the intricate waters of interpersonal relations. You need to know how to confront the whispers in the hallways, the challenges of navigating office politics—both in physical offices and digital spaces—and the sting of exclusion or stereotyping. These experiences, while uncomfortable, are often the litmus test for our personal growth, demanding a blend of tact, assertiveness and empathy.

Yet, there are situations that transcend everyday challenges—moments where ethical boundaries are breached or personal safety and well-being come under threat. How should you confront a workplace bully or address harassment? These are not mere challenges; they're violations that require immediate, assertive action and an understanding of your rights.

Lastly, the inevitability of change—whether personal, such as grappling with mental health concerns or external, such as the departure of a beloved team member—casts its own set of shadows. In these times, self-awareness and adaptability become your most trusted allies, guiding you from uncertainty to a place of understanding and acceptance.

Let's talk about the tough stuff.

# How To Know When To Complain About Something Versus Keeping Quiet

"Remember not only to say the right thing in the right place, but far more difficult, to leave unsaid the wrong thing at the tempting moment."
*Benjamin Franklin*

We all experience times at work when something does not go as expected or as hoped. Maybe there is a misunderstanding between members of your team that delayed a project. Maybe a newly-implemented procedure is causing problems.

You might face a choice regarding how to handle the issue. Should you speak up about the situation or remain silent?

If you decide to speak up, you need to consider when, how and to whom you should address your concern.

### Knowing if you should remain silent or speak up

When determining if you should speak up or remain silent, it can be helpful to ask yourself a few questions.

- **Is the issue impacting your work or well-being?** If the issue is affecting your ability to do your job or is causing you stress or discomfort, it may be worth bringing it up with your boss.
- **Is the issue something that can be resolved?** If the issue is something that can be fixed or improved, it may be worth bringing it up so that steps can be taken to address it.
- **Is bringing up the issue worth the potential consequences?** Consider whether the potential benefits of speaking up

outweigh the potential risks, such as damaging relationships or causing tension in the workplace.
- **Do you have a solution in mind?** If you can offer a solution or suggestion for how to address the issue, it may be more effective to bring it up in a constructive way.
- **Is the situation worth investing your emotional energy?** Some issues may not be worth the emotional energy and time it would take to address them, especially if they are unlikely to be resolved. In these cases, it may be better to let it go and focus on what you *can* control.

## How to handle this situation

Let's take the earlier example cited about a newly-implemented procedure that is not working out.

Before you complain about it, find out who came up with the new procedure and who made the decision to implement it. Was it your boss's idea? If so, you need to put together a solid case to support your concern before going to your boss. You should also think through how issues with the new procedure could be addressed by refining it.

You should then think about the *when, how and to whom* when raising your concern.

If you raise the concern too early, you may not have enough evidence or data to make a solid case. If you wait too long, you could be faulted for not having raised the issue earlier. Before making a complaint, it is often best to wait until you have gathered enough data (statistics, expert opinions and specific examples) to support your concerns.

Nobody likes negative surprises, especially your boss. If you notice a negative trend in quality or productivity with the new procedure, you should collect data and send it to your boss on a regular basis to keep him apprised of the evolving situation.

Keep your boss's personality in mind as you find the best way to phrase your concern. Try to phrase your complaint as impersonally as possible. The focus of the complaint should always be on the team's performance and the company's success. This makes your argument more compelling and deserving of prompt attention. It will seem less like a complaint and more like an opportunity to address an issue for the benefit of the organization.

You may face a situation where it is harder to speak up, such as if you are being subjected to harassment or discrimination. In these cases, it is important to seek support and guidance from a trusted HR representative. Also, keep in mind that for serious or complex issues, it may be necessary to follow your organization's formal complaint or grievance procedures.

# How To Stay True to Your Ethics and Principles at Work

> "Integrity is not a conditional word. It doesn't blow in the wind or change with the weather. It is your inner image of yourself, and if you look in there and see a man who won't cheat, then you know he never will."
> 
> *John D. MacDonald.*

It can feel like a harsh world these days for ethics and principles. The news is rife with headlines about fraud, cover-ups and corruption. It often feels as though we are surrounded by unethical entities and hypocritical leaders, preaching values they themselves fail to uphold. Despite this, there are still businesses and leaders who operate with integrity, honesty and trustworthiness, although they are seldom recognized for doing the right thing.

If you work for a medium-sized or large organization, your company probably has a process and set procedures for reporting ethical violations you may well be required to follow. Knowing about unethical or illegal behavior and keeping your mouth shut is being complicit. To quote *Law & Order*, you're an accessory after the fact, and you could both lose your job and face legal action. Report it.

It's trickier in small organizations, but the basic actions remain the same. If someone is behaving unethically, go to your boss, your boss's boss or the owner of the company. Accepting the behavior is the same as condoning it. Tell somebody who can do something about it.

Personal values and principles are not always so clear cut. You may find some behaviors unprofessional or personally offensive, but they might not be illegal or damaging to the business. Here, you have to make a judgment call about how to respond.

First, you have to determine if you're dealing with professional ethics or personal principles. Honesty, kindness, integrity, fairness, trustworthiness and loyalty are examples of personal principles and values. It's good to be honest; it's bad to lie. It's good to be kind to others; it's bad to be cruel to them.

Ethics, on the other hand, are more a question of right versus wrong. Often, they have important legal ramifications, especially in the workplace. It's bad to lie to your customers. It's wrong and illegal to cheat them out of their money.

Someone who mistreats their partner is unprincipled. Someone who steals from their company is unethical. A racist joke in the breakroom is unprincipled. Racist hiring practices are unethical. They might *all* offend you, but you may have to deal with them differently.

It's easy to become cynical, but as an individual with personal standards of behavior, it's crucial not to succumb to the negativity. You may not be able to right all the unethical behavior in the world, but you possess the power to create a positive impact in your own corner of the working world.

## How to handle this situation

No one wants to work in an environment that feels unsafe or emotionally toxic. Holding to a code of ethics—whether it's personal or set out by the business—helps you to maintain a level of order.

Reporting ethical violations is not about being a snitch; it's about acting responsibly and upholding ethical standards. It can be a challenging decision, especially if the violator is a friend or superior, but it's an essential step to ensure integrity and accountability in the workplace.

Create your own code of behavior. Define lines that you will *never* cross. Once you codify your personal values and principles, you can use them as a guide for decision-making and behavior. Take responsibility and hold yourself accountable for your actions and decisions. Don't compromise your values or principles for short-term gains or "in-the-moment" convenience. Instead, strive for consistency in your actions and decisions, regardless of the circumstances.

Feel free to share your code, but don't get caught up in proselytizing. You don't want to come across as self-righteous or preachy. You're not looking for converts—you can simply let people know how you intend to react to bad behavior. Adopt a tone of openness and understanding. You might say, "I'm happy to share my perspective, but I fully respect that everyone has their own set of values. My intention is not to persuade anyone to adopt my beliefs, but rather to be transparent about how I respond to actions that I find unacceptable." This approach emphasizes respect for diverse viewpoints while clearly communicating your personal stance.

Then walk your talk. If Janet in Operations tells offensive stories and jokes, let her know, calmly and firmly, that you don't appreciate the jokes and then walk away. Janet may not like it, but that's *her* issue. You're not keeping Janet from doing her job, you're following your own code of personal behavior.

Remember: your personal beliefs are your own. They're not your coworkers' or company's beliefs. If you simply can't or won't subordinate your beliefs to your professional duties, you should consider leaving the job. It's hard to do your best work when you are on the horns of this kind of dilemma.

Dealing with ethical violations can be difficult. Following your personal values and principles can take guts. The world and the working world will repeatedly test you. Sometimes the best you can do is fight to a draw. But you don't have to *lose*. You can function at your job and in the larger world and still look at yourself in the mirror each morning and respect who you see looking back at you.

# How To Respond When Others Violate Ethical Standards at Work

> "Ethics is knowing the difference between what you have a right to do and what is right to do."
> *Potter Stewart*

Dubious ethics make for great TV and movies. As humans, we seem to find unscrupulous villains, business executives and politicians wildly entertaining. However, in real life, dubious ethics and amoral behavior are a lot more problematic.

Most of the talk about unethical behavior at work focuses on major corporate scandals such as WorldCom or Tyco. Compared to what happened at Enron, stealing office supplies, inflating expense reports and skimming from the cash register seems like petty theft.

However petty, though, it still constitutes theft. Not only does it add up over time, but unethical behavior creates a culture of mistrust and normalizes offensive behavior. You might convince yourself that the company you work for can afford it. But would you really want to work at a place where cheating and stealing are considered unimportant?

## How to handle this situation

What looks like a minor offense can be the top of a slippery slope. Just like the TSA warning you hear at the airport, if you see something say something.

This means you have to decide who to say something to. This depends upon what unethical behavior you observe. Padding quarter-end sales stats is one thing; defrauding customers is another.

**What's the overall value and impact of what you know or suspect?** The answer to this question will go a long way in deciding how to proceed.

If the stakes are relatively low, talk to the offender first. Chances are he'll get defensive and deny his actions, but he'll also know that his unethical behavior is on the radar and if they continue, he runs the risk of losing his job.

In the case of repeat offenders or in seriously impactful situations, talk to your manager or HR. People who won't comply when confronted with their misdeeds are one thing. If they won't stop on their own, they need to be stopped by someone with the authority to stop them.

In all cases, protect yourself. The U.S. and most states have non-retaliation laws in place. Most midsize and large companies have policies in place to prevent retaliation. It's rare that you'll be faced with something like this, but if you are, take steps to protect yourself. Know your rights.

After all, you're the one acting ethically.

# How To Handle Gossip at Work

> "There is only one thing in life worse than being talked about, and that is *not* being talked about."
> *Oscar Wilde*

It's hard to imagine a workplace where people aren't chatting about what each other are up to, speculating on who's really up for that promotion or who might be hanging onto his job by a thread.

We're social animals—and we're not just curious about what is actually going on. We're looking for connection and validation. Engaging in gossip and rumor let us indulge in both.

*"Did you hear about Shelly in Customer Service? Well, let me tell you . . . "*
Not all gossip and rumors at work are negative. In companies where information tends to be closely guarded or at least poorly shared, informal passing of information can keep you in the loop. You may learn who landed a big account, why the CFO was in New York all week or what kinds of projects are getting approved.

Work gossip and rumor can also be malicious or at the least hurtful and counterproductive. It breeds discontent. It creates bad feelings and suspicion. It drives wedges between coworkers. It spreads lies and misinformation.

### How to handle this situation

The first step in handling gossip and rumor is to decide whether the gossip is malicious or positive.

Most everyone needs to vent now and then. When your coworker fumes about how Jim in Accounting sabotaged his presentation on purpose, he's angry and blowing off steam, not spreading rumors.

However, when comments leave the realm of work and move into people's private lives, it's time to draw the line. Hearing that Lisa got a raise is great. Hearing that she went out for drinks with a married coworker is not.

If the talk crosses the line into negativity or is potentially hurtful, it's time to confront the person spreading it.

If possible, pull the gossip aside and talk with them privately. You don't need to be combative or aggressive, but you do need to be firm. Explain how and why the talk is harmful and the possible consequences. Gossip and rumors can seriously derail someone's reputation and career.

If you're in a crowd of people chatting away maliciously, use redirection. *"You know, that's really interesting, but have you seen the new episode of The Mandalorian? I wasn't expecting that."* Sometimes the change will then happen naturally; sometimes people will get the idea and drop the gossip topic.

You're at work, so change the subject back to something work-related. The point is to make it known that you're not interested in whatever hot rumor is making the rounds.

If all else fails, walk away. You can try your best to change the talk around you, but there will be times when the battle is futile. If a stubborn band of coworkers is intent on discussing who's dating whom or which executive head might be next on the chopping block, you may not be able to dissuade them, no matter how many private talks and conversation deflectors you try.

Take the high road and disengage.

# How To Survive Office Politics

"Office politics are real, and dangerous. [But]… it's less about what other people are doing and more about how you respond."
*Joseph Grenny*

Office politics have been an issue for as long as humans have been working together. They can determine group status and power structures; who gets the glory and who gets the blame.

Office politics can feel slimy, unpleasant and toxic, but they're part of nearly every workplace. And while the ever-increasing movement toward remote and hybrid work has lessened breakroom gossip and elevator espionage, politics are still a part of the job.

Of course, office politics don't have to be all veiled, nefarious and evil. Lobbying for limited resources, putting in a good word for a colleague's promotion and making sure your supervisor's boss knows about your successful project aren't evil. But they're still politics.

*No one* likes workplace politics. They can be corrosive, disruptive and hurtful. They can stifle innovation and productivity. They cause stress and anxiety. Even people who are good at navigating office politics generally wish they didn't have to.

Everyone has to play politics at work. At least sometimes. But that doesn't mean you have to lower yourself into the trenches and declare political warfare. You *can* engage with the workplace politicians and still survive, perhaps even thrive.

## How to handle this situation

**First, assess the political situation and your reaction to it**. Step back and evaluate what happened or what's going on around you. When something happens that affects us, we tend to take it personally. The guy who ran the stop sign and crumpled your car fender may have wrecked your morning, but he didn't hit your car on purpose. Often negative office behavior isn't necessarily nefarious, it's simply ill-considered. You just happened to be present.

**Second, take a deep breath and keep your cool**. Some people thrive on drama and intrigue. You should try not to encourage them or worse, be one of them. How you react can either amplify the problem or help moderate it. Choose to be a moderator.

**Third, you must get comfortable with conflict**. It's a fact of life. Conflict forces people to think about solutions for resolving it. It challenges us to rise up and create, to think of new ways of doing things, because the old way may not work well enough anymore.

**Fourth, office politics aren't always inherently negative**. It's how they're used that makes the difference. Office politics are an informal, behind-the-curtain set of actions undertaken to get things done. So instead of using them for personal glory or power, choose to use them to get others to throw their weight behind your team's project. Use politics to get buy-in from the corner office to increase your budget. Use them to encourage cooperation and communication.

And be open about it. It's okay to say, "I need your support so we can succeed." It's okay to say, "I want to convince you to back this initiative because it will help grow revenue." It's even okay to say, "I want that promotion and here's why I should get it."

Form positive alliances. The idea that ignoring politics and focusing exclusively on your work will be enough to secure your job and career is, sadly, unrealistic. You need to invest some time and energy building connections that can see and champion your good work. Don't think of this as a distraction from your job, but simply another aspect of it.

And while shoring up allies is vital, don't forget about building working relationships with potential adversaries. You may not like them, but if you can work productively with them, it builds up your own political capital and increases your effectiveness.

**Fifth, strive to be open and honest with everyone you work with.** Office politics thrive on mistrust and depend on everyone being suspicious of everyone else. Your openness and honesty are only effective when their target is secrecy and mistrust. This honesty isn't intended to be selfish or manipulative. Think of it as *practicing* honesty in your dealings with your coworkers, not *using* it against your enemies.

**Sixth, take charge of your destiny.** If backstabbing offends you, don't engage in it. Like your grandma always said, if you can't say something nice, don't say anything at all. And that means not tacitly encouraging it by sitting idly by when others are being stabbed in the back.

If gossip is destroying working relationships, refuse to take part in it. If you've been part of cliques or conspiracies, gracefully bow out and walk away. Ease out negative politicians in your inner circles. You don't have to make a production number out of it. This doesn't mean that you can't be a safety valve for a friendly coworker who's blowing off steam, but you need to use your judgment. You know when things have moved on from "getting it off my chest" to character assassination. You know when it's time to change the subject or when it's time to move on to something productive.

Choose not to collude in office politics and focus on your goals and responsibilities instead. What most of us really want out of work is to do a good job and have it recognized and rewarded. We don't want cloak and dagger. We want to work hard, make a contribution, learn, grow and support ourselves and our families.

Ultimately, you can take heart knowing that you've moved on from the petty, underhanded behaviors of office politics. You're making yourself accountable and contributing to a more positive workspace.

Coping with office politics, whether onsite or remote, is less about what *others* are doing in the break room or behind the Zoom window and more about how *you* react to it.

# How To Handle Being Excluded at Work

> "All paradises, all utopias are designed by who is not there, by the people who are not allowed in."
> *Toni Morrison*

Most people remember a time or two from childhood when they stood waiting on the sidelines to be picked for a team. We remember the stress and humiliation it creates. For the kid whose name is called last comes the painful but unspoken message: nobody wanted you, but somebody got stuck with you.

No matter how old you are, it hurts when you discover you're being excluded by other people. FOMO is a real thing in the workplace too, and when it happens at work, it can have a negative effect on your job performance and your morale.

The most prevalent type of exclusion is social, where coworkers may ignore or avoid you, leave you off email chains or company communications or fail to include you in meetings or social gatherings.

## How to handle this situation

*Step back and examine the situation.*
Feeling excluded can cause past insecurities to resurface, so consider whether your feelings of rejection might just be emotional baggage you're still carrying around. Allow yourself some time to process your emotions. Once you've had some time to calm down and sort out how you're feeling, then you can find the best way to articulate it rationally and professionally.

If you feel excluded in social situations at work, reflect on your behavior. This isn't an exercise designed to get you to blame yourself;

it's an opportunity for self-improvement. Do you come across as approachable, or do you tend to keep to yourself and avoid eye contact? Even if you don't mean to, you might be giving off a vibe that makes others think you want to be left alone.

If you think people are misunderstanding who you really are, then be more mindful about how you come across.

*Confirm your reality.*
After reflecting on your situation, you may still come away with evidence that you're being excluded. If it's happened to you, it's very possible it's happening or has happened to others, so check in with colleagues to see if anyone can offer help. For example, if you're feeling excluded by one particular individual, ask a few colleagues if they've ever had any issues with that person. If a colleague says, *Oh yeah, Jim has his favorites and pretty much ignores everyone else,* then you know the problem lies with Jim rather than with you.

If you do reach out to others, you may not find anyone who confirms your feelings. People are often wrapped up in their own feelings and concerns in the workplace, so validation isn't a necessity. You can still get some guidance and perspective by asking them to put themselves in your place.

*Try talking to those who exclude you.*
This may be a little difficult to accomplish, considering the individual has been actively avoiding you. However, you can try to pull him aside after a meeting or in the break room.

Explain that you would like to eliminate whatever barrier exists between you and ask how to do it. You might get what you want: a truthful answer and a suggestion for how to fix things. Or you may get no useful response or worse, an outright denial that a problem exists or that you're just imagining it.

If that's the case, at least you've made the attempt. If things get worse and you need to speak to your manager or HR, you can let him know that you've already attempted to solve the problem yourself.

### Keep track of incidents.

If you're experiencing a clear pattern of ostracism, keep a record of the occurrences—including names, dates, details. If an incident is extreme, then getting comments from witnesses would also be useful. This is especially true if you suspect the reason you're being excluded has to do with your race, sex, gender identity or any other federally protected class.

### Build up your social network.

Workplaces can be as bad as middle school when it comes to cliques, and it's possible that you're being excluded because you're perceived to be different or not worthy of the *in* group. If you experience harassment or bullying or some other clear violation of workplace rules, you should take action with HR. But if people are just being childish, then at least you'll understand why they're excluding you.

Cultivate your friendships with colleagues to minimize your focus on being excluded. By establishing a positive and supportive social group, you'll boost your self-esteem, which will help you confidently navigate more difficult work relationships.

### Make a change.

If despite your best efforts you still feel excluded, it's time to take action. You can transfer to another position in the company or find a new job. If you opt for the latter, make sure you check into what potential employers say about culture and inclusion. Read reviews and social media postings to get insight from current and former employees. If you're going to make a switch, do everything you can to land in an inclusive culture where you're confident you can thrive.

# How To Handle Being Stereotyped at Work

*"Unity, not uniformity, must be our aim.*
*We attain unity only through variety.*
*Differences must be integrated, not annihilated, not absorbed."*
*Mary Parker Follett*

The biology of human beings allows for vast and rich variation in our world population. For many people, that uniqueness is something to be appreciated and valued. Sadly, for others, being different is viewed as undesirable, abnormal or against the natural order.

The wide variety of perspectives on the subject of what's normal or acceptable makes it impossible to fully eradicate bias and stereotyping. Fortunately we have federal and state laws that protect individuals from harassment—but stereotyping seldom rises to that level.

Stereotyping can often be subtle, creeping into conversations and taking us by surprise with words that feel like a sudden, hurtful slap. Maybe it's a remark stemming from the speaker's own unconscious bias, which comes from their life experiences and learned behaviors. Imagine you're in a meeting at work, and the team is discussing who should lead a new project that involves a lot of negotiation. One of your colleagues, perhaps without realizing, says, "Let's have John lead this project; as a guy he'll be better at managing tough negotiations."

This comment is an example of subtle (or maybe not so subtle) stereotyping. It's based on the unconscious bias that men are inherently better at certain tasks than women, a belief likely shaped by life experiences and societal influences. This kind of remark might not be overtly aggressive, but it can feel like a "sudden, hurtful slap" to the women in the room who are aware of the stereotype it perpetuates and the implicit gender bias it reflects.

## How to handle this situation

In the workplace, your employer is responsible for ensuring that employees receive anti-harassment training—and more importantly, that the workplace is a safe space. Unfortunately, when both subtle and overt stereotyping happens, it often falls to the victims to deal with the comments. Soon, the situation morphs into an internal battle between wanting to respond and fearing the fallout that may come from responding.

The safest approach is to respond respectfully and honestly in the hope that you can influence the people in your workplace without alienating them. Here are five steps that can help you build the skills needed to achieve that balanced response.

*Decide if it's worth responding.*

If you're accustomed to receiving unjust comments, it's likely that you automatically make a decision whether to react as soon as you hear them. Recognize that you are in control of whether you want to respond or not. Either way, it's okay. You are not responsible for educating other people all the time unless you choose to.

*Identify your core motivation.*

If you're going to respond to a stereotyping comment, then consider what you hope to get from your response.

- Are you hoping you'll attain a feeling of belonging?
- Are you seeking an honest and open conversation?
- Are you trying to prove that you're capable and worthy?

Whatever your core motivation, you want your words and actions to align to the message you're sending. When you remain calm and professional, you're more likely to capture their attention.

*Pay attention to your own communication style.*
Be the most aware when you're in a situation that makes you feel insecure. When you're judged as a stereotype, it's natural to want to immediately defend yourself. While it might feel good to erupt in the moment, chances are you'll wish you hadn't lost the chance to have a meaningful conversation when you've had time to think about the situation

Rather than immediately switching to a defensive posture, try to shift your mindset into one of inquiry. What caused this person to say what they did? What can you tell them that might make *them* think a little more about how *you* feel?

*Tell them your truth.*
People relate to stories, so let them hear a few of your own past experiences.

Begin by saying something such as, *I don't think you realize how that came across,* and relate other times when you've had similar things said to you. For someone who spoke from a place of unconscious bias, hearing more blatant examples of bias or stereotyping may give them clarity about why what they said was wrong.

By sharing your own experiences, you become living proof that the stereotype used against you doesn't align with who you are. You take a divisive issue and you attach it to a real person, not a political agenda.

*Remember that their perspective isn't your reality.*
Ultimately, you can't force other people to change. If the person in question continues to say and do hurtful things, remind yourself that their perspective is *not* the truth.

Sometimes, people use stereotypes as a way to support their view of the world or because it makes them feel superior to others. No matter what the reason, those words come from their feelings of insecurity or weakness.

# How To Handle a Workplace Bully

> "Not everyone has been a bully or the victim of bullies, but everyone has seen bullying. [In seeing it they have] responded to it by joining in or objecting, by laughing or keeping silent, by feeling disgusted, or feeling interested."
> *Octavia E. Butler*

Many of us have difficult memories of being bullied in our childhood. It can be painful to think back on them. But when you were in elementary school, bullies were usually only interested in taking your lunch money or calling you names on the school bus. Bullies at work, however, have refined tactics. The psychological and emotional fallout of their behavior has far greater impact. Their tactics can interfere with your ability to earn a living.

Workplace bullies exist at any level of an organization, and they generally fall into four types.

- **Aggressive communicators**: people who communicate hostility through any means.
- **Disparaging criticizers**: people who find fault with others and point it out publicly.
- **Information controllers**: people who withhold information or assistance to set others up to fail.
- **Back stabbers**: people who act loyal but who secretly undermine others.

Being bullied at work can be mentally and emotionally overwhelming, but you shouldn't just let it go. You have a right to a safe workplace.

## How to handle this situation

Here are seven specific suggestions to handle being bullied at work.

1. **Stand up for yourself.** Bullies are usually looking to be feared (which they mistakenly equate to being respected) and to get an emotional reaction. If you speak up and confront the bully as soon as you sense you're being mistreated, you send a strong message that you're not a good target. Just taking this step may cause the bully to back off because you're not reacting the way he wanted.
2. **Document everything.** Having a timeline and evidence will be crucial if you need proof later. Keep a detailed record every time you're bullied; write down when it happened, what was said, who was there, where it happened, how you reacted—anything and everything. If your work is being criticized, ensure you also save evidence of your work quality, including praise from clients, other managers or project stakeholders.
3. **Practice self-care.** Being exposed to frequent negative comments, anger or humiliation can make you feel embarrassed, erode your self-confidence and create a sense of instability about your job. Take steps to counteract that negativity. Confide in friends and family about what you're enduring. Do activities that make you happy and restore a sense of calm in your life. Take a walk, join an exercise class or try yoga. You should also consider seeking professional help from counselors who are trained to deal with trauma. They can help you manage your stress and advise you on next steps.
4. **Review your company policy.** If you're being bullied at work, check your company's policies to find out how to report it. Unlike harassment, bullying isn't illegal; however, many organizations rightly have a zero-tolerance policy.

5. **Speak with a manager.** Since managers can be the bullies in an organization, reporting your situation to a manager is tricky. If you're being bullied by your own manager, decide if there's another manager you can trust to help you. You probably want to avoid going to your boss's manager, especially if that person is the one who hired your boss. Then, choose your words carefully and present the situation from a neutral point of view. You can say, *"I've tried to resolve this situation in these ways and it hasn't helped, so I'm hoping you can provide some guidance."*

6. **Go to HR.** If you don't get help from a manager or you choose not to report the issue to management, your next option is HR. If your organization has an HR person responsible for employees and company culture, that's the best person to speak to. Be calm and professional in the conversation and present the situation as a business issue that costs the company in terms of productivity or morale issues. This is where your documentation is valuable because you'll have facts to back up your assertions.

7. **Find another job.** In many cases, people who are bullied end up leaving their job—or worse, they end up getting fired because their performance suffers due to the trauma of persistent bullying. If your bullying situation doesn't get resolved because your company culture isn't equipped to deal with it, then it might be best to cut your losses and begin looking for a new job. Find an employer who considers employee well-being a cornerstone of their culture and put the bully in your rearview mirror.

# How To Handle Harassment at Work

*"One's dignity may be assaulted, vandalized and cruelly mocked, but it can never be taken away unless it is surrendered."*
*Michael J. Fox*

If you like pop culture and entertainment, you might remember the scene in *The Devil Wears Prada* when Miranda harasses Andy about her lack of understanding and appreciation for the fashion industry. Or maybe you remember scenes from *The Office* when Michael Scott harasses Pam Beasley.

Although played up for laughs in these scenes, harassment in the workplace is no joking matter. Workplace harassment can take many forms—including being verbally or physically threatening, leering or staring, bullying and belittling.

Any behavior that makes you feel uncomfortable, threatened or unsafe is not acceptable in the workplace. Your employer has a responsibility to create a safe and respectful work environment, and as an employee, you have the right to speak up if you experience or witness harassment.

## How to handle this situation

Here are five steps to follow if you experience harassment on the job.

### *Speak up to the harasser.*

This is a good first step—as long as the behavior isn't abusive or sexual in nature. For situations where you're the victim of unkind comments, foul language or humiliation, try to resolve it directly with the harasser. A positive response varies greatly depending on the individual and their personality, the relationship between the bully and the victim and the context in which the bullying occurs. Some bullies do respond to a direct appeal, especially if they were unaware of the impact of their actions or if they respect the victim's assertiveness. However, others might not be receptive to such a plea, potentially even escalating their behavior in response to being confronted.

When someone's behavior crosses the line, initiate a conversation to explain that the behavior is unwelcome and you don't want it to continue. You don't need to be threatening; just be clear and straightforward. For example, you can say "I'm not comfortable with your comments/actions. Please stop immediately." Or, "Your behavior toward me is inappropriate. I ask that you respect my boundaries."

If your harasser seems contrite, then you could suggest you both work together to resolve any differences and aim for a better working relationship. If you're met with resistance or denials, it's best to restate that you expect the behavior to stop and be prepared to take the next step if the behavior continues. You might say, "I'd like this behavior to stop, or I will need to take further action." It's important to assess the situation carefully. If the behavior is abusive or if there's a risk of retaliation, it might be safer and more effective to seek assistance from a manager, human resources professional, or another appropriate authority.

*Document all instances.*

Even if you think that talking to your harasser has solved the problem, it's still a wise idea to keep a record of the incidents, including details about what was said or done, who else was there and when it happened. Include details about how you responded to the incident. Keeping track of the early details shows the pattern of behavior and how it has escalated.

If you're tempted to secretly record your harasser, it may be unlawful depending on the state in which you work. It's best to document things in written format, and if you have witnesses, ask them if they would be willing to document what they saw.

*Report the behavior.*
If you are threatened, physically or sexually abused or if you feel unsafe around the other person, report it immediately.

Your organization should have a policy for reporting incidents of harassment. If it doesn't, report the incident to your manager (only if they are not the harasser) or go straight to HR. Harassment in the workplace is a serious issue, and it will receive prompt attention.

*Seek additional support.*
Gather your own support system who can sit in meetings with you and hear what you're being told. This is especially important if the meeting will be upsetting for you.

For incidents that were abusive or threatening, consider seeking counseling. Your employer may even have an employee assistance program that can recommend counselors.

*Carry on as best you can.*
You may find it difficult to go to work each day, even if your harasser has been dismissed from the company. You may be on the receiving end of some whispers or unfriendly looks, especially from the harasser's friends.

You don't owe anyone an explanation.

It's to your benefit to show up every day and continue to do the best job you can. Try to reestablish your regular routine. Seek out your work friends and ask for their support. Getting back to the same reliable and productive employee you've always been will quiet the gossip and put the negativity into your past.

# How To Overcome Embarrassment at Work

> "I learned that there's a certain character that can be built from embarrassing yourself endlessly. If you can sit happy with embarrassment, there's not much else that can really get to you."
>
> *Christian Bale*

All of us have been in an embarrassing situation at work at least once. After rushing to work in the morning heat, you realize that you forgot to put on deodorant. During the team meeting you start to feel self-conscious as you notice your shirt becoming soaked with sweat. You try to keep your arms down but notice a few awkward stares. You feel your face flush with embarrassment.

Let's look at the difference between being embarrassed and being ashamed.

Shame is what you feel when you've done something egregious and is generally associated with willfully doing something wrong or wildly inappropriate. Think of things such as mocking a coworker in a meeting in front of the rest of the team. You *should* feel ashamed.

Embarrassment is nearly always the result of inadvertently doing something momentarily humorous or briefly mortifying. It usually has only short-term effects, if any. Think of things such as realizing your fly was open while presenting in a team meeting. You'll *probably* feel foolish, but you don't need to—at least, not for long.

## How to handle this situation

When something embarrassing happens, don't freak out. If you treat it casually, so will most everyone else. Most embarrassing situations at work pass quickly.

Acknowledge it, own it and if possible, laugh at yourself. You should always be willing to laugh at your inadvertent goofs. It's charming, it's disarming, it's humanizing. If you don't let them laugh with you, they'll laugh at you. And that's far more embarrassing than whatever you probably just did.

It's better to have your colleague Jack say to you, *"Remember that time you tripped on the stairs when you were called up to receive your employee of the month award?"* rather than to have Jack remind the whole team, *"Remember when Sheila tripped on the stairs to get her award and then angrily ran out of the room?"*

We've all been there: tripping in the hallway, sneezing loudly on Zoom, calling Raheem by Ed's name, making a joke about New Jersey in front of Kelly, who proudly hails from Hoboken. Everybody laughs, then everybody moves on.

It's certainly no fun to embarrass yourself no matter where it happens. It may *feel* worse at work, in a meeting, in front of your boss. Yes, they may all laugh. Laugh right along with them, because they've all done something similar. Put it behind you and move forward.

# How To Talk to Your Boss About Your Mental Health

> "When you struggle with your mental health, it doesn't just impact how you feel. It impacts your physical health as well. It impacts how you show up at work."
> *Dr. Vivek Murthy*

Maybe you've always been a strong performer but lately, you've been feeling overwhelmed and anxious at work. Your sleep is affected, you're finding it difficult to concentrate and you've even experienced a few panic attacks.

Despite your struggles, you try to hide your mental health challenges from your colleagues and boss, worrying that it may negatively impact your career. But the pressure of trying to appear normal is taking a toll—and you find yourself calling in sick more often. You wonder when the right time is to talk to your boss about the situation.

Mental health is a legitimate health concern. In fact, mental illnesses are among the most common health conditions in the United States. According to the CDC, more than 50 percent of Americans will be diagnosed with a mental illness or disorder at some point during their lifetime. Still, nearly 60 percent of employees have never spoken to anyone at work about their mental health status.

### How to handle this situation

Here's the hard truth: the only way to know how each of us is feeling is by talking to each other.

You may feel that talking about your struggles makes you seem weak, but it takes a strong person to admit their vulnerabilities and challenges. Open communication with your boss can help you receive the necessary accommodations or resources to perform at your best.

It can also break the stigma around mental health and encourage a more supportive and understanding workplace culture.

Studies show that people are twice as likely to be willing to give support for a colleague's mental health than talk about their own challenges. Below, I've created a handy checklist to follow when deciding why, when and how you should talk with your boss about your mental health struggles.

- ☑ Do some self-reflection and prepare yourself to consider what you're experiencing and the impact that your struggles are having on your job performance.
- ☑ Think about how much you need to share in order to achieve the outcome you're looking for.
- ☑ Write down exactly what you want to say, even if it's just a list of bullet points.
- ☑ Choose the best time and place for the meeting. Always choose a private location and at time when your boss can give you their full attention.
- ☑ Gather your courage and start talking. Speak your truth, as concisely as possible, using your prepared notes or straight from your heart and include how issues are impacting your job.
- ☑ Move on to specifics about the accommodations you're asking for.
- ☑ Give your manager some time to work with HR and senior management before getting back to you with options or next steps.
- ☑ Set a time to follow up, and consider setting up a regular check-in time.

Now that you've opened the conversation, it won't feel as stressful to keep your boss informed about your progress and future development.

Speaking up about your mental health challenges takes courage and strength, but it also shows your boss that you are committed to taking care of yourself and being the best version of yourself at work.

Remember, your mental health and well-being is just as important as your physical health, and there's no shame in seeking support. Seeking support is a sign of strength, not weakness. Write that down.

# How To Handle Anxiety About Potential Job Loss

"There is only one way to happiness and that is to cease worrying about things which are beyond the power of our will."
*Epictetus*

When you read about rising inflation rates, an increase in the unemployment index or significant lay-offs at high-profile organizations, you might feel anxious and insecure about your own employment.

While you might not like how reading or hearing about negative economic news keeps you up at night, a low level of anxiety can offer some benefits. Some anxiety enables you to direct your attention to what is most important. It can help you push yourself to accomplish more at work.

However, if anxiety about the economy or an impending economic recession is left unchecked, it can distract you at work and make achieving your goals harder.

### How to handle this situation

I've found four effective approaches to help manage the anxiety about impending recession and the potential for job loss.

*Acknowledge your feelings.*
It's normal to have some anxiety about what is happening in the economy or how a recession might negatively impact your job security. Allow yourself to experience the emotions; don't try to suppress them. It can be helpful to share your fears with family, friends and trusted coworkers who might share similar fears. You will realize that you are not alone in your feelings.

*Focus on what you can control*

You are not in control of what happens in the economy or how events will unfold. You're not in control of your company's financial vulnerabilities. Worrying about them robs you of the energy you need to be productive in your job. Focus on what you *can* control, which is the progress you make at work every day and your own performance. Don't think too far ahead. Take the situation one week, even one day, at a time.

*Don't catastrophize.*

Remind yourself that there is a difference between what's possible and what is likely to happen. In most circumstances, the worst-case scenario is *not* the most likely.

There is a possibility that the organization you work for will be negatively impacted in an economic downturn. If that happens, it is possible that the company might need to lay off some employees. If there is a layoff, your job might be affected. All of those events are possible, but are they likely? Try not to let your mind rush to the worst-case scenario. Check your negative thought patterns. Think about the best-case and likely-case scenarios too.

Maybe your company will weather an economic downtown better than the competition. Maybe your company will implement a hiring freeze or eliminate bonuses instead of laying people off. Maybe the department you work in will be spared from experiencing any lay-offs.

*Practice gratitude.*

If you are worried about an economic recession and the prospect of losing your job, ask yourself what you would still be grateful for even *if* and that's a big if, the worst-case scenario comes to pass. Reflect on all the positive things that you would still have in your life.

Whether it is your health, family, friends, pets, hobbies, future job prospects or your education, we can always be grateful even when we face a significant challenge. That's the power of gratitude.

# How To Make Two Jobs Work for You

> "Good things happen to those who hustle."
> *Anais Nin*

Did you know that 44 percent of Americans work at least one extra job to make ends meet? On average, side hustlers spend thirteen hours a week on their second job.

Juggling two jobs at the same time can feel like a never-ending balancing act, with each role pulling you in different directions. From the rise in your stress levels to the feeling of accomplishment, there are both challenges and rewards to working two jobs. But how do you manage the demands of both employers *and* keep the rest of your life in balance?

### How to handle this situation

Let's explore seven key considerations that can help you successfully integrate a second job into your life.

1. **Be thoughtful in choosing your second job**. You should seriously contemplate whether you're physically, mentally and emotionally able to take on a second job, even as a part-time gig. Your current and prospective employers will expect a certain level of work from you, so you need to seriously consider what you're capable of handling.
2. **Examine your reason for wanting a second job**. Is it to earn additional money? If so, consider finding a job where you can apply your current skills to the new job. You may be able to secure a higher hourly rate. If you're trying to acquire new skills, then you'll want to look for a job that aligns with your career interests.

3. **Don't put your primary job at risk**. Before you accept a second job, ensure you're not putting your primary job in jeopardy. Review the paperwork and look for any rules regarding conflicts of interest. The best way to convince your primary employer that you're still committed is to make sure there's no change in the hours or quality of your work.
4. **Become a time management expert**. When you're working multiple jobs, time becomes your opponent. In order to prevail, you have to manage the hours in your day. The most efficient way to do that is to find a good time-management app. You'll end up with a clear view of your available time and responsibilities for each week, and then you can plan around them accordingly. You may be busy, but you'll be organized.
5. **Make self-care a priority**. If you don't prioritize your physical and mental health, then your top-notch time management skills won't matter. After a while, your body won't let you get away with ignoring its basic needs of food and sleep.
6. **Schedule at least one full day off from work every 60 days so you can let your mind rest**. Consider regular meals, adequate sleep and physical exercise as non-negotiables in your schedule. It might mean your meals are at unusual times, or your workout time is now at the crack of dawn instead of after work. Your bedtime might shift too. Finally, don't overlook the other crucial part of self-care: enjoying time with family and friends. They are your support network, and you need to nurture those relationships as much as they nurture you.
7. **Keep an eye on your financial picture**. You're working a second job for a reason and if it's to pay off debt or pay your monthly bills, then you already have a plan for the extra money when it hits your bank account. Make it a habit that as soon as you get paid, you pay somebody else. Also keep an eye on the cost of your second job. If you find

that you're putting more than half your paycheck into your gas tank or other expenses such as child care, then you need to reconsider whether that particular second job is the best one for you.

Ideally, taking on a second job is just a temporary means to help you solve a money problem. Good money management will help you reach your financial goals quickly and perhaps allow you to leave your second job and regain some leisure time.

# How To Cope When You Survive a Layoff

> "Storms don't come to teach us painful lessons,
> rather they are meant to wash us clean."
> *Shannon L. Alder*

Layoffs, especially widespread layoffs, create an enormous amount of turmoil in an organization. The entire staff waits to learn their fate. During that time, workers feel anxiety regardless of the outcome.

Many long-standing relationships and vast amounts of institutional knowledge are lost with each person who packs up his desk and walks out the door. It's life-changing for those who are laid off.

Organizations typically offer support and resources to help ease the sting. If you're one of those who were retained, your experience will be jarring in a whole different way. You're in a comfortably familiar workplace but friends are gone and desks are empty. A terrible storm has blown through and changed the landscape . . . forever.

There's a name for the way you feel: survivor's guilt. It's not uncommon. Not knowing why you were retained while others were let go can make you feel vulnerable. You may even fear that the company made a mistake by keeping you, because lots of people who got laid off had more skills or more experience than you.

## How to handle the situation

You can navigate your way through survivor's guilt and come out better on the other side.

1. **Do your best to stay calm**. After surviving a layoff, your anxiety and stress levels are bound to be higher than usual, so seek out ways to help yourself relax. Sign up for a yoga or

meditation class. Get a massage. Go for a swim. Find a quiet spot, close your eyes and focus on breathing.

2. **Understand that it's okay to feel guilty.** When you survive a layoff, other people may say things such as, *"Wow, you're lucky it wasn't you."* Yes, you might feel lucky in the sense that you still have a job, but you may also feel guilty that you were spared. Your feelings of loss, sadness and guilt are appropriate. Don't try to push them down or ignore them because the longer you refuse to acknowledge them, the longer they'll eat away at you.

3. **Be strategic with your workload.** Given that your organization's workforce has been reduced, it's likely your workload will increase. Your manager will make decisions about how to divide the work, so it's a good idea to do some strategic thinking and prepare yourself for that conversation. Figure out how many responsibilities you can realistically manage while still meeting your performance goals. Put together your game plan and make sure you explain your reasoning for what you're proposing. Don't go in with a fixed idea of what you're willing to take—you're not haggling with a car salesman. By choosing to negotiate fairly, you show your manager that you're very interested in staying on and know what you're capable of achieving.

4. **Disconnect your self-esteem from your organization.** Your self-esteem can take a big hit during a layoff, even if you're a survivor. A simple counteraction is to not let your job define you. Instead, find other things in your life that boost your self-esteem. If you're an occasional runner, sign up to run a half marathon and train for it. If you play a musical instrument or sing, get up on stage during open mic night. You're more than your job, so build your sense of value through the things that truly matter to you.

5. **Build your skills and your network.** Consider adding a few credentials and certifications to your resume. It's also a good time to go through your contacts and broaden your network. Get in touch with some of your former colleagues who are active in the job market and offer to be a personal reference. You never know—the next opportunity to advance your career might come from a former colleague who tips you off to a new position because you helped him land one.
6. **Move from uncertainty to opportunity.** Layoffs tend to be a broad stroke, typically focused on realigning the company's cost and organizational structures—not a careful selection process for eliminating jobs. Once revenue starts to recover and customers are buying again, new positions will start to open up. Keep an eye on your employer's job listings. You may see something in another department that sounds like a great next step.

Surviving a layoff may initially knock you down, but you now know what it takes to not only recover, but to thrive.

# How To Cope With a Beloved Team Member's Departure

"*When Devi left, everybody else started thinking about it, too. It wasn't that she was so good at her job, even though she was. It wasn't that she was always able to lift everybody's mood simply by walking into the room or turning on her mic and camera, though she did. It wasn't just that she was unfailingly kind, funny, and supportive, though she was all of those things.*

*It was that she felt like the heart and soul of the team. When she left for that job in Atlanta, it's like she took all of the oxygen with her. It was like the whole team went into mourning.*"

If it's lucky, every team has someone who becomes everyone's favorite. Neil and Krystal can barely tolerate each other, but they *both* loved Devi.

However, when that person leaves, there's bound to be fallout, sadness and a sense of loss. That's natural. Remember that she didn't leave you, she left the job, the company or maybe the workforce in general. Regardless of the reason, it's important to keep this in mind, as well as a few other things.

## How to handle this situation

- **Don't take it out on the person leaving**. Keep the disappointment and bitterness to yourself. Assuming that leaving is *her* choice, be happy for her, offer congratulations and focus on all she brought to your work life.
- **Be part of the going away celebration, if there is one**. Your teammate is probably going to miss you too. Let her leave with a sense of warmth and how much she's appreciated, not how much she'll be missed.

- **Don't do anything rash**. No matter how much gloom settles over the team, remember that it will eventually pass. Let yourself go through a period of mourning before you take any other action. Don't let your sadness and frustration lead you to make any rash work or career decisions that you may regret later. Bad times don't last.
- **Support each other**. You're probably not the only one grieving. Share stories and memories with your fellow mourners. Laugh together about that time when Jack came to work in a Cookie Monster costume. Remember that time on the video call when Carol did one of her standup comedy routines. If someone doesn't want to share or reminisce, be okay with it. He isn't being cold, he's experiencing the loss in his own way. Everyone grieves differently.
- **Welcome the new person with warmth and respect**. The new person is probably going to be nervous. Help him feel at home. Comparing him to someone he's likely never met is not going to do that. You don't have to hide your appreciation and affection for your departed colleague, but muzzle it a little when the new person's around. Show some restraint no matter how sad or frustrated you feel about your loss.
- **If your now-former-teammate meant something to you outside of work, make the effort to keep in touch**. A lot of people we get close to at work quickly fade into a warm memory. For many of us a close working relationship doesn't translate into a close long-term relationship outside of work. And no matter how much you may not want it to happen, without the commonality of the job, these friendships can fall away.

Everyone processes loss differently. Some people will be morose. Some will seem to shrug it off and move on quickly. Whatever way you cope with the loss of your teammate, remember that the emotions you feel are *yours*. And so are the happy memories you shared. You'll always have those to reflect on.

# Index

## A

abrasiveness, of management, 215–218
accountability, verifying, 304
achievements
   monitoring, 323–325
   showcasing your, 247–249
   tracking your, 251
achievers, as a working style, 26
action plans
   creating, 408
   feedback and, 89–90
actionable examples, in feedback, 246
active listening skills, as a foundational skill for attention to detail, 64, 65
activities
   finding, 377
   outside of work for relationship-building with peers, 124–125
adaptability, at new roles, 363–364
advice, requesting from toxic co-workers, 167
advocacy
   about, 227–228
   asking for feedback from bosses, 242–244
   asking for promotions, 250–252
   asking for raises, 253–256
   asserting yourself, 232–234

advocacy (*continued*)
   being your authentic self, 229–231
   gaining respect, 235–238
   getting more constructive feedback, 245–246
   managing not getting promotions, 257–258
   managing someone taking credit for your work, 261–263
   managing unfair treatment, 259–260
   playing up achievements, 247–249
   preventing unfair blame, 264–266
   taking initiative in performance appraisal process, 239–241
affirming yourself, 171
after-work ritual, developing, 402–403
aggressive communicators, as workplace bullies, 430
all or nothing thinking, as a cognitive distortion, 73, 75
alliances, forming at new roles, 362
alternatives, decision-making and, 51
amplifying your game
   about, 33
   demonstrating charisma, 67–69
   facing uncertainty, 35–37
   getting to the root of problems, 47–49

453

amplifying your game (*continued*)
  learning from failure, 41–43
  making sound decisions, 50–54
  managing disappointing news, 38–40
  owning the details, 64–66
  owning your mistakes, 44–46
  responding to questions, 58–60
  speaking up in meetings, 61–63
  taking initiative, 55–57
analytical skills, as a foundational skill for attention to detail, 64, 66
anecdotes, demonstrating charisma by using, 68
Angelou, Maya, 67, 281
anxiety
  about potential job loss, 441–442
  managing, 395–397
  urgent work and, 389
anxiety-response ritual, 396–397
apologies, 234
appearance, when meeting colleagues for the first time, 184
appreciation, showing, 225, 283–284
arguments
  effectiveness of, 158–159
  persuasive, 251
assertive modesty, 262
assertiveness, 232–234
attention to detail, 64–66
attention-getting statement, to help management listen to you, 204

attitude
  demonstrating charisma with a positive, 67
  fear of trying new things and, 92
  reflecting on your, 345
authentic self, being your, 229–231
awareness, of nonverbal signals, 118

# B

back stabbers, as workplace bullies, 430
behaviors
  changing, 94–97, 118
  documenting, 407
"beyonds," self-doubt and, 80
black hat, in six thinking hats technique, 53, 54
blame, preventing unfair, 264–266
blue hat, in six thinking hats technique, 54
body language, 233
boredom, managing job-related, 336–338
boss issues. *See* management
boundaries
  creating for colleagues, 138–140
  maintaining, 231
  recognizing crossed, 162
  setting clear, 130, 149, 180, 330, 340, 375
  setting for dating coworkers, 177
  setting physical, 115
bragging, jealousy and, 225

## Index

breaking barriers
- about, 71
- accepting less than perfection, 82–84
- becoming more confident, 104–106
- being patient, 111–113
- being receptive to feedback, 88–90
- changing behaviors that hold you back, 94–97
- changing others' perceptions of you, 117–119
- developing new work habits, 99–100
- eliminating negative thought patterns, 73–78
- finding a sense of purpose, 101–103
- keeping your commitments, 107–108
- letting go of what other people think, 85–87
- maintaining composure, 109–110
- overcoming fear of trying new things, 91–93
- overcoming self-doubt, 79–81
- succeeding as an introvert, 114–116

breaks
- outside, 403
- taking, 400–401

Buffett, Warren, 281

burnout
- managing during remote work, 402–403
- steps to reduce, 398–401
- urgent work and, 389

business hours, setting formal, 402
busy times, getting through, 329–332

## C

calendars
- organizing, 314
- setting up access to invitations, 358

calming your mind, 392–393
calming yourself, practicing, 110
career aspirations, in performance appraisal, 240

career growth/progression
- about, 267–268
- becoming an intrapreneur, 295–297
- building personal power, 289–291
- capturing attention of senior executives, 278–280
- challenging workplace status quo, 292–294
- finding mentors, 281–285
- growing in a dead-end job, 298–300
- identifying hidden keys to success, 271–272
- increasing visibility, 286–288
- intelligence, 269–270
- keeping skills current, 273–275
- in performance appraisal, 240
- selling your ideas, 276–277

Career Limiting Move (CLM), 276
career path, for advancement, 353
catastrophizing, 442

challenges
   for roles, 352
   seeking new, 298–299
   tackling, 10–11
   taking on new, 20
challenging conversations, engaging in, 135–137
changes, implementing, 217–218, 426
charisma, 33, 67–69
chat functionality, in video conferences, 62
checklists, 100
clarity
   for conflict resolution, 136
   delivering in meetings, 61
Clinton, Bill, 67
closed-ended promises, 108
cognitive distortions, negativity and, 73–78
collaboration
   with others, 24–26
   skills needed for, 25
colleagues. *See* coworker dynamics
comments, strategizing in meetings, 62
commitments
   demonstrating, 279
   maintaining, 107–108
common ground
   finding with new management, 196
   identifying areas of, 134

communication
   about urgent work, 389
   as an introvert, 116
   consistency of, 124
   with facts, 210
   frequency of, 124
   with lazy colleagues, 145–146
   with management, 193
   for relationship-building with peers, 124
   styles of, 429
commute, planning when meeting colleagues for the first time, 184
companies, switching, 348
company intelligence, activating, 269–270
company policy, in workplace bullies, 431
company purpose, connecting with your, 19
company-sponsored events, attending for relationship-building with peers, 124
compensation, negotiating, 349, 354–356
competencies, developing relevant, 289–290
composure, maintaining, 109–110
compromise, conflict resolution through, 134
conclusions, jumping to, as a cognitive distortion, 74, 76

Index 457

confidence
- building, 104–106
- delivering in meetings, 61
- demonstrating charisma by projecting, 68

conflict
- engaging in challenging conversations, 135–137
- identifying type of, 133
- resolving, 28, 156–159
- resolving with colleagues, 132–134
- in team settings, 24–25

conformity. *See* status quo

connections
- with people outside work, 373
- staying connected, 403

conscientiousness
- developing grit and, 8
- of employees, 15–17

consequences, about urgent work, 389

consistency, perceptions and, 119

contrasts, demonstrating charisma by using, 68

contributions, reflecting on, 253–254

control
- focusing on what you can, 442
- lack of, 393
- seizing, 399

conversations, about toxic coworkers, 165

coping skills
- for managing annoying colleagues, 142
- for managing toxic coworkers, 168

courage, developing grit and, 7

coworker dynamics
- about, 121–122
- as allies in meetings, 62–63
- for being a conscientious employee, 17
- building relationships with peers, 20, 123–125
- collaboration with coworkers, 24–26
- constructive feedback from coworkers, 246
- counteracting negativity, 153–155
- creating boundaries for chatty colleagues, 138–140
- deepening workplace relationships, 126–128
- engaging in challenging conversations, 135–137
- getting on same page with coworkers, 132–134
- introducing yourself to, 358
- maintaining professional relationships with personal friends, 129–131
- managing annoying coworkers, 141–143
- managing conflict, 156–159
- managing coworker gossip, 151–152

coworker dynamics (*continued*)
  managing coworkers always asking for help, 148–150
  managing coworkers who dislike you, 160–162
  managing dating a coworker, 175–178
  managing jealousy of coworkers, 169–171
  managing slacker coworkers, 144–147
  managing toxic coworkers, 163–168
  managing work when they quit, 333–335
  meeting colleagues for the first time, 183–184
  meeting virtually, 185–187
  mending relationships, 172–174
  priorities of, 358
  resolving conflict with, 132–134
  support from, 210
  switching from buddy to boss, 179–182
  talking to, 405
credit
  misassigned, 261–263
  sharing, 225, 249
critical job elements, in performance appraisal, 240
cultural expectations, aligning to at new roles, 363
cultural fit, 348–349
culture of inclusivity and inquiry, creating, 180
curiosity, showing, 296
custodians, as a working style, 26

## D

data gathering, 385
dating coworkers, 175–178
dead-end jobs, growing in, 298–300
deadlines
  delivering on, 28
  meeting, 320–322
decision-making
  about new assignments, 386–387
  for new taking positions, 345–350
  tips for successful, 50–54
defending yourself, from toxic coworkers, 166
detail, attention to, 64–66
devices, changing, 403
digital distractions, disabling, 312, 314
directness, for conflict resolution, 136
disappointing news, handling with grace, 38–40
discipline, approaching new ideas with, 297
discomfort, tolerance for, 93
discounting positives, as a cognitive distortion, 74, 76
disparaging criticizers, as workplace bullies, 430

documenting
　bullying situations, 431
　harassment, 434
　issues with toxic coworkers, 166
　success, 263
　unfair treatment, 260
　your work, 265
downtime, scheduling regular, 115
dress, confidence and, 105

# E

effect-cause analysis, 49
effective arguments, 158–159
efficiency, focusing on, 341
ego, appealing to a colleagues, 161–162
Eisenhower Matrix, 318, 341
emails, responding to, 315
embarrassment, handling, 436–437
emotional expressiveness, demonstrating charisma by showing, 68
emotional reasoning, as a cognitive distortion, 74, 76–77
emotional self-control, demonstrating charisma by maintaining, 69
emotional sensitivity, demonstrating charisma by showing, 68
emotional state, conflict and, 133–134
emotions
　addressing your, 312
　in arguments, 158
　controlling, 12–14, 234
　swallowed, 164–165

empathy
　for abrasive management, 216
　from management, 209–211
employees, conscientiousness of, 15–17
empowerment
　of colleagues, 149–150
　of teammates, 28
entrepreneurial mindset, 296
equitable treatment, 400
ethics
　conflict and, 156
　responding to violations of, 417–418
　staying true to, 414–416
evidence, gathering, 293
excluded, handling being, 424–426
expectations
　clarifying, 306–308
　clarifying for new roles, 357
　realistic, 284
　resetting with bosses, 376
　for roles, 351
　setting clear, 180, 390
　setting realistic, 113
experience, in performance appraisal, 240
extroverts, 114–115

# F

face-saving, in arguments, 158
failure
　embracing for growth mindset, 4

failure (*continued*)
  learning from, 41–43
  negative aspects of past, 83
family, support from, 105
fears
  acknowledging your, 290
  examining your, 230
  overcoming, 91–93
feedback
  asking for from management, 242–244
  constructiveness of, 245–246
  encouraging unbiased, 118
  establishing goals to address, 258
  from managers, 274
  for mistakes, 45–46
  negative, 240
  in performance appraisal, 241
  receptiveness to, 88–90
feelings, acknowledging, 441
fence-mending, in arguments, 159
files, setting up access to, 358
finances, well-being and, 373
fishbone diagrams, 48–49
Five Whys analysis, 47–49
flexing, 26
focusing
  maintaining, 314–316
  on what you can control, 442
  on work, 165
  on your team, 249
  on yourself, 170–171
follow-up
  in performance appraisal, 241
  showing, 283–284
foundational skills, for attention to detail, 64–66
freelance work, 299–300
friendliness, for relationship-building with peers, 123–124
friends
  defining workplace friendships, 130
  managing professional relationships with, 129–131
  support from, 105
fulfillment, finding in your work, 101–103

# G

Game Changers
  about, 1
  becoming a conscientious employee, 15–17
  becoming a proactive networker, 30–32
  being a team player, 27–29
  being open to others' ideas, 21–23
  collaborating with others, 24–26
  controlling emotions, 12–14
  developing grit, 6–9
  embracing growth mindsets, 3–5
  finding daily purpose, 18–20
  handling everyday challenges, 10–11
Gandhi, Mohandas, 67

Index   461

gaslighting, from management, 212–214
Gates, Bill, 6, 281
goals
　confirming joint, 134
　designing, 83
　establishing to address feedback, 258
　for new roles, 352
　prioritizing, 28
　for teams, 353
goal-setting clarity
　abrasive management and, 216
　for being a conscientious employee, 17
Google Workspace, 325
gossip
　avoiding when meeting colleagues for the first time, 184
　from colleagues, 151–152
　managing, 419–420
　managing annoying colleagues and, 143
gracefully losing, in arguments, 159
gracefulness, when not receiving a promotion, 257–258
grass is greener, as a cognitive distortion, 74–75, 78
gratitude
　practicing, 171, 442
　showing, 127
green hat, in six thinking hats technique, 53, 54
greeting people, 126
grit, developing in your personal life, 6–9
grit scale, 8
ground rules, setting clear, 330
grounding yourself, 36
group spirit, improving, 400
growth mindset
　embracing a, 3–5
　maintaining, 290

# H

habits
　developing new, 98–100
　modifying, 314
harassment, handling, 433–435
hardware, setting up access to, 358
harmonizers, as a working style, 26
haters, dialing down, 87
help
　asking for, 11, 309–310
　offers to, 284
high road, taking with colleagues, 162
high-impact tasks, prioritizing 341
honesty, in feedback, 88–89
hooks, finding, 62
hours, number worked, 339–342
human resources (HR)
　consulting with, 211, 214, 432
　unfair treatment and, 260
humanity, 230–231
hypotheticals, 36

## I

"I" statements, 233
ideas, selling at work, 276–277
impatience, acknowledging, 112
improvement, identifying opportunity for, 293
incidents, tracking, 426
inclusivity, culture of, 180
industry networking, 299
industry skills, 274
industry standard, for salary, 254
influence, sharing your, 225
information
    acquiring for decision-making, 51
    bringing to meetings, 63
information controllers, as workplace bullies, 430
information-sharing, with teammates, 28
initiative, taking, 33, 55–57, 234, 239–241
inner critic, 86–87
innovators, as a working style, 26
inquiry, culture of, 180
integrating, into teams at new jobs, 365–367
intent
    awareness of, 118
    understanding, 60
interactions
    changing your, 345–347
    with management, 357

internal network, as a key to success, 272
interruptions
    controlling, 340
    skills of, 139
intrapreneur, becoming an, 295–297
introductions, offering, 127
introverts, success tips for, 114–116
investing in yourself, 238

## J

jealousy
    of coworkers, 169–171
    of management, 224–226
Jefferson, Thomas, 323
job titles, roles compared with, 349
jobs. *See also* roles
    first week at new, 357–359
    handling anxiety about potential loss of, 441–442
    questions to ask to ensure a job match, 351–353
    taking new, 345–350
    working two, 443–445
Jobs, Steve, 281
Johnson & Johnson, 19
judgment
    of management, 199
    of others, 87
jumping to conclusions, as a cognitive distortion, 74, 76
Jung, Carl, 114

## K

Kennedy, John F., 68
kindness, to yourself, 408

## L

labeling, as a cognitive distortion, 74, 77
laughter, 110
layoffs, handling, 446–448
laziness, of colleagues, 144–147
learning
  from failure, 41–43
  to say no, 377
  from your network, 279
legal and compliance issues, conflict and, 157
likability
  about, 290
  demonstrating charisma by being, 68
  when negotiating compensation, 356
likely-case scenarios, 76
limits, setting, 381–383
LinkedIn, 282
loyalty, demonstrating, 28
Luther King, Martin, Jr., 67

## M

management
  about, 189
  abrasive, 215–218
  asking for a raise, 253–256
  asking for feedback from, 242–244

management (*continued*)
  being comfortable around, 198–200
  bringing problems to, 201–202
  building rapport with, 191–194
  communication with, 193
  constructiveness of feedback from, 245–246
  empathy from, 209–211
  first impressions with, 195–197
  gaslighting from, 212–214
  honesty with, 193
  identifying pet peeves of, 193
  informing about toxic coworkers, 167–168
  interactions with, 357
  jealousy from, 224–226
  judging, 199
  knowing on a personal level, 193–194
  lack of support from, 221–223
  making them hear you, 203–205
  meeting with, 217
  onboarding new, 196
  performance appraisals, 239–241
  problem-solving for, 192
  rudeness of, 219–220
  sharing ideas with, 192–193
  showing your value to, 192
  speaking with about bullying, 432
  speaking with about lazy colleagues, 146–147
  unpredictability of, 206–208

manners, when meeting colleagues for the first time, 184
mantras, personal, 83–84
measured language, for conflict resolution, 136
meetings
    to discuss new assignments, 385–386
    for mentors, 282–283
    overloading of, 314–315
    speaking up in, 61–63
mending fences, in arguments, 159
mental filters, as a cognitive distortion, 73, 76
mental health
    managing, 438–440
    safeguarding your, 213
mentors
    finding, 281–285
    as a key to success, 272
metaphors, demonstrating charisma by using, 68
Microsoft Office, 325
mind, calming your, 392–393
mind traps, 393
Miranda, Lin Manuel, 6
mission, of teams, 27
mistakes
    learning from failure, 41–43
    owning your, 44–46, 265
morale, improving, 400
motivation
    identifying core, 428
    maintaining, 378–380

move, making a, 36

## N

needy colleagues, 148–150
negative feedback, in performance appraisal, 240
negative self-talk, identifying and challenging, 104–105
negative thought patterns, eliminating, 73–78
negativity, of colleagues, 153–155
networking
    within industry, 299
    proactivity in, 30–32
networks
    building, 448
    learning from your, 279
neutral tone, for conflict resolution, 136
news, sharing, 127
no, saying, 233, 384–387
non-confrontational manner, for managing annoying colleagues, 142
nonverbal signals, awareness of, 118
norms, challenging existing, 279–280
note-taking, feedback and, 89
notifications, turning off, 314

## O

Obama, Barack, 67
observational skills, as a foundational skill for attention to detail, 64, 65–66

obsessing, about colleague relationships, 161
office hours, 140
office politics, managing, 421–423
onboarding, new management, 196
open-ended promises, 108
open-mindedness
　for feedback, 89
　to ideas of others, 21–23
　at new roles, 363–364
opinions, seeking, 293
opportunities, urgent work and missed, 389
organization skills
　for being a conscientious employee, 16
　as a foundational skill for attention to detail, 64, 65
outcomes
　decision-making and, 51
　reflecting on, 113
overdelivering, 108
overgeneralizing, as a cognitive distortion, 73, 75
owning your mistakes, 44–46

# P

part-time work, 299–300
passions
　developing grit and, 7
　investing in, 102
passive voice, for conflict resolution, 136–137
passiveness, 232
patience
　for growth mindset, 4
　importance of, 111–113
　perceptions and, 119
Pelosi, Nancy, 6
people, greeting, 126
perceptions
　changing others' of you, 117–119
　reality *versus,* 94–97
perfectionism
　accepting less than, 82–84
　expecting, 312
performance
　evaluating and measuring, 353
　measuring, 304, 305
　taking initiative in appraisal process, 239–241
permanence, self-doubt and, 80
perseverance
　developing grit and, 6–7
　for growth mindset, 4
personal life
　for busy times, 331
　developing grit in your, 6–9
personal mantras, 83–84
personal power, building, 289–291
personal situation, assessing, 375
personal style, assessing your current, 233
personalization
　as a cognitive distortion, 74, 77
　self-doubt and, 80

perspective
   maintaining, 394
   reality *versus*, 429
persuasive arguments, 251
pervasiveness, self-doubt and, 80
phone calls, responding to, 315
physical boundaries, setting, 115
physical well-being, 372–373
planning tasks, 318–319
plans
   creating, 293
   presenting to leadership, 293
playfulness, demonstrating charisma by having, 69
Pomodoro Technique, 324–325
positive self-talk, 83–84, 290
positives, discounting, as a cognitive distortion, 74, 76
positivity, maintaining after not receiving a promotion, 258
pre-commitment, 312
preparation, for conflict resolution, 136
present, staying in the, 80–81
pride, in mastering your craft, 102
principles
   responding to violations of, 417–418
   staying true to, 414–416
prioritizing
   asking for, 307
   clarifying, 348–350

prioritizing (*continued*)
   small tasks, 312
   tasks, 318
   urgent work, 388–390
proactivity
   commitments and, 108
   in networking, 30–32
probing questions, 296
problems, getting to the root of, 47–49
procrastination, avoiding, 311–313
product integrity, conflict and, 157
productivity
   about, 301–302
   accomplishing more, 323–325
   asking boss for role clarity, 303–305
   asking for help, 309–310
   avoiding procrastination, 311–313
   clarifying expectations, 306–308
   effect of location on, 312
   increasing by upskilling, 325
   increasing task completion, 317–319
   managing busy times, 329–332
   managing hours worked, 339–342
   managing job-related boredom, 336–338
   managing more work when co-workers quit, 333–335
   maximizing during remote work, 326–328
   meeting deadlines, 320–322
   staying focused, 314–316

professional development, participating in, 299
professional goals, in performance appraisal, 241
professionalism
  about, 33
  in management interactions, 225
  when not receiving a promotion, 257–258
progress
  acknowledging for managing annoying colleagues, 143
  evaluating after not receiving a promotion, 258
  evaluating for behavioral change effort, 97
  tracking as motivation, 379
project integrity, conflict and, 157
promotions
  asking for, 250–252
  managing, 179–182
  managing not receiving, 257–258
protecting yourself, from toxic co-workers, 166
purpose, finding a sense of, 101–103
purposefulness
  finding in your daily work, 18–20
  for growth mindset, 4

## Q

quality of work, 389
questions
  about new assignments, 386
  to ask to ensure a job match, 351–353
  asking, 280
  probing, 296
  responding to, 58–60
quick wins, establishing at new roles, 362–363

## R

rapid teaming, 25
Reagan, Ronald, 67
reality
  confirming, 425
  perception *versus*, 94–97
  perspective *versus*, 429
recalibration, for being a conscientious employee, 16
recognition, for your work, 299
red hat, in six thinking hats technique, 53, 54
reframing situations, 113
relationship-building
  as an introvert, 116
  with colleagues, 20
  for growth mindset, 4
  with peers, 123–125
  starting at a new job, 361

relationships
  dating coworkers, 175–178
  deepening, 126–128
  investing in positive, 103
  managing professional, 129–131
  mending, 172–174
  monitoring, 196
  respectful, 237–238
  urgent work and, 389
reliability, for being a conscientious employee, 16–17
remote work
  managing burnout during, 402–403
  maximizing productivity, 326–328
  visibility and, 286–287
reports, 407–408
reputation
  conflict resolution and, 156
  maintaining for quality work, 265
research
  conducting, 293
  for new positions, 349
resilience, developing grit and, 7
resource allocation, conflict and, 157
resources, for skill development, 274–275
respect
  gaining, 235–238
  showing to others, 237
responding to questions, 58–60
responsibilities
  conflict and clarity of, 157

responsibilities (*continued*)
  delivering on, 28
  prioritizing, 130–131
  seeking new, 298–299
  taking on more, 280
  verifying, 304
rewards
  for completing work, 313
  as motivation, 379
  seeking for effort, 399
risks, of dating coworkers, 175–176
role model, being a, 237
roles
  about, 343–344
  asking boss for clarity about, 303–305
  asking questions regarding job match, 351–353
  clarifying expectations for new, 357
  conflict and clarity of, 157
  deciding whether to accept new, 345–350
  expectations for, 351
  first week of new, 357–359
  integrating into new teams, 365–367
  job titles compared with, 349
  maintaining professionalism, 130
  managing with confidence, 360–361
  negotiating compensation for new, 354–356
  relationship with purpose, 18
  success tips for new, 362–364

Index    469

roles (*continued*)
  switching, 348
  tackling new, 360–361
  tweaking, 345
  typical workdays for, 352
routines, developing, 359, 372
rudeness, of management, 219–220
rules and policies
  for dating coworkers, 176
  explaining after a promotion, 180

## S

safety and well-being, conflict and, 156
salary expectations, 254. *See also* compensation
Samsung, 19
scheduling your day, 327, 358
second jobs, 443–445
self-awareness
  authenticity of, 229–231
  building, 118, 321
  practicing, 95
self-care
  bullying situations and, 431
  practicing, 290–291
self-confidence, when negotiating compensation, 356
self-doubt, overcoming, 79–81
self-esteem
  disconnecting from your organization, 447
  nurturing your, 210–211

self-reflection
  about, 95
  to help management listen to you, 203–204
  for managing annoying colleagues, 142
self-reliance, 149, 309
self-talk
  identifying and challenging negative, 104–105
  positive, 83–84, 290
senior leaders. *See* management
sensitivity, letting go of, 85–87
sharing credit, 262–263
sidebars, avoiding when meeting colleagues for the first time, 184
situational analysis, of abrasive management, 216
situations
  addressing with colleagues, 161
  exploitation of, 131
six thinking hats technique, 51, 53–54
skill gaps, identifying, 347–348
skills
  for attention to detail, 64–66
  building, 448
  coping, 168
  to develop at new roles, 363
  developing new, 20
  developing relevant, 289–290
  interruption, 139
  inventorying, 274

skills (*continued*)
   maintaining, 273–275
   needed for collaboration, 25
   for team members, 352–353
social events, visibility and, 287–288
social media connections, 127–128
social network, building your, 426
software, setting up access to, 358
solutions, focusing on, 28
speaking up
   as an introvert, 115–116
   in meetings, 61–63
special situations
   complaining *versus* keeping quiet, 411–413
   ethics and principles, 414–416, 417–418
   handling workplace bullies, 430–432
   managing a team member's departure, 449–451
   managing anxiety about potential job loss, 441–442
   managing being excluded, 424–426
   managing embarrassment, 436–437
   managing gossip, 419–420
   managing harassment, 433–435
   managing layoffs, 446–448
   managing mental health, 438–440
   managing office politics, 421–423
   managing stereotypes, 427–429
   working two jobs, 443–445
specificity, for conflict resolution, 136

stakeholders
   about, 48–49
   finding who they are, 307
   knowing at new roles, 364
standing up for yourself, 236–237
status quo, challenging, 292–294
status quo bias, 293
stereotypes, handling, 427–429
stories, demonstrating charisma by using, 68
strategy, for changing behaviors, 96
strengths
   identifying, 347–348
   leveraging as an introvert, 116
stress management
   for busy times, 331
   in the moment, 391–394
   urgent work and, 389
success
   celebrating, 28, 81
   as a finite resource, 171
   identifying hidden keys to, 271–272
   monitoring metrics for, 99
support
   after gaslighting, 213
   for behavioral change effort, 96
   from bosses, 341–342
   from colleagues, 210
   from friends and family, 105
   getting more, 404–405
   for harassment, 435

support (*continued*)
  lack of from management, 221–223
  of management team, 225
  seeking, 403
support system
  creating a, 408
  as motivation, 379–380
supporters, building up, 87

# T

tasks
  completing, 317–319, 320–322
  documenting, 318
  prioritizing high-impact, 341
  taking on tough, 299
teaching, for growth mindset, 4–5
team members
  handling departure of, 449–451
  integrating into at new jobs, 365–367
  meeting with after a promotion, 179–180
  for new roles, 352
team player, being a good, 27–29
teamwork, 24–25
temporizing, 385
texts, responding to, 315
thinking patterns, unproductive, 393
thought patterns, eliminating negative, 73–78
three Ps, self-doubt and, 80

time
  dedicating to projects, 323–324
  efficient use of, 376
  prioritizing, 376
  for reflection, 350
  using to maximum benefit, 324–325
time management skills, as a foundational skill for attention to detail, 64, 65
timeframe, for raises, 254–255
timeliness, for being a conscientious employee, 16–17
timing, to help management listen to you, 204
Tolstoy, Leo, 406
toxic coworkers, 163–168
toxic environment, managing, 406–408
track record, 289
training and development
  participating in, 299
  in performance appraisal, 240
  for roles, 352
transportation, planning when meeting colleagues for the first time, 184
triggers
  for impatience, 112
  knowing your, 110
trust-building, 125, 405
truth, telling your, 429
Twain, Mark, 110

two-sided conversations, for conflict resolution, 137
Tyco, 417

## U

uncertainty, facing at work, 35–37
under-promising, 108
understanding, of abrasive management, 216
unfair treatment, handling, 259–260
Unilever, 19
unpredictability, of management, 206–208
upskilling, increasing productivity by, 325
urgency, of work, 388–390

## V

values
　demonstrating your, 236
　estimating your value to a company, 354–355
　identifying, 348–350
venting, 110
virtual meetings
　with colleagues, 185–187
　constructive feedback in, 246
visibility, increasing, 286–288
vocabulary, broadening your, 14
volunteering, visibility and, 287

## W

well-being
　about, 369–370
　achieving work-life balance, 374–377
　getting more support, 404–405
　maintaining motivation, 378–380
　managing anxiety, 395–397
　managing burnout during remote work, 402–403
　managing stress, 391–394
　optimizing, 371–373
　prioritizing urgent tasks, 388–390
　reducing burnout, 398–401
　saying no, 384–387
　setting limits, 381–383
　toxic work environments, 406–408
white hat, in six thinking hats technique, 53, 54
Williams, Serena, 6
Winfrey, Oprah, 67, 281
wishful thinking, as a cognitive distortion, 74, 77
"withins," self-doubt and, 80
words and actions, professionalism with, 131
work arrangement, changing, 376
work environment, physical, 358–359
work ethic, developing your, 16
work situation, assessing, 375

workflow, establishing a, 330–331
working styles, 26
work-life balance
  achieving, 374–377
  establishing, 372
workload
  being strategic with your, 447
  reducing, 398–399
workplace bullies, handling, 430–432
workplace politics, managing, 421–423
workplace rights, conflict and, 157

workspace
  establishing a regular, 327
  setting up, 358
WorldCom, 417
worth. *See* values

## Y

yellow hat, in six thinking hats technique, 53, 54

## Z

Zuckerberg, Mark, 281

Milton Keynes UK
Ingram Content Group UK Ltd.
UKHW022059190224
438095UK00016B/600